Unveiling the NIST Risk Management Framework (RMF)

A practical guide to implementing RMF and managing risks in your organization

Thomas Marsland

Unveiling the NIST Risk Management Framework (RMF)

Group Product Manager: Pavan Ramchandani

Publishing Product Manager: Neha Sharma

Book Project Manager: Ashwini Gowda

Senior Editor: Runcil Rebello

Technical Editor: Rajat Sharma

Copy Editor: Safis Editing

Proofreader: Runcil Rebello

Indexer: Manju Arasan

Production Designer: Nilesh Mohite

DevRel Marketing Coordinator: Marylou De Mello

First published: May 2024

Production reference: 1050424

Published by Packt Publishing Ltd.

Grosvenor House

11 St Paul's Square

Birmingham

B3 1RB, UK

ISBN 978-1-83508-984-2

www.packtpub.com

To my wife, Jennifer, for being my support through everything – for your encouragement, understanding, and unwavering love.

To my daughter Brianna – you are a strong, amazing, and remarkable woman – I love seeing the woman and mother you've become. I am so proud of you.

To my daughter Chloe for your strength and independence. I love you.

To my son Cooper and your love of LEGO – I love seeing your creativity.

Finally, to my son Colin and your love of Fortnite and Minecraft – I love you with all my heart

I am so glad I'm here with all of you to watch you grow.

– Thomas Marsland

Foreword

In the ever-evolving domain of cybersecurity, frameworks such as those developed by the **National Institute of Standards and Technology (NIST)** serve as crucial navigational beacons, guiding practitioners through the complexities of securing digital assets. The NIST **Cybersecurity Framework (CSF)**, **Risk Management Framework (RMF)**, and others are indispensable tools for organizations striving to establish resilient cybersecurity postures. It is against this backdrop that Thomas Marsland presents his comprehensive exploration of NIST frameworks within his book *Unveiling the NIST Risk Management Framework (RMF)*, offering readers a detailed roadmap to mastering these pivotal standards.

Tom Marsland is not just an author; he is a fervent advocate for empowering veterans to transition into the field of cybersecurity. His commitment to this cause is rooted in a rich tapestry of experiences and an unwavering dedication to service. With over two decades of distinguished service in the US Navy's nuclear power field, Tom has demonstrated an unparalleled commitment to excellence and a deep understanding of the technical and leadership skills that are highly transferable to the cybersecurity domain.

Beyond his military service, Tom has been an active participant and leader within the cybersecurity community. His role on the board of directors for VetSec, a non-profit organization dedicated to helping veterans enter the cybersecurity field, underscores his passion for supporting those who have served. Moreover, as the vice president of technology at a leading cybersecurity training company, Tom is at the forefront of developing and delivering cutting-edge training content, ensuring that the next generation of cybersecurity professionals is well equipped to face the challenges of the digital age.

I had the privilege of meeting Tom through our shared involvement with VetSec, where his enthusiasm for technology and his commitment to veteran support were immediately apparent. His ability to translate complex technical concepts into accessible knowledge makes him an invaluable mentor and educator. Tom's unique blend of technical expertise, leadership experience, and genuine desire to contribute to the cybersecurity community makes him the ideal guide for navigating the intricacies of NIST's frameworks.

Unveiling the NIST Risk Management Framework (RMF) is not merely a technical manual; it is a testament to Tom's belief in the power of education and community support to transform lives. As you delve into the pages that follow, you will gain not only a comprehensive understanding of NIST's cybersecurity frameworks but also insights into the principles of leadership, dedication, and service that define true excellence in the field.

Whether you are a veteran looking to carve out a new career path in cybersecurity, a seasoned professional seeking to deepen your knowledge of NIST standards, or simply someone with a passion for technology and security, this book offers valuable lessons and guidance. Through Tom Marsland's expertise and experience, you will find not only a path to mastering NIST's frameworks but also the inspiration to pursue excellence in all your endeavors.

Welcome to a journey of discovery, learning, and empowerment.

Jaclyn "Jax" Scott

Combat Veteran and Cybersecurity at Outpost Gray

Contributors

About the author

Thomas Marsland is a cybersecurity leader with a focus on designing systems and processes that embrace security at their foundations, while protecting scalability and minimizing technical debt. He enjoys working on problems in operations and technology, delivering value to organizations with a mission-focused mindset. A 22-year veteran of the United States Navy, his work history includes nuclear power, information technology, cybersecurity, and executive leadership in the cybersecurity and technology fields, including for the US Navy and Cloud Range. He has a bachelor's degree in IT security and a master's degree in cybersecurity, along with numerous industry certifications.

In his spare time, he leads VetSec, a 501c3 nonprofit with the mission to "*create a world where no veteran pursuing a career in cybersecurity goes unemployed.*" Originally from Port Ludlow, Washington, Tom, the proud father of four children, currently resides in Ravensdale, Washington, with his wife and children. In his free time, he enjoys home automation, backpacking in the Olympic and Cascade mountains, and enjoying the land he's settled on with his family.

The writing of this book has been a new challenge for me. First, this, along with so much of my life, wouldn't be possible without the love and support of my wife, Jennifer. She has supported me through my service in the US Navy and every extra project I've undertaken. Second, I'd also like to dedicate this book to my children – Brianna, Chloe, Cooper, and Colin. I'm so proud of all of you and look forward to watching you grow and see your accomplishments. Third, a big thank you to the Packt Publishing team for working with me and believing in me in this process. Fourth, to my dad, Tom Marsland, for teaching me the value of hard work – and for always being there for me.

Finally, to all of the veterans of the armed forces – to my brothers and sisters in arms, those I've stood shoulder to shoulder with wearing the submarine dolphins, those I've met through my work in VetSec, and those that still serve – your sacrifice makes our nation stronger. Thank you for continuing to stand watch. VetSec will always be here for you when the need arises.

About the reviewers

Jason Brown's passions are data privacy, cybersecurity, and continuous education. Brown has spent his career working with small to medium-sized businesses to large international organizations, developing robust data privacy and cybersecurity programs. Brown has held titles such as chief information security officer, virtual chief information security officer, and data privacy officer.

Brown is also a distinguished public speaker, having given talks on regulatory and cybersecurity topics throughout the US. He has provided material on **Payment Card Industry Data Security Standard (PCI DSS)**, risk management, privacy, and the development of cybersecurity programs. Brown currently holds several industry-leading certifications and holds a master's degree in information systems management.

Rajat Dubey, a cybersecurity expert with 13+ years of experience, safeguards global enterprises. He has expertise in risk assessment, compliance, threat modeling, incident response, ethical hacking, digital forensics, cloud security, AI, blockchain, IoT, and quantum computing. He did an MEng in cybersecurity policy and compliance at George Washington University, USA, and an MBA from Rotman, University of Toronto. He works with Fortune 500 clients across various industries. He is a senior member of **Institute of Electrical and Electronics Engineers (IEEE)** and a fellow of **Cloud Security Alliance (CSA)**. He publishes research papers and articles and peer-reviews books. He is a trusted advisor, navigating complex challenges and developing innovative solutions.

Table of Contents

3

Benefits of Implementing the NIST Risk Management Framework   23

Part 2: Implementing the NIST RMF in Your Organization

4

Preparing for RMF Implementation   35

5

The NIST RMF Life Cycle   55

6

Security Controls and Documentation   65

7

Assessment and Authorization   93

Part 3: Advanced Topics and Best Practices

8

Continuous Monitoring and Incident Response   123

9

Cloud Security and the NIST RMF   151

10

NIST RMF Case Studies and Future Trends   181

11

A Look Ahead   193

Index   201

Other Books You May Enjoy   216

Preface

Welcome! Let's face it, if you're reading this book, you probably weren't too excited about the task you may have been given; implementing the NIST **Risk Management Framework** (**RMF**) in your organization is truly a difficult undertaking and not one everyone would enjoy. Even for me, sometimes cracking open and browsing a NIST Special Publication is something that can put me to sleep.

That's why I wrote this book. This book introduces risk management and the NIST RMF. I've attempted to break down the framework into easy-to-understand topics. This book will not go into every detail, or provide every possible way you could implement the framework; to do so would cover many volumes and be very technology stack and industry dependent. However, once you've read this book, you should have a great understanding of the framework from a big-picture perspective, and know where to focus your attention to successfully implement the NIST RMF in your organization.

Who this book is for

This book is for information technology and cybersecurity professionals who are exploring the world of governance, risk, and compliance. Perhaps you've donned the management hat for the first time, leaving some of your technical abilities behind in favor of writing policy. This book is meant for you – the person who needs an understanding of NIST, risk, and how to manage it via policies and technical controls.

What this book covers

Chapter 1, Understanding Cybersecurity and Risk Management

What good is building a house without a foundation? In this case, our foundation is cybersecurity and risk management. This chapter will kick things off, getting us on the right foot so we can move forward on the same level together.

Chapter 2, NIST Risk Management Framework Overview

NIST is a cool organization – no, really! They are! Before we dive into the framework, let's talk about where it came from. The main topics we touch on here are the history of the NIST RMF, the stages and crucial components, and finally, the roles and responsibilities of the team that will utilize it in your organization.

Chapter 3, Benefits of Implementing the NIST Risk Management Framework

It's useless to do something and truly own it if you don't even know why you're doing it, right? This chapter aims to solve just that. Covering the advantages of adopting the NIST RMF, some regulatory considerations, as well as the whole purpose for doing this in the first place (risk reduction!), we'll start to dive into this topic together and have some fun.

Chapter 4, Preparing for RMF Implementation

How can you do something if you don't prepare first? One might call that "winging it," and in the context of risk management, it's not something I really recommend. This chapter will discuss how to put your team together, set goals, create a strategy, and start implementing the framework.

Chapter 5, The NIST RMF Life Cycle

Here, we take an in-depth look at the stages of the framework – *Prepare, Categorize, Select, Implement, Assess, Authorize*, and *Monitor*. You, the reader, will understand how the RMF is laid out and the importance of each step, with clear breakdowns.

Chapter 6, Security Controls and Documentation

This chapter gets into the so-called meat and potatoes of every **governance, risk and compliance (GRC)** person's life – the controls themselves, and just as important, the documentation of those controls. This chapter discusses the importance of controls, not just for security's sake but also from the perspective of business enablement. We will also discuss documentation and automation as keys to truly making your life easier.

Chapter 7, Assessment and Authorization

Moving on, we set out to equip you with the skills to conduct a security assessment (or even more than one), navigate the assessment and authorization process, and prep for the inevitable audits. Fear not the auditor – they're here to help (we hope).

Chapter 8, Continuous Monitoring and Incident Response

Despite all of the controls in the world you may have implemented, the human factor will still play a role. Eventually, you may find yourself conducting incident response. But how can you do that without a solid plan? In this chapter, we'll discuss how to develop an incident response plan and how to use it. We'll also touch on verifying your controls with continuous monitoring.

Chapter 9, Cloud Security and the NIST RMF

We'd be remiss if we didn't talk about the revolution that has been the cloud and the unique ways that risk can rear its head here. We'll discuss how we might adapt the NIST RMF for cloud environments and some challenges (and solutions), and even have a brief chat about compliance.

Chapter 10, NIST RMF Case Studies and Future Trends

What good is learning about a framework unless you can also learn from others' experiences? Sometimes the best way to do something is to follow in the footsteps of those who've come before you. In this chapter, we'll do just that.

Chapter 11, A Look Ahead

As we draw to a close, we'll reflect on the journey we've taken, discussing lifelong learning and the role of all of us as cybersecurity leaders in excellence.

Conventions used

There are a number of text conventions used throughout this book.

Bold: Indicates a new term or an important word.

> **Tips or important notes**
> Appear like this.

Get in touch

Feedback from our readers is always welcome.

General feedback: If you have questions about any aspect of this book, email us at customercare@ packtpub.com and mention the book title in the subject of your message.

Errata: Although we have taken every care to ensure the accuracy of our content, mistakes do happen. If you have found a mistake in this book, we would be grateful if you would report this to us. Please visit www.packtpub.com/support/errata and fill in the form.

Piracy: If you come across any illegal copies of our works in any form on the internet, we would be grateful if you would provide us with the location address or website name. Please contact us at copyright@packt.com with a link to the material.

If you are interested in becoming an author: If there is a topic that you have expertise in and you are interested in either writing or contributing to a book, please visit authors.packtpub.com.

Share Your Thoughts

Once you've read *Unveiling the NIST Risk Management Framework (RMF)*, we'd love to hear your thoughts! Scan the QR code below to go straight to the Amazon review page for this book and share your feedback.

https://packt.link/r/1835089844

Your review is important to us and the tech community and will help us make sure we're delivering excellent quality content.

Download a free PDF copy of this book

Thanks for purchasing this book!

Do you like to read on the go but are unable to carry your print books everywhere?

Is your eBook purchase not compatible with the device of your choice?

Don't worry, now with every Packt book you get a DRM-free PDF version of that book at no cost.

Read anywhere, any place, on any device. Search, copy, and paste code from your favorite technical books directly into your application.

The perks don't stop there, you can get exclusive access to discounts, newsletters, and great free content in your inbox daily

Follow these simple steps to get the benefits:

1. Scan the QR code or visit the link below

https://packt.link/free-ebook/978-1-83508-984-2

2. Submit your proof of purchase
3. That's it! We'll send your free PDF and other benefits to your email directly

Part 1: Introduction to the NIST Risk Management Framework

We have to start somewhere, and that somewhere, when learning a new topic, makes me think of building a house. In the world of cybersecurity, and more specifically, in the world of governance, risk, and compliance, it's important to start with frameworks. Frameworks are, well, like the frame of the structure. They won't tell you what goes inside the structure or what colors to paint your walls, but they will help you support it with all of the details you plan to add.

To start in this endeavor of learning about the NIST Risk Management Framework, we're going to make no assumptions about the foundation, which, in this case, is cybersecurity and risk management. We'll start by diving into the knowledge you need to build upon a solid foundation. We'll then provide an overview of the RMF as a whole and what some of the benefits may be for you and your organization to consider.

Cybersecurity is a team sport, and as the old adage goes, "*A rising tide lifts all ships.*" I can't wait to get started.

This part has the following chapters:

- *Chapter 1, Understanding Cybersecurity and Risk Management*
- *Chapter 2, NIST Risk Management Framework Overview*
- *Chapter 3, Benefits of Implementing the NIST Risk Management Framework*

1

Understanding Cybersecurity and Risk Management

In the modern digital landscape, cybersecurity stands as the shield guarding against an ever-evolving array of cyber threats. It is a battlefield of paramount importance, and the industry encompasses the strategies, practices, and technologies necessary to safeguard the digital realm. At its core, cybersecurity is not merely a specialized discipline for experts but increasingly a fundamental skill and awareness that every individual and organization must possess.

In this chapter, we're going to cover the following main topics:

- Introduction to cybersecurity fundamentals
- Overview of risk management concepts
- Identifying common cyber threats
- Recognizing vulnerabilities
- NIST frameworks – compare and contrast

By the end of this chapter, you will possess a clear comprehension of essential cybersecurity concepts, setting the stage for our exploration of risk management, common threats, vulnerabilities, and the various **National Institute of Standards and Technology (NIST)** frameworks.

Introduction to cybersecurity fundamentals

In today's interconnected world, cybersecurity has become the linchpin in preserving privacy, trust, and the integrity of digital systems. This section serves as your introduction to the fundamentals of the cybersecurity landscape. We'll begin by examining the core concepts that underpin this critical field.

The digital revolution

The last few decades have witnessed a digital revolution that has transformed the way we live, work, and communicate. The internet, once just a research and communication network, has grown into a sprawling ecosystem connecting billions of devices worldwide. Our personal lives, businesses, governments, and critical infrastructure all rely extensively on digital technologies.

As the digital landscape expanded, so did the avenues for cyber threats. Imagine a world without cybersecurity measures – the consequences would be dire. Personal data would be constantly exposed, financial systems would falter, and critical infrastructure could be compromised. Cybersecurity is not a choice; it's a necessity in this digital age.

Defining cybersecurity

At its core, cybersecurity is the practice of safeguarding digital systems, networks, and data from unauthorized access, damage, or theft. It involves a multifaceted approach, employing technologies, processes, and best practices to shield against cyber threats and vulnerabilities. Cybersecurity is not a once-and-done task; it is an ongoing process and requires adapting to the ever-changing threat landscape. It's a critical awareness that should be woven into the fabric of our daily lives and operations to safeguard our digital landscape.

The cybersecurity imperative

Understanding the significance of cybersecurity is imperative. Picture a world without these protocols and practices in place – cybercriminals would run rampant (even more so than it seems they are now), exploiting vulnerabilities and causing untold damage. Personal privacy would be a thing of the past, and trust in digital systems would erode. It would be likely that society would not even use digital systems.

The necessity of cybersecurity extends beyond individual interests; it encompasses global security, the world's economic stability, and the preservation of critical services. Government agencies, private enterprises, and every person all share a common responsibility to uphold cybersecurity best practices.

The journey begins

This chapter marks the beginning of your journey into the realm of cybersecurity and risk management. We will explore the fundamental concepts and terminologies that serve as the bedrock of all cybersecurity efforts. Whether you are new to the field or seeking to reinforce your knowledge, the principles you'll learn here will lay a strong foundation for our subsequent exploration and implementation of the NIST **Risk Management Framework (RMF)**.

Our journey commences with a deep dive into the core elements that constitute the cybersecurity landscape. We'll scrutinize the anatomy of cyber threats, investigate common vulnerabilities, and equip you with the foundational knowledge needed to recognize the risks and challenges we face.

From there, we will build upon this foundation, guiding you toward the practical implementation of cybersecurity practices within the framework of the NIST RMF.

With that said, let's embark on this trek through cybersecurity, where understanding the fundamentals is the first crucial step toward helping fortify the digital world against emerging threats and challenges.

In the next section, we'll delve deeper into the process section of cybersecurity by exploring the core principles of risk management, a vital component of effective cybersecurity practices.

Overview of risk management concepts

In the realm of cybersecurity, the adage that *knowledge is power* holds immense significance. While understanding the fundamentals of cybersecurity provides a solid foundation, grasping the principles of risk management is equally vital. After all, risk is at the heart of cybersecurity, and effective risk management is the compass that guides our efforts to safeguard digital assets.

The nature of risk

Before we dive into risk management concepts, let's explore what *risk* truly means in the context of cybersecurity. **Risk**, in this context, is the likelihood of a cyber threat exploiting a vulnerability, leading to potential harm or damage. In simpler terms, there's a chance that something could go wrong in the digital world, and the consequences could range from minor inconveniences to catastrophic breaches.

Understanding risk is essential because it helps us make informed decisions. In the cybersecurity context, these decisions involve prioritizing security measures, allocating resources, and determining the appropriate level of protection. **Risk management**, therefore, is the systematic process of identifying, assessing, and mitigating these potential threats.

The risk management process

Effective risk management in cybersecurity follows a structured process. While different frameworks and methodologies exist, they generally encompass these key steps:

1. **Risk identification**: The first step involves identifying potential risks. This includes recognizing vulnerabilities within your systems and understanding the various threats that could exploit them. It's akin to scanning the battlefield before the battle begins, knowing the lay of the land and potential adversaries.

2. **Risk assessment**: Once risks have been identified, they are assessed to understand their potential impact and likelihood of occurrence. A risk assessment quantifies the risks, allowing you to prioritize them based on their severity. Essentially, this step involves evaluating the strengths and strategies of your adversaries.

3. **Risk mitigation**: With a clear understanding of the risks, the next step is to implement measures to mitigate or reduce these risks. These measures can include security controls, policies, procedures, and best practices. Think of this as fortifying your defenses to minimize the vulnerabilities and potential for exploitation.

4. **Risk monitoring and review**: Risk management is an ongoing process. After mitigation measures are in place, it's essential to continually monitor the threat landscape, assess the effectiveness of controls, and adapt to emerging risks. This is equivalent to maintaining vigilance in the face of evolving adversaries.

5. **Risk communication**: Effective risk management also involves transparent communication. Stakeholders need to be informed about the identified risks, the measures in place to mitigate them, and the residual risks that remain. Think of this as briefing your team before a mission.

Now that we've identified the key risk management processes, let's look at them in the context of cybersecurity.

Risk management in cybersecurity

In the cybersecurity context, risk management takes center stage because of the constantly evolving nature of cyber threats. As technology advances, so do the methods and tactics of cybercriminals and **advanced persistent threats** (**APTs**). Therefore, cybersecurity professionals must be proactive in identifying and mitigating risks to stay one step ahead.

The goal of cybersecurity risk management is not to eliminate *all* risks – such a feat is impractical and often impossible. Instead, it aims to manage risks to an acceptable level, balancing the cost of mitigation measures with the potential consequences of a cyber incident. This elimination of all risks is impractical for numerous reasons – cost, time, resources, and even that the risk is purely reasonable to accept.

NIST and risk management

As we dive deeper into the NIST RMF later in this book, you'll find that risk management is at its core. The RMF provides a structured approach to managing risk throughout the system development life cycle. By adopting the RMF, organizations can systematically identify, assess, and mitigate risks, ensuring the security of their digital assets.

Understanding the fundamentals of risk management is pivotal in your journey toward becoming a proficient cybersecurity practitioner. It equips you with the knowledge needed to assess and prioritize risks effectively, laying the groundwork for the practical implementation of cybersecurity practices within the NIST RMF.

In the following sections of this chapter, we'll delve deeper into the world of cyber threats, vulnerabilities, and the critical task of risk assessment. These concepts will further sharpen your understanding of the challenges and opportunities presented by the cybersecurity landscape.

Identifying common cyber threats

In the ever-evolving realm of cybersecurity, identifying common cyber threats is a crucial skill. Awareness of the threats that lurk in the digital landscape empowers you to proactively protect your systems and data. In this section, we will explore some of the most prevalent cyber threats, understand their modus operandi, and learn how to recognize their telltale signs.

Types of cyber threats

In this section, we'll review the common types of cyber threats to develop a common framework to build on:

- **Malware**: Malware, which is short for malicious software, is a type of software designed to infiltrate, damage, or exploit computer systems without the user's consent or knowledge. Malware comes in many forms, such as viruses, worms, ransomware, spyware, and adware, each with its unique characteristics.

  Example: Ransomware, such as the notorious WannaCry, encrypts files and demands a ransom for decryption keys, crippling organizations' operations.

- **Phishing**: Phishing attacks use the art of deception, typically via email or SMS/text messages, to trick the end user into giving away sensitive information, such as their financial account information or login details.

  Example: A phishing email impersonating a legitimate bank requests the recipient to click a link and provide their account login credentials.

- **Denial of service (DoS) and distributed denial of service (DDoS) attacks**: These attacks are meant to take down one leg of the **Confidentiality-Integrity-Availability (CIA)** triad, *availability*, by overwhelming a target with too much traffic, typically making it inaccessible or knocking it completely off of a network.

  Example: A DDoS attack against a popular eCommerce website floods it with traffic, causing it to crash during a high-traffic holiday shopping season.

- **Insider threats**: An insider threat refers to the threat of damage or harm to an organization's assets, perpetrated by individuals who have authorized access to the organization's resources.

  Example: An employee with privileged access intentionally leaks sensitive company data to a competitor.

- **Zero-day vulnerabilities**: This is a type of vulnerability that has no currently available fix, and is not publicly known to the software vendor.

  Example: An attacker exploits a previously unknown vulnerability in a widely used web browser to gain unauthorized access to a user's system.

- **Man-in-the-middle (MitM) attacks**: In MitM attacks, an attacker intercepts network communication between two parties, allowing them to modify the message in transit or listen in on the communications.

  Example: A hacker sets up a rogue Wi-Fi hotspot at a cafe, intercepting the communication between users and the cafe's Wi-Fi network to capture sensitive data.

- **Social engineering**: Social engineering involves using human nature and deceptive techniques to convince individuals to give up information they would not otherwise share with unauthorized individuals.

  Example: An attacker calls a target, posing as a technical support representative, and convinces them to share their login credentials.

Now that we've seen the different types of cyber threats, let's learn how to recognize these threats better.

Recognizing the signs

Recognizing common cyber threats involves being vigilant for signs and indicators that something may be amiss. Here are some practical examples of how to recognize these threats:

- **Malware**: Frequent system crashes, unexpected pop-up ads, and unexplained changes in system settings can be indicative of malware infections

- **Phishing**: Look for misspelled URLs, generic greetings in emails, and suspicious requests for personal or financial information

- **DoS/DDoS attacks**: A sudden, significant decrease in network performance, inability to access websites, or unusual traffic patterns can indicate such attacks

- **Insider threats**: Unusual or unauthorized access to sensitive data or systems by employees may signal an insider threat

- **Zero-day vulnerabilities**: Keep systems and software updated to patch vulnerabilities as soon as fixes become available

- **MitM attacks**: Be cautious when connecting to public Wi-Fi networks, especially if they lack password protection or encryption

- **Social engineering**: Always verify the identity of individuals requesting sensitive information or access to your systems

Cyber threats are not static; they evolve continuously. Staying informed about the latest threats, vulnerabilities, and attack techniques is essential. Online resources, security news websites, and threat intelligence reports, as well as professional organizations such as **InfraGard**, **CISA**, and **US-CERT**, and information-sharing organizations, are invaluable resources for staying up to date.

In the next section, we'll turn our attention to vulnerabilities – weaknesses in systems or processes that can be exploited by cyber threats. Understanding these vulnerabilities is key to effective risk management and cybersecurity.

Recognizing vulnerabilities

In the landscape of cybersecurity, recognizing vulnerabilities is akin to identifying weak links in a chain – knowing where your defenses may be breached is a critical aspect of effective risk management. Vulnerabilities can exist in software, hardware, configurations, and even human processes. In this section, we'll delve into the common vulnerabilities and discuss tools that can aid in their identification.

Common vulnerabilities

Let's look at some of the common vulnerabilities:

- **Software vulnerabilities**: Software, including operating systems and applications, often contains vulnerabilities that can be exploited by attackers. These may result from coding errors, insufficient testing, or outdated software. Vulnerability scanners such as Tenable's **Nessus** or **OpenVAS** can help identify known software vulnerabilities in your systems.

- **Weak or default passwords**: Many security breaches occur due to the use of weak or default passwords. Attackers can easily guess or crack such passwords. Password auditing tools such as **John the Ripper** can assess the strength of passwords in your environment. Additionally, the use of **two-factor authentication** (**2FA**) can provide an exponential increase in security in this regard.

- **Unpatched systems**: Failing to apply security patches and updates promptly leaves systems susceptible to known vulnerabilities. Vulnerability management tools, such as **Qualys**, can help identify unpatched systems and missing updates.

- **Misconfigured systems**: Incorrectly configured systems can create security holes. These misconfigurations may allow unauthorized access, data leaks, or other security issues. Security configuration assessment tools such as **CIS-CAT**, developed by the **Center for Internet Security** (**CIS**), can scan systems for misconfigurations.

- **Lack of encryption**: Failing to encrypt sensitive data during storage or transmission can lead to data breaches. Network scanning tools, such as **Wireshark**, can be used to see if current network traffic is passing unencrypted.

- **Outdated hardware**: Aging hardware may no longer receive security updates, even at the firmware level, making it vulnerable to known exploits. Inventory management and monitoring tools can help identify hardware that is past its shelf life in your environment.

- **Insider threats**: Employees with excessive access privileges or those acting maliciously can introduce vulnerabilities. User and access management solutions can help monitor and limit access to sensitive systems and data. Implementing policies around the concept of only granting the minimum access needed is important to mitigate the potential impact of an insider threat.

Next, we'll look at some of the tools we mentioned previously.

Vulnerability scanning tools

Vulnerability scanning tools play a crucial role in identifying weaknesses in your digital ecosystem. These tools automate the process of discovering vulnerabilities, allowing you to proactively address them. Here are a few widely used vulnerability scanning tools:

- **Nessus**: Nessus is a comprehensive vulnerability scanner that can identify security issues across a wide range of devices, systems, and applications.
- **OpenVAS**: OpenVAS is an open source vulnerability scanner that helps assess the security of networks and web applications. Others include **Wazuh/OSSEC** and **Security Onion**.
- **Qualys**: Qualys offers cloud-based vulnerability management and assessment services, enabling organizations to identify and remediate vulnerabilities effectively.
- **CIS-CAT**: The CIS provides the CIS-CAT suite, which includes tools for assessing system configurations and identifying misconfigurations.
- **Wireshark**: While primarily a network protocol analyzer, Wireshark can also be used to identify unencrypted data transmissions, revealing potential security vulnerabilities.

Understanding vulnerabilities and actively seeking them out with the assistance of these tools is a proactive approach to risk management. By addressing vulnerabilities promptly, you can mitigate the potential for cyber threats to exploit weaknesses in your systems and infrastructure.

In the following section, we will delve into the NIST **Cybersecurity Framework** (CSF) and the NIST RMF, comparing and contrasting them to gain insights into how they can be leveraged to manage cybersecurity risks effectively.

NIST frameworks – compare and contrast

Within the realm of cybersecurity, two prominent frameworks developed by the NIST stand as cornerstones for managing risk and enhancing security: the NIST CSF and the NIST RMF. While both frameworks share the overarching goal of bolstering cybersecurity, they serve different purposes and operate at distinct stages of the cybersecurity life cycle. In this section, we will delve into a comprehensive comparison between these two frameworks to understand their key features, purposes, and how they can be leveraged effectively.

NIST CSF

First, let's delve into the NIST CSF.

Purpose

The NIST CSF, officially titled the *Framework for Improving Critical Infrastructure Cybersecurity*, was created to provide organizations, particularly those in critical infrastructure sectors, with a flexible framework for enhancing their cybersecurity posture. It is designed to help organizations manage and reduce cybersecurity risk while fostering a culture of cybersecurity awareness and resilience.

Key components

The NIST CSF is built around five core functions: *Identify*, *Protect*, *Detect*, *Respond*, and *Recover*. These functions provide a structured approach to cybersecurity activities. Within each function, various categories and subcategories outline specific cybersecurity activities and outcomes. Organizations can select and implement relevant subcategories based on their needs.

Organizations can create cybersecurity profiles to align their current and target cybersecurity postures, facilitating risk management and prioritizing improvements. The framework also includes four implementation tiers (*Partial*, *Risk Informed*, *Repeatable*, and *Adaptive*) that help organizations assess their current cybersecurity practices and set goals for improvement.

Application

The NIST CSF is widely used by organizations across various sectors to enhance their cybersecurity posture. It helps organizations identify and prioritize cybersecurity activities, assess their current state, and develop a roadmap for improvement.

NIST RMF

Next, let's delve into the NIST RMF.

Purpose

The NIST RMF, as outlined in NIST Special Publication 800-37, provides a structured approach to managing and mitigating risk throughout the system development life cycle. It is primarily used by federal agencies and government contractors to secure information systems and achieve compliance with federal regulations.

Key components

The NIST RMF is built around seven core phases:

- **Prepare**: In this phase, an understanding of the organization's risk environment is developed, along with establishing the necessary resources, policies, and procedures to manage risk

- **Categorize**: In this phase, information systems are categorized based on their sensitivity and importance, determining the level of security required

- **Select**: Security controls are selected based on the system's categorization and risk assessment

- **Implement**: Chosen security controls are implemented within the system

- **Assess**: Security controls are assessed for effectiveness and compliance

- **Authorize**: Based on the assessment results, the system is authorized for operation, or further action is taken to address deficiencies

- **Monitor**: Continuous monitoring of security controls and ongoing risk management ensure the system remains secure throughout its life cycle

Application

The NIST RMF is primarily used by the US federal government and its contractors to manage and secure information systems. It helps ensure that federal agencies and organizations adhere to a structured process for assessing, authorizing, and maintaining the security of their systems.

Comparison and contrast

Now, let's compare and contrast both frameworks.

Scope and applicability

First, let's look at their scope and applicability:

- **CSF**: The NIST CSF primarily focuses on helping organizations manage and improve their cybersecurity posture through risk reduction. It provides a set of guidelines and best practices to help organizations identify, protect, detect, respond to, and recover from cybersecurity threats and incidents. It applies to a wide range of organizations, including critical infrastructure sectors such as energy, healthcare, finance, and transportation, as well as non-critical infrastructure organizations.

- **RMF**: The NIST RMF is designed primarily to guide **state, local, tribal, and territorial** (SLTT) government organizations in managing the security and privacy risks associated with their information systems. It is specifically tailored to the federal government and its contractors, although the underlying principles, and even the framework itself, have a significant amount of applicability outside the government. It is mandated for all federal information systems and is used to assess and authorize the security of these systems.

Functions versus phases

The NIST CSF is organized around functions (*Identify, Protect, Detect, Respond, Recover*), while the RMF is organized around phases (*Categorize, Select, Implement, Assess, Authorize, Monitor*).

Flexibility

While the NIST CSF is highly flexible and allows organizations to tailor the implementation based on their unique needs, the RMF adheres to a more rigid, standardized process that ensures federal requirements are met.

Primary goal

The CSF's primary goal is to enhance cybersecurity, promote resilience, and foster risk management awareness. The RMF's goal is to achieve compliance with federal regulations and secure federal information systems.

Adoption

The NIST CSF is widely adopted across industries globally, while the RMF is still primarily used within the United States federal government and its contractors.

In summary, while both the NIST CSF and the NIST RMF share the goal of enhancing cybersecurity, they differ in scope, application, and approach. The CSF is a versatile tool for organizations seeking to bolster their cybersecurity posture, while the RMF is more specific to federal agencies and their compliance requirements. Understanding the distinctions between these frameworks is crucial for selecting the appropriate approach to managing cybersecurity risks based on your organization's context and goals.

Summary

In this opening chapter, we embarked on a journey to explore the foundational principles of cybersecurity and risk management, two essential pillars in safeguarding your digital realm. We began by understanding the fundamental concepts of cybersecurity and gained insight into the importance of cybersecurity in our world, both at an individual and organizational level. We delved into the essence of risk management, learning how to identify, assess, and mitigate risks. Understanding risk is a crucial step in making informed decisions about security measures. You explored the world of cyber threats, from malware to insider threats. Recognizing these threats and their telltale signs equips you to proactively protect systems and data. Then, you learned how to identify vulnerabilities in systems and processes using tools such as vulnerability scanners to proactively address weaknesses. Finally, we compared the NIST CSF and the NIST RMF, highlighting their purpose, components, and applicability.

These foundational lessons are the building blocks of your journey toward becoming a proficient cybersecurity practitioner. Understanding the fundamentals equips you to identify, assess, and mitigate cybersecurity risks, protecting digital assets from a wide range of threats. Knowledge of risk management and the NIST frameworks lays the groundwork for future chapters, where you will explore practical implementation and the application of these concepts.

In the next chapter, we will take the next logical step by delving into the practical implementation of cybersecurity controls. Building upon your foundational knowledge, you will learn how to put these concepts into action, fortifying your digital defenses and ensuring resilience against emerging threats. This hands-on journey begins with the application of security controls, setting the stage for effective risk management and cybersecurity operations.

NIST Risk Management Framework Overview

In the intricate landscape of cybersecurity, effective risk management is paramount. The **National Institute of Standards and Technology (NIST) Risk Management Framework (RMF)** is a structured approach that stands as a guiding light for organizations, helping them navigate the complex journey of securing digital assets and managing cybersecurity risks. In this chapter, we embark on an enlightening exploration of the NIST RMF, unraveling its history, key components, stages, and the pivotal roles played by individuals in this critical framework.

In this chapter, we're going to cover the following main topics:

- The history and evolution of the NIST RMF
- The key components and stages of the RMF
- Roles and responsibilities in the RMF

The history and evolution of the NIST RMF

The NIST RMF didn't emerge overnight; its historical evolution is a testament to the ever-growing importance of effective cybersecurity practices. To gain a comprehensive understanding of the framework, we must delve deeper into its historical context, examining the key developments and factors that led to its inception and evolution.

Precursors to the RMF

Before the establishment of the NIST RMF, several significant precursors laid the groundwork for a more systematic approach to cybersecurity. These early initiatives and regulations were pivotal in shaping the principles and practices that underpin the RMF today:

- **The Trusted Computer System Evaluation Criteria (TCSEC)**: Commonly referred to as the **Orange Book**, TCSEC emerged in the 1980s as a pioneering initiative in the field of computer security. It aimed to evaluate the security of computer systems and provided a framework for this evaluation. TCSEC introduced the concept of security levels, each with specific requirements, to guide system developers and evaluators. This precursor established the foundation for evaluating and classifying the security of computer systems, an essential aspect of the later NIST RMF.

- **The Computer Security Act of 1987**: The Computer Security Act of 1987 marked a pivotal moment in recognizing the importance of securing federal computer systems. Enacted by the United States Congress, this act authorized the NIST to develop standards and guidelines for securing these systems. This legislative action reflected a growing awareness of the need for enhanced cybersecurity practices in the federal government, paving the way for NIST's involvement in the development of the RMF. It established the computer systems security and privacy advisory board to provide guidance and advice on computer security matters.

- **The Federal Information Security Management Act (FISMA)**: In 2002, the FISMA was enacted, reinforcing the emphasis on securing federal information systems. FISMA mandated that federal agencies protect their information systems by developing and implementing security programs. Crucially, it highlighted the importance of risk management and compliance with established security standards. FISMA and its requirements aligned closely with the principles that underlie the NIST RMF, emphasizing risk management and the development of security programs.

The emergence of the NIST RMF

The NIST RMF, in its current form, can be traced back to these early initiatives and the growing recognition of the need for a more comprehensive and flexible approach to managing cybersecurity risks. Several key developments and publications played a significant role in the framework's evolution:

- **NIST Special Publication 800-37**: One of the foundational documents in the development of the NIST RMF is NIST Special Publication 800-37, titled *Risk Management Framework for Information Systems and Organizations: A System Life Cycle Approach for Security and Privacy*. Published by NIST, this guide introduced the core concepts and principles of the RMF. It presented a systematic approach for managing risks throughout the system development life cycle and emphasized the importance of assessing and authorizing information systems.

- **Alignment with FISMA**: The NIST RMF was developed in close alignment with the requirements of the FISMA. This alignment ensured that federal agencies had a structured and consistent framework for meeting their obligations under the law. It underscored the RMF's role as a key tool in enabling agencies to comply with federal regulations while effectively managing cybersecurity risks.

- **Ongoing updates and refinements**: In recognition of the ever-evolving threat landscape and the rapid advancements in technology, the NIST RMF has undergone a series of updates and refinements over the years. These updates are crucial to ensure that the framework remains relevant and effective. They allow the RMF to address emerging challenges and adapt to changing technology environments, ensuring that it continues to provide valuable guidance for managing cybersecurity risks.

Why it matters

Understanding the historical evolution of the NIST RMF is not merely an exercise in tracing its origins but a means to appreciate the framework's growing relevance and the challenges it seeks to address. The RMF's historical context underscores the mounting awareness of the critical need for robust cybersecurity practices in an increasingly digital world.

As cyber threats continue to evolve, the RMF's adaptability and unwavering commitment to risk management remain vital. By gaining insight into its historical development, you're better equipped to appreciate the framework's significance and how it can be effectively applied in the contemporary digital landscape.

In the next section, we will get into the core components and stages of the NIST RMF. This exploration will lay the groundwork for practical implementation and risk management, providing the essential tools and knowledge needed to navigate the complex landscape of cybersecurity.

The key components and stages of the RMF

The NIST RMF consists of essential core components and well-defined stages that collectively form a structured approach to managing cybersecurity risks within an organization. These components and stages guide the organization through the process of identifying, assessing, and mitigating risks effectively.

The core components of the NIST RMF

NIST Special Publication 800-37 Revision 2 provides comprehensive guidance on the NIST RMF. It's essential to understand the core components outlined in this document, which serve as the foundation for effectively managing cybersecurity risks within an organization.

RMF overview and context

NIST 800-37 begins with an introduction and context-setting section. It outlines the overarching framework and its applicability, providing a clear understanding of the RMF's purpose and scope. The document emphasizes the importance of adopting a risk management approach to secure information systems effectively.

Stages

The stages of the NIST RMF are discussed in detail in the *The stages of the NIST RMF* subsection. The stages are *Prepare*, *Categorize*, *Select*, *Implement*, *Assess*, *Authorize*, and *Monitor*, and they are a key piece of this book.

Interconnections and interdependencies

NIST 800-37 acknowledges that the RMF is interconnected with other frameworks, standards, and processes. This component explores the interconnections and interdependencies between the RMF and various factors such as organizational risk management, security engineering, and continuous monitoring. It highlights the need to integrate these elements seamlessly into the RMF process.

Supporting guidance and appendices

Throughout the publication, readers can find valuable supporting guidance, references, and appendices that provide additional information, examples, and templates to assist organizations in implementing the RMF effectively. These resources offer practical insights into applying the RMF principles and processes.

NIST 800-37 Revision 2 is a comprehensive guide that provides a structured approach to managing cybersecurity risks. Understanding these core components is essential for organizations aiming to implement the RMF successfully, as they form the basis for securing information systems and safeguarding critical assets. Next, we take a deeper look at the stages of the NIST RMF.

The stages of the NIST RMF

In 2018, *NIST 800-37* was revised to include an additional step. Let's examine the seven steps of the RMF:

1. **Prepare for RMF execution**: This initial step involves preparing for the RMF process. It includes establishing the context and the boundaries of the system, defining the roles and responsibilities, and ensuring that the necessary resources are in place to support the RMF process.

2. **Categorize system and information**: In this step, the system is categorized based on its potential impact on organizational operations, assets, and individuals. This categorization helps determine the appropriate security controls that need to be implemented.

3. **Select and tailor controls**: Once the system is categorized, specific security controls are selected from the *NIST Special Publication 800-53*, which provides a comprehensive set of security controls. The selection is based on the categorized impact level and tailored to the system's unique requirements.

4. **Implement controls**: The selected security controls are implemented in the system during this step. This involves configuring hardware and software, establishing security policies and procedures, and deploying security technologies to ensure that the controls are correctly integrated.

5. **Assess controls**: Security control assessments are conducted to evaluate the effectiveness of the implemented controls. This step includes activities such as vulnerability scanning, penetration testing, and other security tests to identify vulnerabilities and weaknesses.

6. **Authorize system or controls**: The authorization step involves reviewing the results of the security control assessments, assessing residual risks, and making a formal decision on whether to grant **authorization to operate (ATO)**. An **Authorizing Official (AO)** plays a crucial role in this decision-making process.

7. **Monitoring the system's controls**: The final step involves the continuous monitoring of the system's security controls. This ongoing process includes real-time threat detection, incident response, and regular security assessments to ensure that the controls remain effective, as well as monitoring whether the system maintains its security posture over time.

These seven steps together create a structured and systematic approach to risk management and cybersecurity within an organization, ensuring that information systems are secured and compliant with established standards throughout their life cycle.

As we move into the final section of this chapter, we will look at the roles and responsibilities of individuals in the RMF process.

Roles and responsibilities in the RMF

There are numerous stakeholders involved in implementing the RMF in your organization. In this section, we'll give a breakdown of each role and what their responsibilities are as it pertains to the implementation of the NIST RMF.

Authorizing Official

The AO plays a pivotal role in the NIST RMF process. Their primary responsibility is to make the final decision regarding ATO for an information system. This decision is based on a comprehensive review of the results of security control assessments and an assessment of residual risks. To execute this role effectively, the AO must have a profound understanding of the RMF process, organizational security policies, and the system's specific requirements. They must be able to weigh the assessment findings against security standards and acceptable risk levels.

In carrying out their responsibilities, the AO should communicate effectively with other RMF stakeholders, such as the **Chief Information Officer (CIO)** and **Information System Owner (ISO)**, to gather the necessary information and insights. The AO's decision plays a pivotal role in ensuring the security and compliance of the information system. Therefore, it's crucial that the AO remains impartial, unbiased, and well-informed throughout the process.

Chief Information Officer

The CIO holds a strategic position in the RMF process and is responsible for overseeing the organization's broader information technology and cybersecurity strategy. To execute this role effectively, the CIO must align the RMF process with the organization's overarching IT strategy. This alignment includes resource allocation, budgeting, and ensuring that the RMF supports the organization's mission and goals.

To fulfill these responsibilities, the CIO should work closely with the AO and other RMF stakeholders to understand the specific security requirements of the information system and to ensure that the RMF process is adequately resourced. This includes collaborating with the ISO to define the system's security requirements and security control selection. The CIO plays a crucial role in ensuring that the RMF process is not only effective in securing the information system but also aligns with the organization's strategic objectives.

Chief Information Security Officer

The **Chief Information Security Officer (CISO)** is a high-ranking executive responsible for the organization's overall cybersecurity strategy, including the RMF process. The CISO plays a pivotal role in ensuring the organization's information systems are secure, compliant, and resilient against evolving threats. Their responsibilities encompass strategic leadership, risk management, and the alignment of the RMF process with the organization's broader security objectives.

For the effective execution of their responsibilities, the CISO should possess a deep understanding of cybersecurity principles, risk management, and the RMF process. They need to stay current with evolving cyber threats and security technologies and be able to translate technical security concepts into business-relevant terms. Collaboration with other RMF stakeholders, such as the AO and ISO, is critical to ensure that the RMF aligns with the organization's strategic goals and security requirements. The CISO should also have strong leadership and communication skills to convey the importance of cybersecurity and risk management to the organization's executive leadership and staff.

Information System Owner

The ISO holds a key operational role in the RMF process. Their primary responsibility is to oversee the day-to-day operation and security of the information system. To fulfill this role effectively, the ISO should define the system's security requirements, select appropriate security controls, and ensure that the system operates securely.

Collaboration is essential for ISOs, as they work closely with other RMF stakeholders, such as the **Security Control Assessor (SCA)**, to define security requirements and select controls. They must also collaborate with the **Security Officer (SO)** to ensure that security controls are correctly implemented and that the system maintains its security posture. ISOs should have a deep understanding of the information system's operation, as well as a strong knowledge of security principles and controls.

Security Control Assessor

SCAs play a critical role in the RMF process by conducting security control assessments. Their primary responsibility is to evaluate the effectiveness of the security controls that have been implemented. This involves assessing whether the controls are correctly configured and functioning as needed.

To perform their duties effectively, SCAs need to possess in-depth knowledge of security control specifications, assessment methodologies, and relevant testing techniques. They should have the ability to identify vulnerabilities and weaknesses in security controls and provide recommendations for mitigation. SCAs must be meticulous in documenting assessment results and working closely with other RMF stakeholders, including the ISO, to gather information and support.

Security Officer

SOs are responsible for implementing and overseeing security measures for the information system. Their responsibilities include ensuring that security controls are correctly implemented, monitoring their ongoing operation, and managing incident response procedures.

To execute these responsibilities effectively, SOs need to have a deep understanding of security policies and procedures, security technologies, and incident response protocols. They should collaborate closely with the **System Administrator** (**SA**) to ensure that access to assessments is provided and to address technical questions. SOs are key in maintaining the system's security posture, making ongoing monitoring and response to security incidents critical aspects of their role.

These roles, each with their specific responsibilities, collectively form a structured approach to managing cybersecurity risks within the RMF process. Collaborative efforts and a strong understanding of the RMF's principles are essential for the effective execution of these responsibilities.

Summary

In this chapter, we began the comprehensive journey toward grasping the fundamentals of the NIST RMF. We began by tracing the historical roots of the RMF, understanding its evolution from earlier frameworks and its adaptation to the evolving landscape of cybersecurity threats. This helps us to appreciate the context in which the RMF operates and how it continues to be refined to meet contemporary challenges. The second part provided a deep dive into the core components and stages of the RMF. These stages form the backbone of the RMF, ensuring a structured approach to managing cybersecurity risks across an information system's life cycle. Finally, we unveiled an array of key roles within the RMF and discussed their distinct responsibilities. Understanding these roles and their functions is vital to understanding the process various stakeholders play in the RMF process.

In the next chapter, we will explore the substantial advantages of implementing the RMF. You will discover how the RMF enhances compliance, reduces risk, and contributes to business continuity while meeting regulatory requirements.

3

Benefits of Implementing the NIST Risk Management Framework

In today's dynamic digital landscape, cybersecurity, compliance, and business continuity are paramount. The NIST **Risk Management Framework** (**RMF**) is your key to navigating this complex terrain effectively. This chapter unpacks the diverse advantages of adopting the RMF and equips you with practical skills for maximizing its potential. By this chapter's conclusion, you'll hold the keys to a fortified cybersecurity strategy, streamlined compliance, and resilient business continuity. Practical insights empower you to make the most of the NIST RMF, ready to secure your organization against evolving threats and regulatory demands.

In this chapter, we're going to cover the following main topics:

- Advantages of adopting NIST RMF
- Compliance and regulatory considerations
- Business continuity and risk reduction

Advantages of adopting NIST RMF

In the dynamic realm of cybersecurity, organizations face a constant barrage of threats and vulnerabilities. To effectively safeguard their networks, systems, and users, they require a strategic, structured approach that delivers a robust defense against a diverse array of risks. The NIST RMF stands as a powerful ally in this ongoing battle, offering a host of tangible advantages for organizations that seek to fortify their cybersecurity posture.

Structured approach to risk management

A fundamental advantage of the NIST RMF is the structured and systematic approach it takes to managing cybersecurity risks. It leads organizations through a well-defined sequence of steps, from the crucial initial categorization of information systems to continuous monitoring and reauthorization. By navigating this roadmap, organizations gain a comprehensive understanding of their security posture. They can meticulously identify, assess, and mitigate risks, fostering a proactive stance against vulnerabilities and emerging threats.

Alignment with industry standards

The NIST RMF is not an isolated framework; it integrates seamlessly with other cybersecurity standards and best practices. The harmonization between NIST Special Publication 800-53 and other industry benchmarks, such as ISO 27001 and the **Center for Internet Security** (**CIS**) Critical Security Controls, ensures that organizations are adhering to well-recognized and widely accepted security guidelines. This alignment not only simplifies efforts to become compliant but also leverages established knowledge to enhance cybersecurity effectiveness.

A holistic approach to risk management

What sets the NIST RMF apart is its holistic approach to risk management. Unlike ad hoc security strategies, the RMF tightly integrates information security into an organization's fabric. It doesn't view cybersecurity as a separate, compartmentalized effort but as an inherent component of every operational facet. This holistic approach ensures that security is not an afterthought but an integral part of the organization's mission, culture, and strategic decision-making. By following this process, organizations can have a more comprehensive understanding of their risk posture, which enables them to make informed decisions about resource allocation.

Efficiency through standardization

Standardization is a cornerstone of the NIST RMF. It instills a common language, methodology, and set of controls for managing security across the organization. By adhering to standard procedures and control sets, organizations can reduce complexity, avoid duplication of efforts, and optimize resource allocation. The framework encourages the reuse and inheritance of information assurance controls, reducing the need for redundant assessments and creating a more efficient, cost-effective security approach.

Enhanced security posture

Implementing the NIST RMF leads to a notably strengthened security posture. The framework's systematic approach requires organizations to implement security controls and continuously monitor their effectiveness. This proactive stance results in reduced vulnerabilities and a faster response to potential threats, ultimately leading to a more resilient security posture.

Compliance and regulatory alignment

The structured nature of the NIST RMF simplifies compliance with various regulatory requirements and standards. The framework's meticulous documentation of security controls, assessments, and authorizations serves as a robust foundation for meeting compliance mandates. Organizations, whether operating in highly regulated sectors or navigating complex industry-specific regulations, find the RMF a valuable ally in their compliance endeavors.

Risk reduction and resilience

An essential aspect of the NIST RMF is its focus on continuous monitoring and assessment. By proactively identifying emerging threats and vulnerabilities, organizations can be aware of them, implement controls, and significantly reduce risks in their environment. Moreover, a vigilant security stance builds resilience, enabling organizations to recover swiftly from security incidents, maintain business continuity, and mitigate potential financial and operational impacts.

Cost efficiency

While the initial implementation of a robust security framework might appear resource-intensive, the NIST RMF offers long-term cost-efficiency. By identifying and mitigating security risks, organizations reduce the potential financial impact of security incidents. Additionally, the standardization and automation of security processes lead to resource optimization, minimizing redundancy, and streamlining security operations.

Informed decision-making

In the NIST RMF, informed decision-making is a guiding principle. The structured approach ensures that decisions regarding system authorization are based on data-driven assessments of security controls. **Authorizing officials (AOs)** have access to comprehensive information, enabling them to make well-informed decisions about **Authorization to Operate (ATO)**. This empowers organizations to grant ATOs based on a thorough understanding of the security posture and risk mitigation strategies.

Flexibility and adaptability

The NIST RMF is not a one-size-fits-all approach; it can be adapted to an organization's unique needs. It accommodates various information systems, risk profiles, and mission requirements. This flexibility makes it suitable for a wide range of organizations, from government agencies to private enterprises, from small businesses to large corporations.

In conclusion, the adoption of the NIST RMF presents a multitude of advantages, from a structured risk management approach to enhanced security, regulatory compliance, cost-efficiency, and risk reduction. By aligning with industry standards, taking a holistic approach to risk management, and emphasizing efficiency through control inheritance and reuse, organizations can fortify their cybersecurity strategy. The NIST RMF empowers organizations to confront the dynamic and ever-evolving cybersecurity landscape with confidence, ensuring the protection of networks, systems, and, most importantly, their users. Now that we've examined the advantages, let's dive into the compliance and regulatory considerations of the NIST RMF.

Compliance and regulatory considerations

In the intricate world of cybersecurity, compliance with regulations and standards is an ever-present concern. Organizations, whether they operate in highly regulated sectors such as healthcare and finance or are subject to general data protection requirements, face a constant challenge to align their cybersecurity practices with an ever-evolving landscape of compliance and regulatory considerations. The NIST RMF emerges as a powerful tool to not only enhance cybersecurity but also streamline the journey toward compliance.

A common compliance challenge

One of the significant challenges organizations encounter is navigating the myriad of compliance requirements imposed by various regulatory bodies and industry standards. Healthcare organizations must adhere to the **Health Insurance Portability and Accountability Act (HIPAA)**, financial institutions must follow the **Gramm-Leach-Billey Act (GLBA)** and **Sarbanes-Oxley Act (SOX)**, and businesses that handle European Union citizens' data need to comply with the **General Data Protection Regulation (GDPR)**. Each of these regulations has its set of cybersecurity and privacy requirements, often leading to a convoluted web of obligations for organizations.

The role of the NIST RMF

The NIST RMF enters this complex landscape as a valuable navigator. While the RMF is not a regulation in itself, it functions as a comprehensive framework for managing cybersecurity risks in a structured, organized, and efficient manner. By adopting the RMF, organizations can streamline their approach to compliance with a wide array of regulations, enabling them to efficiently align their cybersecurity practices with the complex web of regulatory requirements.

Holistic compliance alignment

A notable advantage of the NIST RMF is its ability to holistically align an organization's cybersecurity practices with a variety of compliance requirements. This alignment takes place on multiple fronts. We'll discuss some of these here.

Control inheritance and alignment

The NIST RMF provides a standard set of security controls in *NIST Special Publication 800-53*, which encompass a wide range of security and privacy requirements. By implementing these controls, organizations inherently address numerous compliance obligations. This practice of control inheritance significantly simplifies the process of demonstrating compliance. For instance, the RMF's control set includes control families that cover access control, data protection, incident response, and audit and accountability – topics that are relevant to a multitude of regulations.

Standard documentation

Compliance often involves meticulously documenting security practices and control implementation. The NIST RMF inherently emphasizes the documentation of security control assessments, authorizations, and continuous monitoring. These documentation requirements not only support risk management but also serve as a foundational resource for demonstrating compliance. Organizations can utilize this documentation to illustrate their adherence to security controls and compliance mandates efficiently.

Risk management focus

Compliance efforts are closely intertwined with risk management. The RMF's risk-based approach means that organizations prioritize security controls and compliance measures based on their specific risk profile. This targeted approach ensures that resources are allocated efficiently, emphasizing control implementations that align with the most significant risk factors.

Specific regulatory considerations

Let's delve into a few specific examples to illustrate how the NIST RMF facilitates compliance with key regulations.

HIPAA compliance

HIPAA imposes stringent requirements for the protection of sensitive patient data. The NIST RMF's controls related to access control, audit and accountability, and encryption, among others, align closely with HIPAA's requirements. Organizations can confidently demonstrate their HIPAA compliance by adopting the RMF's security controls and aligning their security documentation with HIPAA mandates.

GDPR compliance

The GDPR mandates strict data protection and privacy requirements for organizations handling EU citizen data. The RMF's emphasis on data protection controls, audit trails, and incident response aligns naturally with GDPR requirements. By implementing RMF controls and documentation practices, organizations can efficiently demonstrate their compliance with GDPR's stringent privacy regulations.

Financial industry compliance

The financial sector is subject to a range of regulatory requirements, including the GLBA and the SOX. The RMF's controls related to financial data protection, audit trails, and internal controls align closely with these regulations. Organizations can leverage their RMF-aligned cybersecurity practices and documentation to streamline compliance with GLBA and SOX.

Compliance and the RMF life cycle

The NIST RMF life cycle – *Prepare, Categorize, Select, Implement, Assess, Authorize*, and *Monitor* – provides a structured approach to managing cybersecurity risks. This structured approach inherently supports compliance efforts by emphasizing the documentation of control implementations and assessments. Additionally, continuous monitoring within the RMF ensures that organizations maintain compliance over time, evolving alongside changes in regulatory requirements.

Efficiency through RMF compliance

An often-underestimated advantage of the NIST RMF is the efficiency it brings to compliance. By embracing control inheritance and alignment, organizations can significantly reduce the effort required to demonstrate compliance. The standard documentation practices of the RMF simplify the process of illustrating adherence to security controls and regulatory mandates. As a result, organizations can allocate their resources more effectively and minimize the effort required for compliance reporting and audits.

The NIST RMF serves as a great tool to help you navigate the intricate web of compliance and regulatory considerations. By adopting the RMF, organizations can holistically align their cybersecurity practices with a variety of regulations and standards. The RMF's focus on control inheritance, documentation, and risk management fosters an efficient and effective approach to compliance, streamlining the process of demonstrating adherence to security controls and regulatory mandates. As organizations grapple with the evolving landscape of compliance, the RMF stands as a valuable resource for building a resilient and compliant cybersecurity foundation. In the next section, we'll discuss strategies for business continuity and risk reduction using the NIST RMF.

Business continuity and risk reduction

In today's digital landscape, where cyber threats loom large and disruptions are a matter of *when*, not *if*, organizations must be equipped with robust strategies to ensure business continuity and mitigate risks effectively. The NIST RMF extends its influence beyond compliance and security enhancement, playing a pivotal role in fortifying business continuity and reducing risks.

Risk reduction with the NIST RMF

Risk management is at the heart of the NIST RMF, and the latest version of the framework incorporates evolving risk perspectives and best practices. Implementing the RMF empowers organizations to reduce risks in the following ways:

- **Proactive threat identification**: The RMF encourages organizations to take a proactive stance in identifying threats and vulnerabilities. This is achieved through the ongoing process of categorization and control assessments. By understanding and addressing potential threats before they escalate, organizations significantly reduce the likelihood of security incidents.

- **Systematic vulnerability management**: Vulnerabilities are inevitable in the constantly changing cybersecurity landscape. The RMF helps organizations manage vulnerabilities systematically by guiding them through the selection and implementation of security controls. This not only mitigates known vulnerabilities but also ensures that new vulnerabilities are promptly addressed through continuous monitoring.

- **Data-driven decision-making**: The RMF promotes data-driven decision-making, particularly during the authorization stage. AOs make informed decisions about system authorization based on risk assessments and control effectiveness. This approach ensures that security risks are adequately managed and aligned with organizational objectives.

- **Control inheritance and alignment**: By inheriting and aligning security controls from *NIST Special Publication 800-53*, organizations embrace a comprehensive set of controls that cover a wide array of security domains. This approach streamlines the implementation of controls, reducing the potential gaps in security and enhancing risk management.

- **Continuous monitoring**: Continuous monitoring is a cornerstone of the RMF. It ensures that organizations are continually aware of their security posture and can respond swiftly to emerging threats. This real-time awareness significantly reduces the window of opportunity for potential threats to exploit vulnerabilities.

- **Risk-centric approach**: The RMF adopts a risk-centric approach, where security controls and practices are tailored to an organization's specific risk profile. By focusing resources on areas with the highest risk, organizations maximize the efficiency of their risk reduction efforts.

- **Efficiency through standardization**: Standardization of control sets, documentation, and processes within the RMF enhances efficiency. Standard documentation practices ensure that security controls are consistently assessed and implemented, reducing the potential for errors and vulnerabilities.

Business continuity and disaster recovery

The NIST RMF is not solely about reducing risks but also about building resilience and ensuring business continuity. Let's look at several key aspects that contribute to business continuity and disaster recovery.

Incident response and recovery planning

The RMF integrates incident response and recovery planning, emphasizing the importance of preparing for and responding to security incidents. By implementing robust incident response plans, organizations can minimize the potential impact of security breaches and swiftly recover.

Business impact analysis

As part of risk management, the RMF encourages organizations to conduct a business impact analysis. This process involves identifying critical business functions, assessing the impact of disruptions, and developing strategies to maintain business continuity.

Disaster recovery techniques

Disaster recovery is a vital component of business continuity planning. The RMF promotes the development of disaster recovery plans that outline how an organization will restore critical systems and data in the event of a disaster. These techniques enhance an organization's ability to recover and continue operations in the face of adversity.

Policy framework

The RMF framework calls for the development of comprehensive security policies and procedures. These policies often include disaster recovery and business continuity elements, ensuring that these critical aspects are incorporated into an organization's security posture.

Testing and exercises

The RMF advocates for the regular testing and exercising of disaster recovery and incident response plans. By conducting tabletop exercises and simulations, organizations can identify weaknesses in their plans and make necessary improvements. These exercises ensure that the plans are effective and can be relied upon during actual incidents.

Resource allocation

The RMF emphasizes resource allocation as part of risk management. Allocating resources to business continuity and disaster recovery planning ensures that these critical functions receive the necessary support and attention to maintain operations during disruptions.

Business continuity as part of the RMF

For organizations that implement the RMF, business continuity is not a separate entity but an integral part of their risk management strategy. This integration ensures that an organization's risk reductions and business continuity efforts are tightly aligned, offering a comprehensive approach to resilience.

Benefits of business continuity and risk reduction

The integration of business continuity and risk reduction within the NIST RMF offers an array of benefits:

- **Enhanced resilience**: Business continuity planning and disaster recovery techniques bolster an organization's ability to withstand disruptions, ensuring that essential functions continue with minimal interruption.

- **Reduced downtime**: Effective business continuity measures reduce downtime in the event of security incidents or disasters, minimizing the potential financial and operational impact.

- **Stakeholder confidence**: Business continuity planning instills confidence in stakeholders, including customers, partners, and regulators. Knowing that an organization can maintain operations while conducting incident response builds trust.

- **Regulatory compliance**: Business continuity planning is often a regulatory requirement in various industries. By integrating it within the RMF, organizations can ensure compliance with these mandates.

- **Cost-efficiency**: Effective business continuity and risk reduction measures ultimately lead to cost-efficiency. By minimizing the impact of disruptions and reducing recovery time, organizations save resources that would otherwise be spent on recovery efforts.

The NIST RMF offers more than compliance and security enhancement; it presents an opportunity for organizations to build resilience, reduce risks, and ensure business continuity. By adopting a risk-centric approach, aligning security controls, and integrating business continuity and disaster recovery techniques, the RMF empowers organizations to navigate the dynamic and challenging cybersecurity landscape with confidence. As the RMF continues to evolve, its role in enhancing business continuity and risk reduction becomes even more pronounced, positioning it as a valuable asset in the pursuit of organizational resilience.

Summary

In this chapter, we explored the multifaceted advantages of implementing the NIST RMF beyond the realms of compliance and security enhancement. By delving into the world of business continuity and risk reduction, we uncovered a comprehensive approach that empowers organizations to fortify their resilience in the face of cybersecurity threats and disruptions. The skills gained we've gained here include a proactive risk reduction strategy, efficient compliance alignment, integration of business continuity, resource allocation for resilience, and the importance of testing and exercises. These skills are invaluable in safeguarding sensitive data, maintaining operational integrity, streamlining compliance efforts, reducing downtime, and saving resources, making them crucial for organizations navigating today's dynamic and threat-laden cybersecurity landscape.

As we continue our exploration of the NIST RMF, the next chapter, *Preparing for RMF Implementation*, takes us on a journey from theory to the practical application of the framework within an organization. There, we'll delve into the intricate process of building a proficient security team, setting clear organizational goals, developing a comprehensive risk management strategy, and guiding you through each step of the RMF implementation. The next chapter equips you with the essential tools and knowledge to navigate the complexities of preparing for a successful RMF implementation, providing you with a robust foundation for effectively securing your organization's digital assets and mitigating cybersecurity risks.

Part 2:
Implementing the NIST RMF in Your Organization

An overview is all well and good, but by now I'm sure you're asking, "*But I'm a <insert org-type here>! How do we implement this whole thing?*"

I'm with you. It's time to dig deeper. All too often in cybersecurity, we see loads of technical documentation; we see just as many tools that have been procured for our environment, and it can be overwhelming to even think about how to start. Rest assured, we're going to start easy here. This part of the book focuses on individual sections of the NIST RMF, but still from a high level. When you finish this part, you'll have a good understanding of the overall framework, its individual parts, and how you might be able to adapt this framework for your own use.

This part has the following chapters:

- *Chapter 4, Preparing for RMF Implementation*
- *Chapter 5, The NIST RMF Life Cycle*
- *Chapter 6, Security Controls and Documentation*
- *Chapter 7, Assessment and Authorization*

4

Preparing for RMF Implementation

In this pivotal chapter, we'll embark on a comprehensive journey to prepare organizations for the effective implementation of the NIST **Risk Management Framework** (**RMF**). The RMF, a cornerstone of modern cybersecurity practices, offers a structured process for managing organizational risks in an ever-evolving threat landscape. The focus of this chapter lies in laying the groundwork for a successful RMF application, a task that involves several critical steps: assembling a competent security team, setting clear organizational goals, developing a tailored risk management strategy, and understanding the RMF life cycle from preparation to authorization.

As we navigate these areas, you will gain practical insights and actionable guidance on each step of the preparation process. You will learn how to formulate and assemble an effective security team, define precise organizational security objectives, and develop a risk management strategy that aligns with your organization's unique needs and constraints. Furthermore, we will delve into the intricacies of the RMF process, providing you with a clear understanding of each phase, from preparation to continuous monitoring.

The lessons in this chapter are not just theoretical; they are steeped in the practical realities of implementing RMF in diverse organizational contexts. By the end of this chapter, you will have acquired the knowledge and skills necessary to kick-start the RMF in your organization. This includes an appreciation of the critical role of team dynamics in cybersecurity, an understanding of how to set achievable and relevant security goals, and the ability to craft a risk management strategy that is both robust and adaptable.

In this chapter, we're going to cover the following main topics:

- Building a security team
- Setting organizational goals
- Creating a risk management strategy
- Implementing the framework

Building a security team

In the context of the NIST RMF, building a robust security team is not merely a preliminary step but a critical foundation for successful framework implementation. The effectiveness of RMF hinges on a team's capability to interpret, apply, and manage the framework's intricacies tailored to the organization's unique security requirements. This section delves into the nuances of assembling a competent team equipped with the right blend of skills, roles, and dynamics to navigate the RMF effectively.

Detailed roles and skills

A comprehensive RMF team composition should encompass a range of roles, each with specialized skills and qualifications:

- **RMF program manager**:

  - **Key responsibilities**: Leads the RMF implementation, coordinates between various stakeholders, and ensures adherence to the NIST guidelines.

  - **Required skills**: Strong leadership qualities, extensive knowledge of cybersecurity, and proficiency in project management. The ability to translate technical risks into business impacts is crucial.

- **Security control assessor (SCA)**:

  - **Key responsibilities**: Conducts thorough assessments of security controls, evaluates compliance with standards, and identifies potential vulnerabilities

  - **Required skills**: Expertise in various assessment tools and techniques, a deep understanding of security architectures, and the ability to document and report findings effectively

- **System owner**:

  - **Key responsibilities**: Manages the security aspects of specific information systems, ensuring they align with organizational objectives

  - **Required skills**: In-depth knowledge of the system's technical framework and risk management abilities, and a clear understanding of the system's operational context

- **Authorizing official (AO)**:

  - **Key responsibilities**: Makes the final decision on system authorization, balancing operational needs with security risks

  - **Required skills**: Strategic decision-making abilities, risk evaluation expertise, and a broad understanding of organizational risk tolerance

- **Additional team roles**:

  - Consider including roles such as cybersecurity analysts, network engineers, compliance specialists, and legal advisors to address specific aspects of the RMF process

Forming and managing the team

In building the security team, an organization should provide the following:

- **Internal resource assessment**: Evaluate current staff's skills and potential for role adaptation or advancement

- **External recruitment**: When necessary, hire externally to fill gaps in expertise

- **Diversity and inclusion**: Aim for a diverse team in terms of skills, backgrounds, and perspectives to enhance problem-solving and innovation

- **Team integration**: Facilitate team-building activities and regular meetings to foster cohesion and align goals

Enhancing team dynamics

The following are two suggestions to improve team dynamics as you build your team:

- **Communication channels**: Establish clear, open lines of communication for sharing information, feedback, and collaborative decision-making

- **Conflict resolution**: Implement strategies for managing disagreements constructively, ensuring they lead to productive outcomes

Continuous education and training

In cybersecurity, a robust training program is critical to staying in front of the threat landscape and the myriad of policy changes that could affect your organization. A solid training program should include the following:

- **Training programs**: Regularly scheduled training sessions should be a staple, focusing on new RMF updates, emerging cybersecurity trends, and advanced risk management techniques

- **Professional development**: Encourage team members to pursue certifications, attend workshops, and engage in continuous learning

- **Knowledge-sharing sessions**: Organize internal seminars where team members can share insights and lessons learned from their professional experiences and external engagements

Assembling a well-rounded security team is a pivotal step in preparing for RMF implementation. This team should not only encompass a broad spectrum of technical and managerial skills but also demonstrate a commitment to continuous learning and adaptability. By investing in the right people and fostering a culture of collaboration and ongoing education, an organization can effectively navigate the complexities of the RMF, thereby enhancing its overall security posture in an ever-evolving cyber landscape.

Setting organizational goals

The establishment of organizational goals is a pivotal step in the implementation of the NIST RMF. These goals are not mere statements of intent; they are the guiding force that directs the selection and application of security controls, shapes the risk management processes, and defines the overall cybersecurity posture of an organization. Ideally, these goals should be intertwined with the organization's broader mission and operational needs, while also addressing specific cybersecurity risks. They act as the bridge that connects the technical aspects of RMF with the strategic objectives of the organization.

Assessing organizational context for goal setting

The process of setting goals begins with a comprehensive assessment of the organization's current cybersecurity state. This initial step involves identifying existing security measures, pinpointing critical assets and data, and recognizing potential vulnerabilities that might impact the organization. Additionally, understanding the business objectives is crucial. For instance, an organization that prioritizes customer data privacy should reflect this in its RMF goals, emphasizing stringent data protection controls.

Stakeholder engagement is another critical aspect of this assessment. It's important to involve various groups, including management, IT staff, and end users, in discussions to gather a broad perspective. Their insights can provide valuable inputs in setting goals that are not only technically sound but also align with the expectations and needs of different segments within the organization.

Crafting and aligning RMF goals with business objectives

Creating goals for RMF should follow the **SMART** framework – **Specific, Measurable, Achievable, Relevant, and Time-Bound**. For example, a specific and measurable goal could be the implementation of multifactor authentication across all user accounts within a set timeframe. Such goals should not only focus on enhancing the security of customer data or achieving compliance with industry regulations but should also consider the operational impact and user experience.

Aligning these goals with business objectives is a strategic endeavor. It involves understanding the organization's risk appetite and defining goals that reflect this appetite. For instance, a financial institution's lower risk tolerance will shape its cybersecurity goals differently from a tech startup. This alignment ensures that RMF goals support the broader business strategy and do not operate in isolation.

Developing, documenting, and communicating goals

Documenting the set goals is crucial for reference and accountability. This documentation should detail the rationale behind each goal, the expected outcomes, and the timelines for achievement. Communicating these goals is equally important. This could range from formal presentations to the leadership to training sessions for IT staff, and even simple communications to the general staff. Such communication helps in fostering a security-aware culture within the organization.

Reviewing and adapting goals

Setting organizational goals for RMF is not a one-time activity. It requires regular reviews to assess progress and adapt as necessary. These reviews could be part of periodic business reviews or annual audits. In a dynamic cybersecurity landscape, the ability to adapt goals in response to changing business environments or emerging threats is crucial. This adaptability ensures that the organization's RMF goals remain relevant and effective over time.

In summary, setting organizational goals for RMF implementation is a multifaceted process that requires a deep understanding of the organization's operational context, stakeholder needs, and risk appetite. These goals should be specific, measurable, and aligned with both the organization's cybersecurity needs and its broader business objectives. Through careful planning, documentation, and communication, these goals lay the foundation for a successful and effective implementation of the RMF, enhancing the organization's overall security posture and resilience against cyber threats.

Creating a risk management strategy

When considering the creation of a risk management strategy to implement the NIST RMF, we must consider some foundational topics and strategies, as well as how to effectively document and communicate.

Risk assessment foundations

The foundation of any robust risk management strategy, especially within the framework of the NIST RMF, begins with a comprehensive risk assessment. This process is integral to identifying and understanding the various cybersecurity threats, vulnerabilities, and potential impacts that an organization might face:

- **Understanding threats and vulnerabilities**: The first step in risk assessment is identifying the threats that could potentially harm the organization's assets. These threats could range from external threats, such as cyberattacks and hacking, to internal threats, such as employee error or system failure. Concurrently, identifying vulnerabilities and weaknesses in systems or processes that could be exploited by threats is essential. This involves examining the organization's IT infrastructure, policies, and procedures to pinpoint areas susceptible to breach or failure.

- **Assessing potential impacts**: After identifying threats and vulnerabilities, the next step is evaluating the potential impact. This involves considering the consequences of a successful threat exploitation. Questions such as *"What would be the impact on our operations if this system were compromised?"* or *"What would be the data loss consequences of a particular vulnerability being exploited?"* help in understanding the severity of different risk scenarios.

Risk response strategies

Developing a risk response strategy is about deciding how to address the risks identified in the assessment phase. There are generally four ways to handle risks:

- **Accepting risk**: Sometimes, the cost of mitigating a risk may outweigh the potential damage. In such cases, an organization might choose to accept the risk, acknowledging and preparing for its potential impacts.

- **Avoiding risk**: This involves changing plans or processes to eliminate a risk or its impacts. For example, if a particular technology is deemed too vulnerable, the organization might decide not to use it.

- **Transferring risk**: Often, risks can be transferred to a third party, such as through insurance or outsourcing certain functions to companies with better capabilities to manage that risk.

- **Mitigating risk**: This is perhaps the most common response and involves taking steps to reduce the likelihood or impact of a risk. This could include implementing new security controls, updating policies, or training staff.

Implementing these strategies often involves a combination of approaches. For instance, an organization might mitigate the risk of data breaches by implementing stronger security measures, transferring some of the risks through cybersecurity insurance, and accepting the residual risk that remains.

Documentation and communication

Once a risk management strategy has been developed, documenting and communicating it becomes critical:

- **Documentation**: This involves creating a formal record of the risk management strategy, including the identified risks, the chosen response strategies, and the rationale behind these choices. This documentation serves as a reference for current and future risk management activities and provides an audit trail for compliance purposes.

- **Communication**: Effectively communicating the risk management strategy to stakeholders is vital. This includes not only the security team and top management but also employees across the organization. Clear communication ensures that everyone understands the risks and their roles in managing them. It also helps in fostering a culture of security awareness within the organization.

Creating a risk management strategy as part of the RMF implementation is a detailed process that requires a thorough understanding of the organization's threat landscape, a strategic approach to addressing these risks, and effective documentation and communication. By carefully assessing risks, choosing appropriate response strategies, and ensuring that these plans are well-documented and communicated, organizations can build a robust foundation for their RMF efforts, enhancing their resilience against cybersecurity threats.

Implementing the framework

Now that we have built our team, selected our organizational goals, and coalesced around a risk strategy, we're ready to implement the RMF. This section will walk through each phase of the RMF and provide an implementation strategy.

Preparation phase

The **preparation phase** is the cornerstone of the NIST RMF, setting the stage for all subsequent actions. This phase involves a series of critical steps designed to ensure a thorough understanding of the system and its environment, alongside a keen awareness of the relevant regulatory compliance requirements. It is during this phase that organizations lay the groundwork for a tailored and effective implementation of the RMF.

Understanding the system and its environment

In the preparation phase, an understanding of the architecture of the organization's environment is crucial. Here are some considerations to keep in mind:

- **System identification and characterization**: The first step involves identifying and characterizing the information system. This means understanding what the system does, the type of data it handles, how it interacts with other systems, and its importance to the organization. For example, a hospital's patient record system would require careful characterization due to how it handles sensitive health data.

- **Technology infrastructure analysis**: Analyzing the system's technology infrastructure is crucial. This includes examining hardware, software, networks, and data storage solutions. The goal is to understand the technical makeup of the system to identify potential vulnerabilities and security needs.

- **Operational environment assessment**: Equally important is assessing the operational environment in which the system functions. This involves understanding the physical and logical connections to other systems, the user base, and the operational processes the system supports. For instance, a financial transaction system in a bank would require an understanding of how it links to other banking systems and its role in daily banking operations.

Regulatory compliance considerations

Regulatory compliance is a major consideration in any cybersecurity strategy but plays a large factor in risk management. The following are some things to keep in mind:

- **Identify relevant regulations and standards**: Different industries are subject to various regulations and standards. Identifying these is a critical step in the Preparation Phase. For a healthcare provider, this might involve ensuring compliance with HIPAA, whereas a financial institution might focus on SOX or **Payment Card Industry Data Security Standard (PCI DSS)** compliance.

- **Compliance gap analysis**: Once the relevant regulations have been identified, conducting a compliance gap analysis is essential. This means assessing the current state of the system against the compliance requirements and identifying areas where the system falls short. This gap analysis helps in pinpointing specific areas that need attention during the RMF process.

- **Legal and ethical considerations**: Beyond technical and operational aspects, legal and ethical considerations must also be taken into account. This includes understanding data privacy laws, intellectual property rights, and ethical implications related to the system's function and data handling.

Preparatory steps for RMF implementation

Before you move forward with implementing the RMF in your organization, you'll want to consider the following factors:

1. **Stakeholder engagement**: Engaging stakeholders early in the process is crucial for successful RMF implementation. This includes system owners, IT staff, end users, and senior management. Their input and buy-in are essential for understanding the system's role, its criticality, and the potential impact of RMF implementation on business operations.

2. **Risk assessment preparation**: Preparing for a comprehensive risk assessment is a key preparatory step. This involves establishing the criteria for evaluating risk, including the likelihood of threat occurrence and the potential impact on the organization. For example, in a manufacturing firm, the risk assessment would focus on the potential for operational disruptions and the impact on production.

3. **Resource allocation**: Allocating the necessary resources – both human and technological – is vital. This includes determining the personnel needed for RMF implementation, the budget for security enhancements, and the tools required for risk assessment and monitoring.

4. **Training and awareness programs**: Implementing training and awareness programs for staff involved in RMF processes and general users of the information system is important. This ensures that all parties understand their roles and responsibilities in maintaining security and complying with RMF requirements.

5. **Developing a communication plan**: A well-structured communication plan is essential to keep all stakeholders informed throughout the RMF process. This plan should outline how updates will be communicated, the frequency of communication, and the channels used.

The preparation phase of the RMF is a comprehensive process that requires a deep understanding of the information system, its operational environment, and the relevant regulatory compliance requirements. Through careful planning, stakeholder engagement, and resource allocation, organizations can lay a solid foundation for the successful implementation of the RMF. This phase not only sets the direction for the entire RMF process but also ensures that the organization's cybersecurity measures are aligned with its operational needs and compliance obligations.

Categorize phase

The categorize phase is a critical step in the NIST RMF where information systems are classified based on the potential impact of a compromise on the **confidentiality, integrity, and availability (CIA)** of the information they process, store, or transmit. This classification guides the selection of appropriate security controls in later phases and is fundamental to establishing an effective risk management strategy.

Understanding the importance of categorization

It's important to understand the purpose of categorizing assets, along with their impact if compromised. Ideally, this should be aligned with the CIA triad, and organizational priorities, as discussed ahead:

- **Purpose of categorization**: Categorization helps in understanding the criticality of the information system to the organization's mission and the potential consequences of security breaches. It lays the foundation for all subsequent RMF steps by providing a clear understanding of what needs to be protected and why.

- **Aligning with organizational priorities**: The categorization process must align with the organization's overall risk management strategy and priorities. For instance, a system handling sensitive customer data in a financial institution will be categorized differently from an internal employee communication system.

Steps in the categorization phase

Now that we've covered the foundations, let's discuss how to accomplish the categorization phase:

1. **Identify information types**: The process begins with identifying the types of information the system handles. This includes classifying data types (for example, personal, financial, and operational) and understanding the context of their use within the system.

2. **Assess impact levels**: Using FIPS 199 standards, each information type is assessed for potential impact levels regarding confidentiality, integrity, and availability. For example, personal data leakage would have a high impact on confidentiality, whereas corruption of financial records would primarily impact integrity.

3. **Determine system categorization**: The overall categorization of the system is determined based on the highest impact level among the information types it processes. If a system handles multiple types of information, each with different impact levels, the system's categorization will reflect the highest of these levels.

Practical examples of system categorization

Let's look at a few examples of organizations and industry verticals and how they accomplished the categorization phase of the RMF:

- **Healthcare organization**: In a hospital's patient management system, the primary concern is the confidentiality and integrity of patient health records. Given the sensitivity of health data and regulatory requirements such as HIPAA, such a system would likely be categorized with a high impact on both confidentiality and integrity.

- **eCommerce platform**: An online retail system would prioritize the availability of the platform to ensure uninterrupted customer access and transaction processing. The integrity of financial transactions and confidentiality of customer data would also be critical, requiring a balanced approach to categorization.

- **Manufacturing control system**: For a manufacturing plant, the **operational technology/ industrial control systems (OT/ICS)** responsible for controlling production processes might prioritize availability to prevent operational disruptions. The integrity of these systems is also crucial to ensure accurate and safe operational commands.

Challenges and considerations in categorization

There are many considerations in categorizing the assets in your organization. Here are just a few:

- **Balancing security and operational needs**: While categorizing systems at higher levels offers greater security, it can also introduce complexity and operational overhead. Organizations must balance security needs with practical considerations of implementation and maintenance.

- **Evolving threat landscape**: The categorization process is not static. As the threat landscape evolves, organizations must reassess the categorization of their systems to ensure continued alignment with current threats and organizational priorities.

- **Regulatory and compliance factors**: Compliance requirements often influence system categorization. Systems must be categorized not only based on impact analysis but also considering the compliance obligations pertinent to the data types and sectors they operate in.

Documentation and validation

Just as important as categorizing assets is documentation. This is vital so team members and leadership alike understand how the process was accomplished. Here are some considerations:

- **Document the categorization phase**: Comprehensive documentation of the categorization process is vital. This includes recording the rationale for impact-level decisions, the methodology used, and any assumptions or constraints considered.

- **Review and validation**: The categorization should be reviewed and validated by relevant stakeholders, including system owners, security experts, and compliance officers. This validation ensures that the categorization accurately reflects the system's security needs and organizational priorities.

The categorize phase of the RMF is a strategic process that requires careful analysis of the information types that are handled by a system and their potential impact on the organization. Through practical examples, we'll see how this phase plays a crucial role in shaping the overall security strategy for information systems. By aligning categorization with organizational priorities, regulatory requirements, and the evolving threat landscape, organizations can lay a solid foundation for the effective and efficient implementation of the RMF. This phase not only guides the selection of appropriate security controls but also ensures that the organization's resources are focused on protecting its most critical assets.

Select phase

After categorizing information systems, the select phase in the NIST RMF involves choosing appropriate security controls. These controls are selected based on the system's categorization and are intended to mitigate identified risks to an acceptable level. Selecting controls is a critical process that requires a deep understanding of the system's security requirements and the organization's risk management strategy.

Understanding security controls

In the select phase, it's important to understand the security controls when choosing which to apply to your assets. Let's review some definitions and resources that can be utilized:

- **Definition of security controls**: Security controls are safeguards or countermeasures to avoid, detect, counteract, or minimize security risks to physical or digital assets. These controls can be managerial, operational, or technical.

- **NIST SP 800-53 security control catalog**: This catalog provides a comprehensive list of security controls that can be tailored to meet the specific needs of an organization. The selection of controls is guided by the system's impact level determined in the categorize phase.

Steps in the select phase

The select phase is tedious and repetitive since you review each asset identified in the categorize phase, and then work to choose the controls. You should do the following for each asset individually and review this process periodically:

1. **Review system categorization**: The selection process begins with a review of the system's categorization to ensure an understanding of the security requirements.

2. **Identify applicable controls**: Based on the system's categorization, relevant controls from NIST SP 800-53 are identified. This involves considering the baseline security controls and tailoring them so that they address specific organizational needs and risks.

3. **Tailor controls**: Tailoring involves adding, modifying, or removing controls from the baseline to suit the specific conditions and environment of the organization. Factors such as regulatory requirements, operational environment, and specific threats play a crucial role in this process.

Practical examples of control selection

Let's look at a few examples:

- **Financial institution**: For a system categorized by a high impact on confidentiality and integrity, such as a banking transaction system, controls related to encryption, access control, and audit logging would be prioritized. This may include advanced encryption methods for data at rest and in transit, multi-factor authentication for access, and comprehensive audit trails for transaction monitoring.

- **Public sector agency**: A public service portal with a high requirement for availability might focus on controls that ensure system uptime and data redundancy. This could involve implementing network resilience measures, backup solutions, and regular testing of disaster recovery procedures.

- **Healthcare provider**: For a healthcare system handling sensitive patient data, controls focused on data confidentiality and integrity would be essential. This might include strict access controls, data encryption, and regular security training for staff handling patient information.

Challenges and considerations in control selection

As much as we can do our best to select the appropriate controls, it can be easy to lose sight of the big picture – that is, that security exists to support the business objectives. Some considerations to keep in mind are as follows:

- **Balancing security and usability**: Selecting the right balance of controls is crucial. Overly restrictive controls can impede usability and efficiency, while insufficient controls can leave the system vulnerable.

- **Cost and resource constraints**: Organizations must also consider the cost and resources required to implement and maintain selected controls. This requires a cost-benefit analysis to ensure that the controls are both effective and feasible.

- **Evolving threats and technologies**: The controls that are chosen must be adaptable to evolving threats and changes in technology. Regular reviews and updates of the selected controls are necessary to ensure ongoing effectiveness.

Documentation and approval

Just as with the previous phase, documenting and approving the selected controls are almost as important as selecting the controls. The following are some thoughts to keep in mind:

- **Document the control selection**: Comprehensive documentation of the selected controls, including the rationale for their selection and any tailoring performed, is essential. This documentation forms part of the system security plan.

- **Stakeholder review and approval**: The selected controls should be reviewed and approved by relevant stakeholders, including system owners, security experts, and compliance officers, to ensure alignment with organizational goals and compliance requirements.

The select phase of the RMF is a critical process where security controls are chosen to protect the organization's information systems based on their categorization. This phase requires careful consideration of the system's security needs, the organization's risk management strategy, and the operational environment. Through practical examples, we see how selecting controls is tailored to address specific requirements and challenges. The effective selection of controls not only mitigates risks but also supports the organization's mission and operational needs, ensuring a secure and resilient information environment.

Implement phase

After selecting the appropriate security controls during the select phase, the RMF progresses to the implement phase. This phase involves deploying and integrating the chosen security controls into the information system and its environment. The effectiveness of the RMF hinges significantly on how well these controls are implemented.

Understanding security control implementation

The following are some considerations related to implementing security controls:

- **Role of security controls in risk management**: Security controls are the tools and practices that reduce risk to an organization's information and systems. Their implementation is crucial to protecting against threats and vulnerabilities and to ensure compliance with regulatory requirements.

- **Integration with system operations**: The implementation process must integrate controls seamlessly into the existing system operations without causing significant disruption. This requires careful planning and coordination with various stakeholders.

Steps in the implement phase

When implementing controls, the team must keep the following key steps in mind. Implementing controls can be very complex, and the tenets of the CIA triad must be kept in mind, as well as the business case for each control:

1. **Develop implementation plans**: Each selected control requires a specific implementation plan detailing the steps, resources, personnel, and timeline needed for effective deployment.

2. **System modifications**: Some controls may necessitate modifications to the system, such as software updates, new hardware installations, or changes to network configurations.

3. **Policy and process development**: Implementation often involves developing or updating policies and processes to support the effective operation of the controls, such as access control policies or incident response procedures.

4. **Training and awareness**: Staff training and awareness are key components of implementation. Employees need to understand the new controls, their purpose, and how to effectively adhere to them.

Practical examples of control implementation

Let's look at a few examples:

- **Implementing access controls in a corporate network**: For a system requiring enhanced access controls, implementation might include deploying a new identity and access management solution, establishing multi-factor authentication for system access, and training employees on new access procedures.

- **Deploying encryption in a healthcare system**: In a healthcare setting where patient data confidentiality is paramount, implementing encryption might involve installing encryption software for data at rest and in transit, encrypting databases, and training staff on handling encrypted data.

- **Setting up intrusion detection systems (IDSs) in a financial institution**: Implementing an IDS in a financial institution might involve installing IDS software or hardware, configuring it to monitor network traffic for suspicious activities, and integrating it with the existing security incident and event management system.

Challenges and considerations in the implement phase

Every phase of the plan will have its challenges, and you will no doubt run into some of the following:

- **Compatibility with existing systems**: Ensuring that new controls are compatible with existing systems and processes is crucial to avoid disruptions

- **Resource allocation**: Adequate resources, including budget, personnel, and technology, must be allocated to ensure successful implementation

- **Change management**: Implementation often requires change management to address resistance and ensure the smooth integration of new controls into the organization's culture and practices

Documentation and assessment

As with the previous phases, documentation is vital. A change management system, or using **Infrastructure as Code (IaC)** to control those changes, is one way to accomplish this task. Consider the following:

- **Documenting the implementation**: Detailed documentation of how each control has been implemented, including any configurations, settings, or procedural changes, is essential for future reference and audits.

- **Preliminary control effectiveness assessment**: An initial assessment of the newly implemented controls' effectiveness should be conducted to ensure they are functioning as intended and to identify any immediate issues.

The implement phase of the RMF is a critical juncture where selected security controls are put into action within the organization's information systems. This phase demands meticulous planning, effective resource management, and thorough documentation. Through practical examples, we've seen the varied nature of implementation across different types of systems and organizations. Successfully implementing these controls is key to strengthening the organization's cybersecurity posture and advancing its overall risk management strategy.

Assess phase

The assess phase is a critical component of the NIST RMF, where the effectiveness of the implemented security controls is evaluated. This phase ensures that the controls are functioning as intended and provides an understanding of the extent to which they reduce or manage risks.

Understanding the assessment of security controls

What good is implementing all of the preceding phases if you don't assess that they are doing what you intended? Here are some details regarding the assess phase of the RMF:

- **Objective of the assessment**: The primary objective of the assess phase is to determine the effectiveness of security controls in meeting the organization's security requirements. It involves a comprehensive review of how controls operate within the system and their impact on the organization's overall risk posture.

- **The assessment process**: The process encompasses various methods, including testing, examining, and interviewing, to gather sufficient evidence about the control's effectiveness.

Steps in the assess phase

Now, let's dive into the steps of the assessment phase. This should be a methodical approach that involves creating a plan, gathering the necessary evidence, and, finally, evaluating the results:

1. **Develop an assessment plan**: The first step involves creating a detailed assessment plan that outlines the objectives, scope, methodology, and criteria for evaluating the security controls.

2. **Gather assessment evidence**: This involves conducting tests, audits, and evaluations to gather evidence on the performance of the controls. This can include automated scans, manual testing, and reviewing policy and procedure documentation.

3. **Analyze assessment results**: The collected evidence is analyzed to determine if the controls are effective in their implementation and operation, and if they meet the organization's risk management needs.

Practical examples of control assessment

Let's look at a few examples:

- **Assessing access controls in an IT system**: For a corporate IT system, assessing access controls might involve reviewing user access logs, testing user authentication and authorization processes, and interviewing staff to understand their awareness of access policies.

- **Evaluating encryption controls in a data storage system**: In a system where data encryption is crucial, the assessment might include testing encryption algorithms, examining key management practices, and ensuring encrypted data is inaccessible without proper authorization.

- **Testing intrusion detection systems in a network environment**: Evaluating the effectiveness of an IDS could involve simulating attacks to see if the system detects and responds appropriately, reviewing incident response records, and checking the configuration of the IDS for proper coverage of the network.

Challenges and considerations in assessment

One of the biggest challenges you may run across when working on the assessment is maintaining objectivity. Some other challenges are as follows:

- **Maintaining objectivity**: The assessment process must be objective and unbiased. This might involve using third-party assessors or ensuring that the assessment team is independent of the control implementation team.

- **Dealing with complex systems**: In complex systems, assessing all controls thoroughly can be challenging. Prioritizing controls based on risk and impact can help manage this complexity.

- **Adapting to evolving threats**: The assessment process should be adaptive to evolving threats and changing organizational contexts. This may require updating assessment methods and criteria over time.

Documentation and reporting

Let's look at some things to keep in mind when reporting on the assessment phase:

- **Document the assessment process**: Comprehensive documentation of the assessment process, including methodologies used, evidence gathered, and findings, is essential for transparency and future reference.

- **Report the assessment process's outcomes**: The results of the assessment should be compiled into a report that includes recommendations for improving control effectiveness. This report is crucial for decision-makers and stakeholders to understand the security posture of the system.

The assess phase of the RMF plays a pivotal role in verifying the effectiveness of implemented security controls. This phase requires detailed planning, objective execution, and thorough documentation and reporting. Through practical examples, we saw the diverse nature of assessments across different systems and control types. The outcomes of this phase not only inform the organization of the current state of its security controls but also guide future actions to enhance the overall security and risk management strategy.

Authorize phase

The authorize phase is a critical decision-making point in the NIST RMF where senior leadership, typically through the **authorizing official** (**AO**), determines whether the risks associated with an information system are acceptable. This phase involves reviewing all the documentation and assessments from previous phases to make an informed decision about the system's authorization to operate.

Understanding the authorization decision

Accepting risk is the nature of every leadership role, and the decisions that are made here can have huge implications. Here are some foundations to help you in those decisions:

- **Purpose of authorization**: The authorization decision is about accepting the risk to organizational operations, assets, or individuals based on the implementation and effectiveness of security controls. It signifies a formal acknowledgment and acceptance of the residual risk.

- **Role of the AO**: The AO, often a senior leader within the organization, is responsible for the authorization decision. They must weigh the security posture of the system against the mission and operational needs of the organization.

Steps in the authorize phase

The following steps in the authorize phase should be followed for every identified deficiency in the assessment conducted:

1. **Review assessment results**: The AO reviews the results of the security control assessments, including any identified deficiencies or weaknesses in the system's security posture.

2. **Examine supporting documentation**: This includes reviewing the **system security plan** (**SSP**), risk assessment report, and **plan of action and milestones** (**POA&M**) to understand the security measures and plans in place for addressing any shortcomings.

3. **Consider risk impact**: The AO evaluates the potential impact of the identified risks on the organization's operations, assets, individuals, and other organizations.

Practical examples of authorization decisions

Let's look at a few examples:

- **Authorizing a financial system**: For a financial system handling sensitive transactions, the AO would review controls related to data protection, transaction integrity, and fraud detection. The decision to authorize would depend on the system's ability to mitigate risks to an acceptable level, considering the potential financial and reputational impact on the organization.

- **Authorizing a healthcare system**: In a healthcare setting, the authorization decision would focus on patient data confidentiality, system availability for critical care, and compliance with health regulations such as HIPAA. The AO must ensure that the system adequately protects patient information while supporting healthcare operations.

- **Authorizing a government agency's data system**: For a government agency, the AO would assess the system's ability to protect classified or sensitive information, ensure data integrity, and support essential public services. The decision would involve balancing security needs with the public's interest and regulatory compliance.

Challenges and considerations in authorization

As we discussed earlier, authorization is extremely important. The decisions that are made on accepting versus mitigating risk can have a large impact, especially if a breach occurs due to a risk you chose to accept. Consider the following:

- **Balancing risk and operations**: One of the key challenges for the AO is to balance the security risks with the operational needs and benefits of the system. This often involves making tough decisions on whether the residual risk is within the organization's risk tolerance.

- **Evolving threat landscape**: The AO must consider the dynamic nature of cyber threats and the system's ability to adapt and respond to these evolving challenges.

- **Stakeholder involvement**: Gaining consensus and input from various stakeholders, including IT staff, security experts, and business unit leaders, is crucial for a well-informed authorization decision.

Documentation and continuous monitoring

A key part of authorization is being able to look back and understand the reason behind the decision to accept risk. Here are some key things to keep in mind and do during this process:

- **Document the authorization decision**: The AO's decision, along with the rationale and any conditions or constraints, should be formally documented. This often results in the issuance of an **Authorization to Operate (ATO)** or an interim authorization.

- **POA&M**: If there are outstanding security issues, a POA&M is developed to document the organization's plan for addressing these deficiencies and improving the security posture.

- **Requirement for continuous monitoring**: The authorization decision is not the end of the RMF process. It requires ongoing monitoring and reassessment of the system's security controls to ensure continued risk management.

The authorize phase of the RMF is a crucial decision point where the AO assesses whether the risks posed by an information system are acceptable and whether the system can be authorized to operate. This phase requires careful consideration of the assessment results, supporting documentation, and the organization's risk tolerance. Through practical examples, we saw how authorization decisions vary across different types of systems and operational contexts. The outcome of this phase is vital not only for the system's operational approval but also for the ongoing management of cybersecurity risk within the organization.

Summary

In this chapter, we embarked on the comprehensive journey of preparing for RMF implementation, laying out the foundational knowledge and practical skills that are essential for implementing the NIST RMF in an organization. This chapter has methodically walked through the crucial preparatory steps, offering a deep dive into each phase of the RMF and providing practical strategies for effective execution.

These are the key lessons we covered:

- **Building a security team**: We explored the significance of assembling a well-rounded security team, highlighting the roles, skills, and dynamics necessary to effectively navigate the RMF process

- **Setting organizational goals**: This section underscored the importance of aligning RMF implementation with the organization's broader objectives, emphasizing the creation of SMART goals that resonate with both cybersecurity needs and business strategies

- **Creating a risk management strategy**: This section discussed conducting a thorough risk assessment, developing tailored risk response strategies, and the importance of documentation and communication in crafting a robust risk management plan

- **RMF process steps – Prepare, Categorize, Select, Implement, Assess, Authorize, and Monitor**: Each phase of the RMF was detailed, offering insights into the practical application of these steps, from understanding the system and its environment in the preparation phase to making informed authorization decisions post-assessment

The skills and knowledge you've gained in this chapter are vital for any organization looking to enhance its security posture by minimizing the risks through the RMF. Understanding and applying these principles will lead to a more structured and effective approach to managing cybersecurity risks.

Looking ahead, the next chapter, *The NIST RMF Life Cycle*, will build upon this foundation. It will guide you through the entire life cycle of the RMF, emphasizing the ongoing nature of risk management. This chapter will also provide valuable advice on tailoring the framework to specific organizational needs, ensuring that the RMF is not just implemented but also effectively integrated and maintained as part of the organization's continuous security and risk management efforts. This progression is the natural next step, moving from preparation and initial implementation to sustaining and optimizing RMF processes over time.

The NIST RMF Life Cycle

In this chapter, we dive into the nuanced journey of the NIST **Risk Management Framework (RMF)**, a journey that is both cyclical and evolving. Unlike the foundational setup discussed in the previous chapter, this segment focuses on guiding you through the life cycle of the RMF, emphasizing the dynamic nature of risk management in the cyber world. Here, we will navigate through a detailed step-by-step breakdown of the RMF stages, not merely revisiting what was covered in *Chapter 4* but expanding on it with a focus on real-world applicability and tailoring the framework to specific organizational needs.

In this chapter, we're going to cover the following main topics:

- Step-by-step breakdown of the RMF stages
- Tailoring the RMF to your organization
- Case studies and examples

Step-by-step breakdown of the RMF stages

This section provides a breakdown of the RMF stages as a reminder of the details we covered in the previous chapter. Utilize this section as a guideline to refer back to as you work through tailoring the RMF to your organization, and learn about how other organizations have implemented the NIST RMF.

Here are the RMF stages:

- **Prepare**:
  - **Scope definition**: Establish the RMF's scope across the organization. This includes what departments will participate in the process, as well as what infrastructure will be evaluated. In some cases, this may not be every network the organization utilizes based on segmentation.
  - **Resource identification**: Identify necessary resources, including personnel and technology. This can also include planning for the time to conduct the process as well as costs.
  - **Risk assessment foundation**: Develop a foundational understanding of risk assessment principles.

- **Categorize**:

  - **System and information valuation**: Evaluate systems and information in terms of criticality and sensitivity.

  - **Impact analysis**: Analyze potential impacts on confidentiality, integrity, and availability.

- **Select**:

  - **Control selection**: Choose appropriate baseline security controls.

  - **Tailoring and supplementing**: Adapt controls to specific organizational contexts and add supplementary measures if necessary.

- **Implement**:

  - **Control implementation**: Put the selected controls into practice within the organizational environment.

  - **Documentation**: Thoroughly document the implementation details.

- **Assess**:

  - **Effectiveness evaluation**: Assess the effectiveness of the implemented controls with meaningful metrics – for example, the number of vulnerabilities present in the network and how that has changed over time.

  - **Documentation of assessment**: Record findings and identify areas needing improvement.

- **Authorize**:

  - **Risk determination**: Evaluate the residual risk against organizational risk tolerance.

  - **Decision-making**: The Authorizing Official makes an authorization decision based on the risk assessment.

- **Monitor**:

  - **Continuous monitoring**: Implement ongoing surveillance of the security controls. This could include audit logging or control dashboards, among others.

  - **Review and update**: Regularly review and update the security controls and risk management strategies.

Each of these stages involves specific activities that collectively form a comprehensive approach to managing organizational risk through the NIST RMF. This breakdown offers a guide for organizations to understand and navigate through each stage, aligning their cybersecurity efforts with their overall risk management and business objectives.

Tailoring the RMF to your organization

Standards can be a useful template for your organization but they have to be tailored to fit correctly. The RMF is no exception. In this section, we'll cover foundational ideas to keep in mind when working to tailor the RMF to your organization.

Understanding organizational context

Understanding your organization's unique context is vital in effectively tailoring the RMF. This multifaceted process begins with a clear understanding of the organization's mission and operational environment. Knowing the mission helps in aligning cybersecurity efforts with the organization's primary objectives and services. The operational environment assessment includes the analysis of workflows, technology infrastructure, and the nature of data handled, which is crucial for identifying critical assets.

Understanding the regulatory landscape is another key aspect, as compliance requirements vary across industries. This involves familiarizing yourself with relevant laws, standards, and guidelines that impact cybersecurity measures.

Assessing current cybersecurity practices is the third crucial element. This assessment should review existing security measures, policies, and procedures to determine their effectiveness and compliance with industry standards and regulatory requirements. It also involves identifying gaps in the current cybersecurity posture, which helps in prioritizing areas for improvement in the RMF process.

Overall, a thorough understanding of these factors provides a strong foundation for tailoring the RMF in a manner that is not only compliant and secure but also aligned with the unique needs and objectives of your organization.

The following are specific thoughts on tailoring the RMF for different industries:

- **Healthcare industry**: For healthcare organizations, where patient data privacy is paramount, the RMF should be tailored to comply with regulations such as HIPAA. Emphasis should be on controls that protect patient information and ensure data confidentiality, integrity, and availability.

- **Financial services**: Financial institutions, governed by regulations such as GLBA or SOX, should tailor the RMF to focus on financial data integrity, fraud prevention, and maintaining customer confidentiality. Robust access controls and continuous monitoring for suspicious activities become crucial.

- **Government agencies**: For government entities, the RMF should align with federal mandates and standards, focusing on protecting sensitive and classified information. Tailoring in this sector often involves strict access controls and rigorous assessment and authorization processes.

- **Retail sector**: Retail businesses handling customer data and conducting transactions should tailor the RMF to protect against data breaches and ensure PCI DSS compliance. Emphasis should be on network security, data encryption, and incident response mechanisms.

- **Manufacturing and industrial**: In sectors such as manufacturing, the RMF should be tailored to ensure both cybersecurity and the safety of industrial control systems. This involves focusing on network segmentation, monitoring operational technology, and protecting against both digital and physical threats.

- **Education sector**: Educational institutions should tailor the RMF to protect student data and research information while accommodating a diverse range of users and technologies. Focus areas might include user education, data privacy, and securing research data.

Customizing based on size and complexity

Tailoring the NIST RMF to accommodate the size and specific needs of an organization is a critical aspect of implementing effective cybersecurity practices. Organizations (depending on their size, mission, or business needs) may require specialized sets of controls to manage their unique risk profiles effectively. The NIST RMF allows for the development of organizationally tailored control baselines for organization-wide use. These tailored baselines complement the standard NIST control baselines by offering the flexibility to add or eliminate controls, thus accommodating the specific organizational requirements while ensuring that the protection of information is commensurate with the associated risks.

Moreover, organizationally tailored baselines are capable of establishing organization-defined control parameter values. These are essential for controls and control enhancements to align with the specific requirements of different communities of interest within the organization. This approach allows for the extension of control parameters beyond the typical NIST guidelines to suit the particular context of the organization, further emphasizing the adaptability of the NIST RMF to various organizational scales and types. Customizing the RMF baselines is beyond the scope of this book and is only recommended for those extremely familiar with the RMF.

However, smaller organizations might focus on implementing essential controls with limited resources, while larger enterprises might have more complex, multilayered cybersecurity needs, which would cause them to implement more controls and areas of the framework.

Regular reviews and adaptation

Tailoring the RMF is not a one-time activity. Regular reviews and adaptation are critical to ensuring the ongoing relevance and effectiveness of the tailored RMF in your organization. This continuous process includes the following:

- **Monitoring emerging threats**: Stay updated with the latest cybersecurity threats and vulnerabilities that could impact your organization

- **Evaluating technological advancements**: Assess new technologies and tools that can enhance your cybersecurity posture

- **Assessing operational changes**: Review any significant changes in your organization's operations, structure, or strategy that could affect your risk profile

- **Updating RMF practices**: Based on these evaluations, update your RMF practices, including revising risk assessments, modifying control implementations, and refining monitoring strategies

- **Stakeholder engagement**: Continuously engage with stakeholders to ensure that RMF adaptations align with organizational objectives and address new or evolving risks effectively

This approach ensures that the RMF remains a dynamic and responsive framework, adapting to the ever-changing landscape of cybersecurity threats, organizational needs, and technological advancements.

Stakeholder engagement and training

Engaging stakeholders in the tailoring process of the RMF is essential for its successful implementation. It involves the following:

- **Involving key personnel**: Engage leaders, IT staff, cybersecurity teams, and end users. Their insights can provide valuable input in setting goals and selecting appropriate controls.

- **Facilitating collaboration**: Encourage collaboration between departments to ensure a holistic approach to cybersecurity.

- **Training programs**: Develop comprehensive training programs for all stakeholders. This should include educating them about the RMF stages, their roles in the process, and the importance of cybersecurity.

- **Feedback mechanisms**: Establish mechanisms for stakeholders to provide feedback on the RMF implementation, ensuring it meets the organization's needs and identifies areas for improvement.

Through stakeholder engagement and training, organizations can ensure that the tailored RMF is well understood, effectively implemented, and receives wide support across the organization.

Documentation and communication

Maintaining comprehensive documentation and effective communication is crucial in the RMF tailoring process. This involves the following:

- **Detailed documentation**: Keep records of decisions made during the tailoring process, including the rationale for selecting specific controls and strategies.

- **Updating policies and procedures**: Incorporate changes into official policies and procedures, ensuring they reflect the tailored RMF.

- **Clear communication**: Develop clear communication strategies to inform stakeholders about the tailored RMF, its implications, and their roles. This can include formal presentations, training sessions, and regular updates.

Effective documentation and communication ensure transparency, facilitate compliance, and foster a culture of cybersecurity awareness across the organization.

Tailoring the RMF requires a thoughtful analysis of an organization's specific needs, risks, regulatory requirements, and operational context. By customizing the RMF, organizations can ensure that their risk management efforts are both effective and aligned with their unique characteristics and challenges.

Case studies and examples

Despite my best efforts, it's not easy to locate organizations telling their story of implementing the NIST RMF. In fact, I was only able to locate one – the University of Florida. Our case study focuses on an implementation at the University of Florida. This was discussed at the *NIST High-Performance Computing Workshop* in 2018. The case study, titled *Applying NIST Risk Management Framework to Controlled Unclassified Information on High-Performance Computing (HPC)*, focuses on the application of the NIST RMF to manage risks associated with **controlled unclassified information** (**CUI**) in a high-performance computing environment.

You can read about it here: `https://www.nist.gov/system/files/documents/2018/03/28/erik_-_rmf-to-cui-for-hpc-lessons-deumens.pdf`.

Here is a summary of the key points and the implementation process.

Background and context

Before we dive into the case study, we have to provide some context and background:

- **CUI**: CUI refers to information that requires safeguarding or dissemination controls as specified by a law, regulation, or government policy
- **Regulatory framework**: The Federal CUI rule and *NIST Special Publication 800-171* provide the foundational requirements for protecting CUI in non-federal information systems and organizations
- **NIST SP 800-171**: This publication focuses on protecting the confidentiality of CUI in non-federal systems and organizations, assuming a confidentiality impact value no lower than moderate

Institutional effort and collaboration

For this implementation, the following stakeholders were present:

- **Collaboration with various stakeholders**: The implementation involved collaboration with the faculty, the Office of Research, information technology departments, the Information Security Office, and other key institutional partners

NIST framework implementation

A rough overview of how the organization implemented the framework is as follows:

- **Risk management**: It utilized the *NIST SP 800* series as guidelines, with a focus on organization-wide risk management, capital planning, and conducting risk assessments

- **System planning and building**: Systems were classified for a moderate baseline, maximizing common controls, and following various NIST SP guidelines for design, engineering, and security controls

- **Project management**: Projects were classified and the NIST CUI process was integrated, ensuring all common controls were inherited

Implementation principles

This implementation of the NIST RMF was tailored in the following focus areas:

- **Meeting researcher needs**: The implementation focused on affordability, reliability, ease of provisioning, and supporting both small and large complex projects

- **Simplifying processes**: A simple process was designed to accommodate the nimble requirements of research and included a simple budget model

Technical implementation

This implementation was done in just one specific environment of the HPC, as discussed ahead:

- **Enclave implementation**: Created a pre-vetted environment for efficient hardware use, project provisioning, and cost efficiency

As a part of the technical implementation, a discussion of the architecture and the approach to technology is required to understand the implementation of the NIST RMF.

Architecture

Let us first look at the architecture:

- **Vertical architecture**: Used in ResShield (2015), focused on dedicated infrastructure and hypervisor-managed VM storage

- **Horizontal architecture**: Implemented in ResVault (2016–2017), typical in HPC, with fast infrastructure and flexibility for demanding workloads

Layered technology approach

Let us look at the different layers in the approach:

- **Physical layer**: Hardware servers and storage, with disaster recovery planning in the public cloud
- **Security layer**: Zero trust end-to-end encryption
- **Work layer**: Research data storage and processing in secure VMs

ResVault components

The RMF implementation provided a multilayered solution with components for work, security, and physical layers, supporting various types of projects and collaborations.

Future directions

The RMF implementation involved the development of multi-user secure VMs, secure clusters, and support for large collaborations, parallel processing, high-throughput computing, big data analytics, and **Message Passing Interface (MPI)** jobs.

Security goals

What use is an RMF implementation if it doesn't make you more secure? The security goals for this implementation were simple but effective.

It was focused on protecting user data from administrators, ensuring security independent of infrastructure, and ease of use despite security measures.

Formal build and compliance processes

As we discussed in the previous chapters concerning documentation, the RMF implementation must follow a formal process, as the team did here.

A formal process was established for designing, reviewing, approving, operating, and auditing, along with a comprehensive compliance process covering policies, architecture, business processes, technical processes, and control outcomes.

In summary, the case study illustrates a comprehensive and multi-faceted approach to applying the NIST RMF in a high-performance computing context, specifically addressing the unique challenges of handling CUI. The integration of NIST guidelines, institutional collaboration, technical architectural choices, and a focus on researcher needs and usability highlights a practical and efficient implementation of the NIST RMF in a specialized environment. In your own implementation, look to *Chapter 4* for a discussion of the specific verticals, and refer here to see how one organization did it themselves!

Summary

In this chapter, we refreshed ourselves on the stages of the NIST RMF, readying ourselves for our own implementation. We took it a step further beyond the foundational aspects covered previously, focusing on the dynamic nature of risk management in cybersecurity. We then examined a detailed case study of the University of Florida's implementation of the NIST RMF in managing CUI. It outlined the background, collaborative efforts, technical implementation, and security goals of the project, providing a practical example of the RMF's application in a specialized context.

Throughout the chapter, we placed an emphasis on understanding organizational context, stakeholder engagement, training, and the importance of documentation and communication in successfully implementing and adapting the RMF. This chapter aims to guide you in applying the RMF, no matter the organizational setting, ensuring that your own cybersecurity efforts will align with your organization's broader business objectives and risk management strategies.

In the next chapter, *Security Controls and Documentation*, we'll provide a comprehensive guide on the selection and application of security controls, the development of necessary compliance documentation, and the advantages of automating control assessments, equipping you with practical skills for enhancing cybersecurity in your organization.

6

Security Controls and Documentation

In today's digital landscape, where threats are constantly evolving, the importance of proper controls and the documentation of those controls cannot be overstated. This chapter is designed to provide you with a comprehensive understanding of how to identify, select, document, and automate security controls within your organization. By engaging in this chapter, you will gain practical skills and knowledge essential for strengthening your organization's cybersecurity defenses and ensuring compliance with regulatory standards. In this chapter, we're going to cover the following main topics:

- Identifying and selecting security controls
- Developing documentation for compliance
- Automating control assessment

Identifying and selecting security controls

The NIST **Risk Management Framework** (**RMF**) serves as a cornerstone in the establishment of a robust cybersecurity posture for organizations. Central to this framework is the meticulous process of identifying and selecting appropriate security controls. These controls are not just technological safeguards but encompass a wide array of measures, including administrative policies and physical protections. The significance of this process cannot be overstated, as the chosen controls form the bedrock of an organization's defense against myriad cyber threats.

In the context of the RMF, security controls are the tools and practices that protect the confidentiality, integrity, and availability of information systems. These controls are categorized broadly into three types: technical, administrative, and physical. **Technical controls** involve the use of technology to enforce security policies, such as firewalls, encryption, and access control mechanisms. **Administrative controls** consist of policies, procedures, and guidelines that govern user behavior, such as security training and incident response plans. **Physical controls** are measures taken to protect the physical premises and the devices within, such as locks, surveillance cameras, and the secure disposal of hardware. This also includes controls such as fences and mantraps to prevent access.

The RMF process mandates a strategic approach to selecting these controls. This approach is not a one-size-fits-all solution but requires a tailored application that aligns with the specific needs and risk profile of an organization. The selection process is influenced by several factors, including the categorization of the information, the assessment of risk, and the operational environment of the organization.

Understanding the types of security controls

In the realm of cybersecurity, particularly within the framework of the NIST RMF, the selection and implementation of security controls are pivotal in safeguarding information systems. These controls are multifaceted mechanisms designed to protect and preserve the confidentiality, integrity, and availability of information systems. Their efficacy lies not only in their individual functionalities but also in how they are synergistically combined within an organization's security architecture. This section delves into the various types of security controls, elucidating their roles, functionalities, and relevance in the context of the RMF.

Categorization of security controls

Security controls are broadly categorized into three types: technical, administrative, and physical. Let us look at these in some detail:

- **Technical controls**: These are primarily concerned with the technology that underpins an organization's information systems. They include hardware and software safeguards designed to detect, prevent, and respond to unauthorized access or alterations to system components, data, and operations. Examples include firewalls, antivirus software, **intrusion detection systems (IDSs)**, encryption, and access control mechanisms. Technical controls are critical in mitigating risks from cyber threats and ensuring the secure operation of digital systems.

- **Administrative controls**: Administrative controls are policies, procedures, and standards that define the organization's cybersecurity framework. These are guidelines for human behavior, staff management, and operational procedures. They encompass security policies, personnel security, training, incident response plans, and security audits. Such controls are pivotal in shaping the cybersecurity culture within an organization, ensuring that employees are aware of security best practices and their roles in maintaining security.

- **Physical controls**: Physical controls pertain to the security of the physical environment where information systems are housed. This includes controls designed to prevent unauthorized access to facilities, protect against environmental hazards, and safeguard physical assets. Examples include locks, security guards, surveillance cameras, and environmental controls such as fire suppression systems and **heating, ventilation, and air conditioning (HVAC)** controls. Physical controls are essential for protecting the tangible assets of an organization and provide a critical line of defense against physical threats.

Types of security controls based on function

In addition to categorization based on their nature, security controls can also be classified based on their function: preventive, detective, and corrective. Let us look at these in greater detail:

- **Preventive controls**: These controls are designed to prevent security incidents before they occur. They establish barriers or safeguards to ensure that potential threats do not materialize into actual breaches. Examples include access control mechanisms, encryption, security awareness training, and the secure configuration of systems and networks. Preventive controls are proactive measures, forming the first line of defense in a comprehensive security strategy.

- **Detective controls**: Detective controls are implemented to identify and detect the occurrence of a security incident in a timely manner. These controls are essential for the early identification of threats, allowing for rapid response and mitigation. Examples include IDS, security audits, and regular system and network monitoring. Effective detective controls are vital for maintaining situational awareness and responding to emerging threats.

- **Corrective controls**: Corrective controls come into play after a security incident has occurred. Their purpose is to restore systems to normal operations and repair any damage caused by the incident. These controls include disaster recovery plans, data backups, and incident response procedures. Corrective controls are crucial for minimizing the impact of security incidents and ensuring business continuity.

The role of security controls in the RMF

Within the RMF, the selection and implementation of these controls are guided by a comprehensive risk assessment process. The framework emphasizes a tailored approach to control selection, where the nature and functionality of controls are aligned with the specific risk profile and operational needs of the organization. This process involves understanding the system's categorization, assessing the likelihood and impact of potential threats, and considering the operational context in which the system operates.

The RMF also advocates for a balanced approach to control selection, ensuring that technical, administrative, and physical controls are effectively integrated. This integration is crucial for establishing a robust security posture, as reliance on a single type of control or functionality can leave gaps in the organization's defenses. For instance, while technical controls may be adept at guarding against cyber threats, they must be complemented with strong administrative policies and physical security measures to address the full spectrum of risks.

Best practices in security control selection

The selection of security controls under the RMF requires a strategic approach that is both comprehensive and adaptable. Best practices in this process include the following:

- **Conducting thorough risk assessments**: Understanding the organization's risk landscape is fundamental to selecting appropriate controls. A thorough risk assessment identifies potential threats and vulnerabilities, guiding the selection of controls that are most effective in mitigating identified risks.

- **Aligning controls with organizational objectives**: Security controls should be chosen not only based on their security efficacy but also on how well they align with the organization's operational goals and objectives. Controls should enable, not hinder, business processes.

By following these best practices and the process outlined earlier, you'll be well equipped to begin the process of planning security control selection. Next, we'll discuss how asset categorization impacts control selection.

Categorization and its impact on control selection

The process of categorizing information systems is a critical first step in the NIST RMF and plays a pivotal role in the selection of security controls. This categorization is governed by the **Federal Information Processing Standard** (**FIPS**) Publication 199, *Standards for Security Categorization of Federal Information and Information Systems*. Understanding this categorization process and its impact on control selection is essential for ensuring that security measures are appropriately tailored to protect the organization's assets in alignment with their value and sensitivity.

Overview of FIPS 199 and system categorization

FIPS 199 is a publication from the Computer Security Division of the National Institute of Standards and Technology (NIST) that addresses one of the tasks passed to NIST by the E-Government Act of 2002; that task was to develop standards by which information systems and data, or information itself, could be categorized by the impact upon that organization were there to be a breach of **confidentiality, integrity, or availability (CIA)**.

The standard identifies three levels of potential impact: low, moderate, and high. The categorization of a system is determined by the highest level of impact for any of the CIA criteria.

This categorization process requires a thorough understanding of the information types processed, stored, and transmitted by the information system, as well as the potential impact of security breaches on organizational operations, assets, and individuals.

The categorization process

Conducting an inventory of information types is the first step in categorization. This involves identifying all types of information that the system handles.

For each information type, the potential impact levels for confidentiality, integrity, and availability breaches are assessed. The impact levels are determined based on predefined criteria that consider factors such as the sensitivity of the information, legal and regulatory requirements, and the potential consequences of unauthorized disclosure, alteration, or unavailability.

The system's categorization is then determined by the highest impact level identified among all information types. For example, if a system processes information where the highest impact level for confidentiality is moderate, for integrity is low, and for availability is high, the system would be categorized as high.

Impact on control selection

The categorization of an information system directly influences the applicable baseline set of security controls. *NIST Special Publication 800-53* provides a catalog of security controls and guidance on tailoring these controls based on the system's categorization.

For a system categorized as low impact, a basic set of controls is applied. As the categorization level increases to moderate or high, the complexity and rigor of the required controls also increase. This ensures that more sensitive systems are subject to stronger protective measures.

Beyond the baseline controls, additional controls may be selected based on a risk assessment that takes into account the specific threats, vulnerabilities, and organizational context.

Tailoring the baseline controls

Tailoring involves adjusting the baseline set of controls to more closely align with the specific conditions and requirements of the organization and its information systems.

This process includes considering factors such as the operational environment, regulatory requirements, and specific threats or vulnerabilities that may not be adequately addressed by the baseline controls.

Tailoring may involve adding controls, modifying control parameters, or implementing alternative controls that provide equivalent or greater protection. In the next section, we'll delve into baseline controls in more detail.

Organizational and system-specific factors in control selection

Factors such as the organization's risk tolerance, mission, and business processes play a significant role in control selection. For instance, systems critical to mission-essential functions may require more stringent controls regardless of their formal categorization.

System-specific factors, such as the architecture, technology used, and connectivity with other systems, also influence control selection. The interoperability of controls across different systems and the potential for cascading effects in interconnected environments must be considered.

Risk assessment in the context of categorization

A comprehensive risk assessment should be conducted to validate the control selection based on the system categorization. This assessment looks at the likelihood and impact of potential threats exploiting identified vulnerabilities.

The risk assessment process aids in identifying areas where the baseline controls may be insufficient and where supplemental controls are necessary.

The role of continuous monitoring in refining control selection

The categorization and initial control selection are not static processes. Continuous monitoring is essential for ensuring that the control selection remains appropriate over time as threats evolve, technologies change, and organizational priorities shift.

Continuous monitoring involves regularly assessing the effectiveness of implemented controls, re-evaluating risks, and making necessary adjustments to control selections and categorizations to ensure processes, controls, and the RMF (as applied) remains effective and relevant.

Documentation and approval of categorization and control selection

The accurate and comprehensive documentation of a categorization process, the rationale behind control selection, and any tailoring of decisions are essential. This documentation is crucial for audit purposes and for ensuring transparency and accountability in the RMF process.

The categorization and control selection must be reviewed and approved by authorized officials within the organization. This approval process ensures that there is organizational consensus and understanding regarding the risks being accepted and the controls being implemented. It also ensures that the security posture aligns with the organization's overall risk management strategy and compliance requirements. Finally, this ensures that the risk management decisions remain transparent, consistent, and compliant with relevant regulations and standards. It enables the organization to demonstrate due diligence and accountability in managing risks.

The approval process typically involves key stakeholders such as information security officers, system owners, and senior management. Their collective agreement on the categorization and control selection underscores the organization's commitment to security and risk management.

Challenges and considerations in categorization and control selection

One of the primary challenges in this process is ensuring that categorization accurately reflects the real-world risks and operational context of the system. Over-categorization can lead to unnecessary costs and operational burdens, while under-categorization can leave systems vulnerable.

Another challenge is the dynamic nature of technology and threats. The categorization and control selection process must be agile enough to adapt to changes in the threat landscape, advancements in technology, and shifts in organizational priorities.

There's also a need to balance security requirements with usability and functionality. Security controls should not impede the primary functions of the information system or create undue complexity for users.

Best practices in categorization and control selection

Let us look at some of the best practices:

- Engage stakeholders from across the organization in the categorization process to ensure a comprehensive understanding of the information system and its context.

- Utilize threat intelligence and historical data to inform the categorization and control selection process. This approach helps understand the likelihood of different threat scenarios.

- Regularly review and update the categorization and control selection in response to changes in the operational environment, technological advancements, and evolving threat landscape.

- Ensure a balance between automated and manual processes in control implementation and monitoring. While automation can enhance efficiency and consistency, human oversight is critical for contextual decision-making.

The categorization of information systems and the subsequent selection of security controls are foundational elements in the implementation of the NIST RMF. This process requires a nuanced understanding of the organization's assets, risks, and operational context. By carefully categorizing systems and tailoring controls to address specific needs and vulnerabilities, organizations can establish a robust security posture that is both effective and adaptable to changing circumstances. The documentation and approval of these processes further reinforce the alignment of security practices with organizational goals and compliance requirements. Through continuous monitoring and periodic reassessment, organizations can ensure that their security controls remain effective in the face of evolving threats and technological changes, thus maintaining the integrity, confidentiality, and availability of their information systems.

Selecting baseline controls

In the context of the NIST RMF, the selection of baseline controls is a critical step in safeguarding information systems against a myriad of cyber threats. **Baseline controls** are the standard protections recommended for an information system based on its categorization.

Baseline controls are predefined sets of security measures recommended by NIST, specifically outlined in *NIST Special Publication 800-53*. They serve as the starting point for securing information systems and are selected based on the system's categorization (low, moderate, or high), as determined by FIPS 199.

The purpose of baseline controls is to provide a foundation of security, addressing general threats and vulnerabilities commonly faced by information systems.

Baseline controls cover various domains, including *"access control, awareness and training, audit and accountability, security assessment and authorization, configuration management, contingency planning, identification and authentication, incident response, maintenance, media protection, physical and environmental protection, planning, program management, risk assessment, system and services acquisition, system and communications protection, and system and information integrity"* (Government Accountability Office, [GAO], 2021).

This section delves into the intricacies of selecting baseline controls, tailoring them to specific organizational needs, and the methodologies involved in making these selections both effective and compliant.

Tailoring baseline controls to the organizational context

Tailoring is the process of modifying baseline controls to suit the specific needs, environment, and risk profile of the organization. This involves adding, removing, or modifying controls based on organizational requirements, operational environment, and technological considerations.

The tailoring process includes the consideration of factors such as regulatory requirements, specific threat intelligence, organizational culture, technology stack, and interoperability with existing systems.

Tailoring should be a collaborative effort involving various stakeholders, including cybersecurity experts, IT staff, system owners, and end-users, to ensure that the controls are practical and effective.

The process of selecting baseline controls

The first step in selecting baseline controls is to thoroughly understand the system's categorization and the baseline control set recommended for that categorization level.

Organizations must then conduct a gap analysis to determine the current state of their security posture against the baseline controls. This helps identify areas where additional security measures are needed.

Following the gap analysis, organizations should assess each control for its relevance, effectiveness, and feasibility within their operational context. This includes evaluating the potential impact of implementing each control on business processes and system functionality.

Considerations in baseline control selection

The security controls should align with the organization's broader risk management strategy and business objectives. Controls should mitigate risks without unduly burdening the organization or impeding business operations.

Cost-benefit analysis is crucial in baseline control selection. While security is paramount, organizations must also consider the financial and operational implications of implementing each control.

Interoperability and integration with existing systems and controls are essential to ensure a cohesive and efficient security posture.

Addressing common challenges in baseline control selection

One of the primary challenges in selecting baseline controls is balancing security needs with operational efficiency. Overly restrictive controls can hinder productivity, while lenient controls may expose the organization to risks.

Another challenge lies in keeping up with the evolving threat landscape and technological advancements. Baseline controls must be continually assessed and updated to remain effective against new and emerging threats.

Ensuring compliance with various regulatory and legal requirements can also be complex, particularly for organizations operating in multiple jurisdictions or sectors.

Documentation and continuous improvement

Documenting the selection and implementation of baseline controls is crucial for several reasons: it facilitates compliance audits, provides a reference for future security assessments, and ensures transparency and accountability in the security process.

Continual improvement should be a core aspect of the organization's cybersecurity strategy. This involves regularly reviewing and updating the baseline controls in response to feedback, security incidents, and changes in the organizational or technological context.

Inclusion of case studies and practical examples

The inclusion of case studies and practical examples can be beneficial in illustrating the real-world application of baseline control selection. These examples can provide insights into how different types of organizations, from small businesses to large enterprises, approach the challenge of selecting and implementing baseline controls.

Integration with advanced security measures

While baseline controls provide fundamental security, organizations often need to integrate these with more advanced security measures, especially in highly dynamic or sensitive environments. This includes incorporating emerging technologies such as artificial intelligence, machine learning, quantum computing, IoT, 5/6G, and blockchain for enhanced security monitoring and response.

The integration process should ensure that advanced security measures complement and reinforce baseline controls without creating redundancy or gaps in the security posture. This requires careful planning and co-ordination across different security domains.

Role of baseline controls in incident response and recovery

Baseline controls play a crucial role not only in preventing incidents but also in an organization's ability to respond to and recover from security breaches effectively.

Controls related to incident response planning, backup and recovery, and system redundancy are particularly critical in minimizing the impact of security incidents and ensuring business continuity.

Leveraging industry frameworks and best practices

Organizations can benefit from aligning their baseline control selection with industry frameworks and best practices, such as the **Cybersecurity Framework (CSF)** by NIST or guidelines from the **Center for Internet Security (CIS)**.

These frameworks provide additional insights and recommendations that can enhance the effectiveness of baseline controls and ensure a more comprehensive security approach.

Best practices in baseline control selection

Regularly update the knowledge base regarding emerging threats, vulnerabilities, and technological trends to ensure that baseline controls are current and effective.

Foster a culture of security within the organization. Employee awareness and adherence to security policies and controls are as important as the technical measures themselves.

Engage in the continuous monitoring and periodic reassessment of the baseline controls to ensure their ongoing effectiveness and to make necessary adjustments in response to changes in the operational environment or threat landscape.

The future of baseline control selection

The future of baseline control selection is likely to see an increased emphasis on adaptive and intelligent security measures. This involves leveraging data analytics and predictive modeling to dynamically adjust controls in response to changing threat landscapes and organizational needs.

The role of automation in baseline control implementation and monitoring will also grow, helping organizations maintain a consistent and effective security posture with greater efficiency.

The selection of baseline controls in the NIST RMF is a complex but essential process that lays the foundation for an organization's cybersecurity defenses. It requires a strategic approach that balances security needs with operational considerations, cost, and compliance requirements. Tailoring these controls to the specific context of the organization, regularly reassessing them in light of new threats and technologies, and documenting the entire process is key to ensuring that these controls remain effective over time. By integrating baseline controls with advanced security measures and aligning with industry frameworks and best practices, organizations can build a robust and resilient cybersecurity posture capable of adapting to the ever-evolving cyber threat landscape.

Risk assessment in control selection

Risk assessment plays a pivotal role in the selection of security controls within the NIST RMF. This process involves identifying, evaluating, and prioritizing risks to the organization's information systems and using this information to inform the selection and implementation of appropriate security controls.

Risk assessment in the context of the RMF is a systematic process for evaluating the potential risks to an organization's information systems and operations. It forms a critical component of the RMF, directly impacting the selection of security controls.

The primary objective of risk assessment is to identify the threats and vulnerabilities that can adversely impact the confidentiality, integrity, and availability of information systems and to estimate the likelihood and impact of these events.

NIST Special Publication 800-30 (`https://csrc.nist.gov/pubs/sp/800/30/r1/final`) provides guidelines for conducting risk assessments, outlining a comprehensive approach that includes **risk identification**, **risk analysis**, and **risk evaluation**.

This section explores the methodologies and best practices in conducting risk assessments and how they directly influence the decision-making process in control selection.

Risk identification

The first step in risk assessment is identifying and listing all of the potential threats and vulnerabilities. This helps to ensure that all possible risks are considered and that no potential threats or opportunities are overlooked. Threats can include cyber-attacks, system failures, natural disasters, and human errors, and vulnerabilities are weaknesses in the system that can be exploited by threats.

This step also involves identifying the information assets that need protection, including hardware, software, data, and processes, and understanding the potential impact of their loss or compromise.

Risk analysis

Risk analysis is a crucial step in the assessment process. It involves evaluating the likelihood of a threat exploiting a vulnerability and the potential impact should this occur. This evaluation considers both quantitative and qualitative factors.

Quantitative analysis involves the use of numerical values to estimate risk, such as the probability of an attack and the potential financial loss. This would involve metrics such as the number of vulnerabilities present, time to respond to alerts or other similar numerical measures. **Qualitative analysis**, on the other hand, uses subjective measures to assess risks based on the severity of impact and likelihood. This measure could be like a sliding scale from 1–5 based on the assessor's feelings on how well the organization complies with facets of the rules.

This analysis helps in prioritizing risks, allowing organizations to focus their efforts and resources on the most significant threats.

Risk evaluation and control selection

Based on the outcomes of the risk analysis, organizations evaluate which risks are acceptable and which require mitigation. This decision is influenced by the organization's risk tolerance and overall risk management strategy.

The selection of security controls is then aligned with the identified risks. Controls are chosen not only to mitigate high-priority risks but also to bring the overall risk to an acceptable level.

This step often involves a cost-benefit analysis to ensure that the cost of implementing controls is proportional to the benefits in terms of reduced risk.

Tailoring controls based on risk assessment

The RMF encourages tailoring baseline controls based on risk assessment findings. This involves adding, removing, or modifying controls to address specific threats and vulnerabilities identified during the risk assessment.

Tailoring also considers the operational context and specific requirements of the organization, ensuring that controls are effective and do not impede business operations.

Addressing residual risk

Residual risk is the risk that remains after controls are implemented. An important aspect of risk assessment is determining the level of residual risk that an organization is willing to accept.

Risk assessment helps identify where additional controls are needed to reduce residual risk further or where it is more cost-effective to accept a certain level of risk.

Continuous risk assessment and control adjustment

Risk assessment is not a one-time activity but an ongoing process. **Continuous risk assessment** is necessary to account for changes in the threat landscape, technological advancements, and changes within the organization. *NIST SP 800-137* goes more in-depth on the subject.

As risks evolve, security controls may need to be adjusted. Continuous monitoring and regular risk assessments ensure that controls remain effective and aligned with the current risk profile.

Documentation and reporting

Documenting the risk assessment process, findings, and decisions regarding control selection is crucial for transparency, accountability, and compliance purposes.

This documentation should include a clear rationale for the selection and implementation of specific controls, as well as for any accepted risks.

Challenges and best practices in risk assessment for control selection

Challenges in risk assessment include keeping up with rapidly evolving cyber threats to identify all relevant risks, managing complex and interconnected information systems, and balancing security needs with operational and budget constraints.

Best practices include using a structured and consistent methodology for risk assessment, involving stakeholders from various parts of the organization, staying informed about emerging threats, and leveraging threat intelligence and industry benchmarks.

Integrating risk assessment with broader organizational processes

Effective risk assessment for control selection is not isolated but integrated with the organization's broader risk management and governance processes. This integration ensures that cybersecurity is aligned with the overall business strategy and objectives.

Collaboration across departments, including IT, operations, finance, and executive leadership, is essential to ensure a holistic and effective approach to risk management and control selection.

This integration also facilitates the sharing of risk-related information and enhances the understanding of cybersecurity risks across the organization. It aligns cybersecurity initiatives with business objectives, ensuring that the security posture supports and enhances business operations.

Engaging senior management and key decision-makers in the risk assessment process helps in securing the necessary support and resources for implementing effective security controls. It also ensures that cybersecurity decisions are made with a clear understanding of their impact on the overall business.

Leveraging advanced tools and techniques

The use of advanced tools and techniques can significantly enhance the effectiveness and efficiency of the risk assessment process. These may include automated risk assessment tools, such as compliance scanners, and products, such as cybersecurity scorecards, cybersecurity frameworks, and data analytics.

Automation tools can help in aggregating and analyzing large volumes of data to identify potential risks more quickly and accurately. Frameworks such as the NIST Cybersecurity Framework can provide structured approaches and best practices for risk assessment and control selection.

Data analytics and machine learning can be used to identify patterns and predict potential risks, enabling the proactive management of cybersecurity threats.

Inclusion of case studies and examples

Including case studies and real-world examples can provide valuable insights into how different organizations approach risk assessment and control selection. These examples can illustrate best practices, common challenges, and innovative solutions in various industry sectors and organizational contexts.

Learning from the experiences of others can help organizations avoid common pitfalls and adopt strategies that have been proven effective in similar situations.

Future trends in risk assessment for control selection

The future of risk assessment in cybersecurity is likely to see increased reliance on predictive analytics and artificial intelligence to anticipate and respond to emerging threats.

There will also be a greater emphasis on integrating cybersecurity risk assessment with enterprise risk management, recognizing the interdependencies between cybersecurity and other organizational risks.

The evolution of regulatory requirements and industry standards will continue to shape how organizations conduct risk assessments and select controls, underscoring the need for agility and adaptability in cybersecurity practices.

Risk assessment is a critical component of the NIST RMF and plays a central role in the selection of security controls. A well-conducted risk assessment provides the foundation for making informed decisions about which controls are necessary to protect information systems against identified threats and vulnerabilities. It involves a continuous process of identifying, analyzing, and evaluating risks and requires the involvement and collaboration of various stakeholders across the organization. By integrating risk assessment with broader organizational processes and leveraging advanced tools and techniques, organizations can develop a dynamic and effective approach to selecting and implementing security controls, ensuring that their cybersecurity posture remains robust in the face of an ever-changing threat landscape.

Supplementing baseline controls

Once baseline controls have been established in the context of the NIST RMF, organizations may find it necessary to supplement these controls. This need arises when the baseline controls do not fully address the specific risks and requirements of the organization. Supplementing baseline controls involves adding, modifying, or enhancing existing controls to provide a more robust defense against threats. This section explores the reasons for supplementing baseline controls, the process of determining appropriate supplements, and best practices in implementing these additional measures.

Understanding the need for supplementing baseline controls

Baseline controls provide a foundational level of security, but they may not cover all the unique risks faced by an organization. The need to supplement these controls arises from factors such as specific threat landscapes, regulatory requirements, unique operational needs, or technological complexities.

For instance, an organization dealing with highly sensitive data or operating in a highly regulated industry might require additional controls beyond the baseline to adequately protect its assets.

Identifying areas for supplemental controls

The process of identifying areas where supplemental controls are necessary typically begins with a thorough risk assessment. This assessment should reveal gaps where baseline controls are insufficient.

Organizations should also consider the results of recent security audits, incident reports, and feedback from cybersecurity teams and end-users to identify areas needing improvement.

Types of supplemental controls

Supplemental controls can be varied and are chosen based on the specific deficiencies identified in the baseline control set. They may include advanced technological solutions, enhanced physical security measures, or more rigorous administrative procedures.

Examples include advanced IDS, **multifactor authentication** (**MFA**), data loss prevention tools, additional encryption measures, or more stringent access control policies.

Risk-based approach to supplementing controls

The selection of supplemental controls should be driven by a risk-based approach, ensuring that the additional controls are proportionate to the level of risk they are mitigating.

This approach involves evaluating the potential impact and likelihood of identified risks and then selecting controls that effectively reduce these risks to an acceptable level.

Cost-benefit analysis in control supplementation

Supplementing baseline controls often comes with additional costs, both financial and operational. Therefore, a cost-benefit analysis is crucial to ensure that the benefits of implementing additional controls justify the investment.

The analysis should consider not just the direct costs of implementing the controls but also the potential costs of not implementing them, such as the risk of data breaches or non-compliance penalties.

Compliance and regulatory considerations

In many cases, the need to supplement baseline controls is driven by compliance requirements. Different industries and jurisdictions may have specific security standards that go beyond the baseline controls recommended by NIST.

It is essential for organizations to stay informed about these regulatory requirements and ensure that their supplemental controls are aligned with them.

Integration with existing controls

When supplementing baseline controls, it is important to ensure that the additional measures integrate seamlessly with existing controls. Poor integration can lead to gaps in security, inefficiencies, and increased complexity.

This integration should be technical, procedural, and administrative, ensuring a cohesive and co-ordinated security posture. In doing this, an audit of procedures and policies should be conducted, for example, the standard operating procedures, the audit guides utilized by the organization, and other various policies the organization may have made with regard to the current controls in place.

Testing and validation of supplemental controls

After the implementation of supplemental controls, testing and validation are critical to ensure they are functioning as intended and effectively mitigating risks.

This process can involve penetration testing, simulated attacks, and regular security audits. Feedback from these tests may lead to the further refinement of the controls.

Training and awareness

Supplemental controls often require changes in user behavior or new processes. As such, training and awareness programs are essential to ensure that all personnel understand the new controls and their roles in maintaining security.

These programs should be ongoing, reflecting any changes or updates in the security controls and policies.

Documentation and record-keeping

Documenting the process of selecting and implementing supplemental controls is crucial for audit purposes, compliance, and future reference. This documentation should include the rationale for the controls, the risk assessment results that prompted their selection, and details of their implementation and testing.

Proper record-keeping also aids in the continuous monitoring and review process, ensuring that the controls remain effective over time.

Continuous monitoring and review

The cybersecurity landscape is constantly evolving, and so should the organization's security controls. Continuous monitoring and regular reviews are necessary to ensure that both baseline and supplemental controls are effective against emerging threats and changing business needs.

This ongoing process should feed back into the organization's overall cybersecurity strategy, informing future risk assessments and decisions about control supplementation.

Challenges and best practices

One of the main challenges in supplementing baseline controls is ensuring that the additional measures do not become overly complex or burdensome, hindering business operations.

Best practices in addressing these challenges include maintaining a balance between security needs and operational efficiency, involving key stakeholders in the decision-making process, and ensuring scalability and flexibility in the implementation of supplemental controls.

Another challenge is keeping up with the rapid pace of technological advancements and the evolving threat landscape. Organizations that work with classified or sensitive data, for instance, may find themselves changing their baseline controls much more frequently due to technology becoming out-of-date or no longer authorized for the transmission of certain classifications of data. The National Security Agency's Commercial Solutions for Classified program maintains a specific vendor and equipment list that must be adhered to as part of baseline controls. This may cause an organization to rapidly change its own adhered-to controls. Organizations must remain agile and responsive, regularly updating their understanding of risks and the effectiveness of both baseline and supplemental controls.

Case studies and practical examples

Incorporating case studies and practical examples can be instrumental in illustrating the application and impact of supplemental controls in real-world scenarios. These examples can demonstrate how organizations in similar industries or with similar risk profiles successfully implemented and benefited from supplemental controls.

Learning from these examples can provide valuable insights into effective strategies and common pitfalls, helping organizations to make more informed decisions about their own control supplementation.

Future trends in control supplementation

The future of control supplementation is likely to see an increased emphasis on adaptive security measures that can dynamically respond to changing threats and business needs.

Emerging technologies such as artificial intelligence, machine learning, and automation will play a significant role in enhancing the effectiveness and efficiency of supplemental controls.

There will also be a greater focus on integrating cybersecurity measures with overall business strategy, ensuring that security controls support and enable business objectives rather than hinder them.

Supplementing baseline controls is a critical aspect of implementing the NIST RMF and ensuring the robustness of an organization's cybersecurity posture. It involves a careful evaluation of risks, a thorough understanding of the organization's unique needs and compliance requirements, and a strategic approach to selecting and integrating additional controls. Through continuous monitoring, regular reviews, and updates, organizations can ensure that their supplemental controls remain effective in the face of evolving threats and changing business environments. By adopting best practices and learning from real-world examples, organizations can navigate the complexities of control supplementation and build a comprehensive, resilient defense against cyber threats.

Documenting control selection

The documentation of the control selection process within the NIST RMF plays a critical role beyond mere compliance—it acts as a vital record for future reference, audits, and security assessments.

Effective documentation captures every facet of the control selection process. It details the types of controls—technical, administrative, or physical—and categorizes them as preventive, detective, or corrective. Furthermore, it elaborates on their functionalities and expected impact on the organization's information systems. This comprehensive record-keeping is essential for understanding and justifying the choices made during the control selection process.

This section outlines the importance of this documentation in providing transparency and accountability for the decisions made regarding cybersecurity controls.

Tailoring controls to organizational needs

A crucial aspect of documentation is the tailoring process, where baseline controls are adjusted to suit the organization's unique context. This process involves documenting any modifications, additions, or removals of controls, providing clarity on how the organization's specific security needs and compliance obligations are addressed.

Change management in documentation

The dynamic nature of cybersecurity necessitates documenting any changes in control selection. This includes recording changes made, the reasons behind these changes, who authorized them, and how they were communicated and implemented within the organization.

Best practices in documenting control selection

Another vital element is the documentation of approvals and authorizations from relevant authorities within the organization. This serves to validate the control selection process and adherence to organizational protocols.

For a holistic view of the organization's security posture, the control selection documentation should be integrated with other cybersecurity documentation. This includes aligning with security policies, incident response plans, and business continuity plans to ensure consistency across all cybersecurity strategies.

Best practices in documenting control selection emphasize clarity, conciseness, and regular updates to reflect the evolving nature of cybersecurity threats and measures. It is crucial that this documentation is both accessible to authorized personnel and securely stored.

Specialized documentation tools and software can aid in maintaining standardization, simplifying updates, and ensuring the security and accessibility of records. They also help in linking different documentation pieces, offering a comprehensive view of cybersecurity measures.

Training and awareness for effective documentation

Training and awareness among staff about the importance and methodologies of documentation are crucial. This extends beyond the cybersecurity team to include other personnel involved in implementing and maintaining security controls.

Preparation for audits and assessments

Preparing documentation for audits and assessments is critical. It should be logically organized, up to date, and aligned with compliance requirements and industry best practices.

Addressing challenges in documentation

While maintaining current and relevant documentation amidst a rapidly evolving cybersecurity landscape can be challenging, organizations must strive to ensure consistency across various documents and align documented controls with actual practices.

Learning from case studies and examples

Incorporating case studies or examples of effective documentation practices provides tangible insights and learning opportunities. These examples illustrate successful strategies, common challenges, and practical solutions in documenting control selection.

Documenting control selection in the NIST RMF is more than a compliance exercise; it's a strategic tool that enhances an organization's ability to manage cybersecurity risks effectively. Adopting best practices in documentation, staying vigilant to cyber threats, and integrating documentation within the organization's broader cybersecurity framework are essential steps in establishing a robust, responsive, and well-documented cybersecurity posture. This approach not only safeguards the organization from potential threats but also reinforces its commitment to high standards of cybersecurity, building trust among stakeholders, customers, and partners.

Case study – Applying control selection in a real-world scenario

To illustrate the practical application of identifying and selecting appropriate controls within the NIST RMF, let's examine a case study involving a hypothetical organization, XYZ Corp, a mid-sized financial services company. This case study will explore how XYZ Corp approached the control selection process, the challenges they faced, and the lessons learned, providing valuable insights into the real-world application of these principles.

XYZ Corp, with its significant holdings in sensitive financial data, faced numerous cybersecurity challenges typical of the financial sector, including threats of data breaches, phishing attacks, and regulatory compliance requirements. The company decided to adopt the NIST RMF to enhance its cybersecurity posture, focusing on the critical step of selecting appropriate security controls. The following is a walkthrough of the process they took to apply the RMF:

- **Categorization of information systems**: The process began with categorizing their information systems based on FIPS 199 standards. Given the nature of their data, most of XYZ Corp's systems were categorized as high impact for confidentiality and integrity but moderate for availability. This categorization was crucial as it set the baseline for selecting the initial controls. Specific to XYZ Corp, by categorizing their information systems based on their criticality and sensitivity, they were able to make more informed decisions about where to allocate their cybersecurity budget. The systems handling customer financial information, for instance, could now be prioritized for stronger security measures, ensuring that investment in cybersecurity would be both effective and cost-efficient.

- **Selecting baseline controls**: XYZ Corp then referred to *NIST SP 800-53* for guidance on baseline controls suitable for their high-impact systems. They selected a range of controls, including advanced encryption methods for data protection, strict access control mechanisms, and comprehensive audit and accountability procedures. In addition to *NIST SP 800-53*, XYZ Corp looked at the various regulatory requirements they were subject to, such as those from the SEC and FDIC, as well as laws such as GDPR and regulations such as SOX. By previously categorizing their systems, they could ensure that the baseline selection verified that each system was compliant with all relevant regulations.

- **Tailoring and supplementing baseline controls**: Recognizing the unique aspects of their operational environment, XYZ Corp tailored the baseline controls. They integrated additional layers of security, such as MFA and real-time IDS, to address specific threats identified in their risk assessment. As financial companies deal with highly sensitive data and transactions, MFA adds an additional layer of security beyond just usernames and passwords, which are increasingly vulnerable to phishing and other forms of attack. This is critical for protecting customer accounts and internal systems from unauthorized access. The addition of a real-time IDS system allowed for the monitoring of network traffic and system activities for signs of intrusion, providing immediate alerts. This helped reduce their time to contain threats and detect APTs earlier. This step demonstrated the importance of not solely relying on baseline controls but adapting and enhancing them to meet specific organizational needs.

- **Challenges faced**: One of the primary challenges XYZ Corp encountered was balancing security needs with operational efficiency. Implementing stringent controls initially led to workflow disruptions and employee pushback. They realized the importance of involving various stakeholders in the control selection process, which helped in fine-tuning the controls for better alignment with operational practices.

An additional challenge was the resource constraints. XYZ Corp and other even smaller financial institutions may find it challenging to allocate their resources effectively. In the case of financial services, many operate on legacy systems, which created yet another challenge, as legacy systems may not easily support the latest security controls or integrate well with modern cybersecurity tools.

Another challenge was the rapidly evolving threat landscape. XYZ Corp found that some controls quickly became outdated, necessitating a continuous review and adaptation process. This highlighted the need for agility in their cybersecurity approach.

- **Documenting the process**: Throughout the control selection process, XYZ Corp maintained detailed documentation. This documentation covered their categorization decisions, the rationale behind each selected control, and the tailoring process. It proved invaluable during internal and external audits, showcasing their compliance with industry standards and regulatory requirements.

- **Training and awareness programs**: To ensure the effectiveness of the implemented controls, XYZ Corp launched comprehensive training and awareness programs for their staff. These programs focused on the importance of cybersecurity, the role of each employee in maintaining security, and how to adhere to the new processes and controls. The training significantly improved compliance with security procedures and reduced inadvertent security breaches. This training was led with a focus on *NIST 800-53* and the specific regulations that a financial firm is subject to. This provided relevant context to the training and raised the investment in learning from the training for all employees.

- **Continuous monitoring and review**: XYZ Corp established a continuous monitoring program to assess the effectiveness of their controls. Regular risk assessments were conducted to identify new threats and vulnerabilities, leading to periodic updates of their control selection. This adaptive approach ensured that their cybersecurity measures remained effective over time.

Lessons learned

The case study of XYZ Corp offers several key lessons:

- **Involving stakeholders**: Involving a broad range of stakeholders in the control selection process can lead to better alignment with operational needs and greater buy-in from staff.

- **Balancing security and efficiency**: Finding a balance between robust security measures and operational efficiency is crucial. Controls should be strong enough to protect assets without impeding business processes.

- **Continuous adaptation**: Cybersecurity is not a set-and-forget process. The continuous monitoring and adaptation of controls are essential in keeping pace with evolving threats and technological changes.

- **Importance of training**: Employee training and awareness are as critical as the technical controls themselves. Staff should be educated and regularly reminded of their role in maintaining cybersecurity.

- **Detailed documentation**: Meticulous documentation is vital not only for compliance and audits but also as a reference for future security decisions and as a historical record of the organization's cybersecurity journey.

The experience of XYZ Corp in applying the NIST RMF for control selection provides a practical perspective on the complexities and nuances of this process in a real-world setting. It underscores the importance of a thoughtful, inclusive, and flexible approach to selecting and implementing security controls. By learning from such case studies, other organizations can gain valuable insights and strategies for effectively managing their cybersecurity risks within the NIST RMF framework. As we move into developing the right documentation for all of our efforts, it's important to look back at what we've discussed. The controls we've selected span technical, administrative, and physical controls, ranging from policies to firewalls and even door locks. The RMF requires that we take a strategic approach to selecting those controls, and this includes the documentation, as discussed in this next section.

Developing documentation for compliance

In the realm of cybersecurity, particularly under frameworks such as the NIST RMF, developing documentation for compliance is not just a procedural necessity but a strategic asset.

Compliance documentation in cybersecurity refers to the comprehensive set of records, policies, procedures, and evidence that demonstrate an organization's adherence to relevant cybersecurity standards and regulatory requirements. This documentation is essential for audits, risk assessments, and maintaining operational continuity in the face of cybersecurity challenges.

This section aims to equip readers with the skills and knowledge to create effective compliance documentation that meets regulatory requirements. This process is crucial for demonstrating adherence to cybersecurity standards and for ensuring that the organization's security practices are both defensible and transparent.

Identifying regulatory requirements

The first step in developing compliance documentation is to identify the specific regulatory requirements applicable to the organization. These requirements can vary based on industry, location, the nature of data handled, and other factors. Common regulatory frameworks include **General Data Protection Regulation (GDPR)**, **Health Insurance Portability and Accountability Act (HIPAA)**, **Payment Card Industry Data Security Standard (PCI-DSS)**, and **Sarbanes-Oxley Act (SOX)**, each with its own set of documentation requirements.

Structuring compliance documentation

Effective compliance documentation should be well-structured and organized. A typical documentation structure may include the following:

- **Policies and procedures**: Clear and concise policies outlining the organization's cybersecurity stance and procedures for implementing these policies.

- **Risk assessment reports**: Detailed reports showing the identification, analysis, and management of cybersecurity risks.

- **Control implementation records**: Records showing which controls have been implemented, how they are managed, and evidence of their effectiveness.

- **Incident response and recovery plans**: Documentation of plans and procedures for responding to cybersecurity incidents and recovering from them.

- **Training and awareness records**: Records of training programs and awareness initiatives conducted to educate employees about cybersecurity.

- **Audit trails and monitoring logs**: Detailed logs that demonstrate the continuous monitoring and auditing of cybersecurity controls.

Developing policies and procedures

The cornerstone of compliance documentation is a set of well-crafted policies and procedures. These should be clear, concise, and easily understood by all stakeholders. They must reflect the organization's commitment to cybersecurity and align with the identified regulatory requirements.

Risk assessment documentation

Risk assessment documentation should provide a comprehensive overview of the risks faced by the organization, the methodology used for risk assessment, and the strategies employed for risk mitigation. This documentation should be updated regularly to reflect the evolving risk landscape.

Documenting control implementation

It's essential to maintain detailed records of all the security controls implemented. This includes not just the description of the controls but also how they are integrated into the organization's systems and processes. Documentation should provide evidence of the effectiveness of these controls in mitigating risks.

Incident response and recovery documentation

Documenting the organization's approach to incident response and recovery is vital. This includes detailed plans outlining the steps to be taken in the event of a cybersecurity incident, roles and responsibilities, communication strategies, and procedures for restoring systems and data.

Training and awareness documentation

Documenting cybersecurity training and awareness initiatives is crucial for demonstrating compliance. This should include details of the training content, the frequency of training, attendance records, and any materials used during training sessions.

Creating audit trails and monitoring logs

Maintaining comprehensive audit trails and monitoring logs is essential for demonstrating the ongoing effectiveness of cybersecurity controls. These logs should be detailed, tamper-proof, and stored securely.

Best practices in developing compliance documentation

When developing compliance documentation, there are things to keep in mind to make the documentation useful and future-proof:

- **Regular updates and reviews**: Compliance documentation should be **living documents** that are regularly reviewed and updated to reflect changes in regulatory requirements, business operations, and the cybersecurity landscape.

- **Stakeholder involvement**: Involving stakeholders from different departments can ensure that the documentation is comprehensive and aligned with all aspects of the organization.

- **Use of standardized templates and tools**: Utilizing standardized templates and documentation tools can help maintain consistency and ensure that all necessary information is captured.

- **Clarity and accessibility**: Documentation should be clear, well-organized, and accessible to authorized personnel. Avoid unnecessary technical jargon to make the documents comprehensible to non-technical stakeholders.

- **Challenges and solutions in compliance documentation**: Developing compliance documentation can be challenging due to the complexity of regulatory requirements and the dynamic nature of cybersecurity. Overcoming these challenges requires a strategic approach, regular training, and awareness initiatives for staff involved in documentation, as well as leveraging the expertise of cybersecurity professionals.

Developing documentation for compliance within the NIST RMF or any cybersecurity framework is a critical skill that requires attention to detail, an understanding of regulatory landscapes, and a commitment to ongoing updates and improvements. Effective compliance documentation not only helps organizations meet legal and regulatory obligations but also strengthens their overall cybersecurity posture by ensuring systematic and well-documented security practices. By adhering to best practices and remaining vigilant to the challenges, organizations can create comprehensive, clear, and effective compliance documentation that serves multiple purposes. It becomes a tool for internal governance, a guide for employees, and a record for external auditors and regulators.

Moreover, well-maintained compliance documentation can provide a competitive advantage by showcasing the organization's commitment to cybersecurity and building trust with customers, partners, and stakeholders. It reflects an organization's proactive stance towards cybersecurity, illustrating not just adherence to mandatory regulations but also a dedication to maintaining the highest standards of data protection and information security.

In summary, the development of compliance documentation is an essential component of a comprehensive cybersecurity strategy. It requires careful planning, ongoing management, and a commitment to best practices. With the right approach, organizations can turn compliance documentation from a regulatory requirement into a strategic asset that enhances their cybersecurity posture and supports their business objectives.

Automating control assessment

In the ever-evolving landscape of cybersecurity, automating control assessment is becoming increasingly vital for organizations. Automation in control assessment not only enhances efficiency and accuracy but also ensures continuous compliance with evolving standards and regulations.

The growing complexity and volume of cybersecurity threats, coupled with the dynamic nature of technological environments, make manual control assessments challenging and time-consuming. Automation aids in regularly assessing the effectiveness of security controls, identifying gaps, and ensuring compliance with regulatory requirements. It enables organizations to respond swiftly to changes in the threat landscape and adapt their security controls accordingly.

This section aims to guide readers on how to implement automation in their organizations for controls assessments, providing a comprehensive understanding of its benefits, methodologies, and best practices.

Benefits of automating control assessments

With any automation comes benefits to the end user. Some of the benefits of automating control assessments are discussed as follows:

- **Efficiency and scalability**: Automated systems can assess controls much faster than manual processes, handling large volumes of data and systems efficiently.

- **Consistency and accuracy**: Automation reduces the risk of human error, ensuring that assessments are consistent and reliable.

- **Real-time monitoring**: Automated tools provide continuous monitoring and real-time analysis, allowing organizations to promptly identify and address security issues.

- **Compliance management**: Automation simplifies compliance management by regularly checking controls against compliance requirements and generating necessary reports.

Starting with a clear strategy

Before implementing automation, it's crucial to have a clear strategy. This includes understanding the organization's specific needs, the controls to be assessed, and the compliance requirements to be met. The strategy should outline the objectives of automation, such as improving compliance, enhancing security posture, or increasing operational efficiency.

Choosing the right tools and technologies

Selecting the appropriate tools and technologies is critical for effective automation. The options range from comprehensive security management platforms to specialized tools focused on specific aspects of control assessment. Considerations include the tool's compatibility with existing systems, its ability to integrate with other security tools, and its ease of use.

Integration with existing systems

Effective automation requires seamless integration with the organization's existing security infrastructure. This includes integration with **security information and event management** (**SIEM**) systems, incident management systems, and other cybersecurity tools. Proper integration ensures that automated assessments provide a holistic view of the organization's security posture.

Developing automated assessment processes

Developing the processes for automated control assessments involves defining the scope, frequency, and methodologies of the assessments. This includes automating the collection of data from various sources, analyzing these data against predefined security standards, and generating reports and alerts based on the analysis.

Training and skills development

While automation reduces the need for manual intervention, it requires skilled personnel to manage and oversee the automated systems. Training and skills development for IT staff are essential to ensure they can effectively implement, manage, and interpret the results of automated assessments.

Testing and validation

Before fully implementing automated control assessments, it's important to test and validate the systems and processes. This involves running pilot tests to ensure that the automation works as intended and accurately assesses the controls. Feedback from these tests should be used to fine-tune the system.

Continuous improvement and adaptation

Automated control assessment is not a set-and-forget solution. It requires continuous improvement and adaptation to remain effective. This involves regularly updating the assessment criteria, refining the data analysis algorithms, and staying updated with the latest cybersecurity threats and trends.

Documenting the automation process

Maintaining comprehensive documentation of the automation process is crucial for several reasons. It aids in troubleshooting, facilitates audits and compliance checks, and ensures knowledge transfer within the organization. Documentation should include the configuration of automated tools, assessment criteria, and any changes or updates made to the system.

Addressing challenges and risks

Implementing automation in control assessment can present challenges, such as the risk of over-reliance on automated systems, potential compatibility issues with existing infrastructure, and the need for ongoing maintenance and updates. Addressing these challenges requires a balanced approach, where automated assessments are complemented with manual oversight and regular reviews.

Case studies and examples

Incorporating case studies or examples of successful implementations of automated control assessments can provide valuable insights and practical guidance. These examples can illustrate how organizations in similar industries or with similar risk profiles have effectively utilized automation, the challenges they faced, and the strategies they employed to overcome them.

Automating control assessment is a crucial step for organizations looking to enhance their cybersecurity posture in an efficient, consistent, and compliant manner. By carefully selecting the right tools, integrating them with existing systems, and continuously improving the processes, organizations can reap the benefits of automation in maintaining a robust and responsive cybersecurity framework. This approach not only streamlines the assessment of controls but also enables organizations to rapidly adapt to new threats and regulatory changes, ensuring a high level of security and compliance.

Summary

In this comprehensive chapter, we have journeyed through the essential aspects of cybersecurity within the framework of the NIST RMF, focusing on three pivotal areas: selecting security controls, developing compliance documentation, and automating control assessments. Each section has imparted crucial skills and knowledge, instrumental for any organization seeking to fortify its cybersecurity posture.

First, we discussed the importance of identifying and selecting appropriate security controls, with an emphasis on the need for a balance between security and business functionality. This forms the basis of a tailored security framework. Second, the vital role of comprehensive documentation in cybersecurity strategy was highlighted, serving both regulatory adherence and as a guide for effective audits, which is crucial for proper governance. Finally, we explored the impact of automating control assessments, which can enhance efficiency, accuracy, and responsiveness to threats and is essential for modern cybersecurity management in a complex digital landscape. Collectively, these elements equip organizations with the essential tools and knowledge for establishing, documenting, and maintaining a robust cybersecurity framework, ensuring asset protection, stakeholder trust, and resilience against cyber threats in today's fast-paced digital environment.

As we move on to the next chapter, *Assessment and Authorization*, we will build upon these foundations. We will delve into the practicalities of security assessments, unravel the intricacies of the risk assessment and authorization process, and strategize on preparing for security audits. This next chapter is a natural progression from the groundwork laid in identifying and selecting controls, documenting compliance processes, and automating assessments. It will focus on operationalizing these elements, transforming them from strategic initiatives into actionable, everyday practices that continuously safeguard the organization's digital assets and reputation.

7

Assessment and Authorization

The realm of cybersecurity is perpetually evolving, demanding continuous vigilance and a proactive stance from organizations and individuals alike. In this dynamic landscape, the implementation of the NIST **Risk Management Framework** (**RMF**) is not just a regulatory requirement, but a strategic imperative. This chapter delves into the practical aspects of security assessments, the intricacies of the risk assessment and authorization process, and the vital preparations needed for security audits.

This advanced chapter aims to equip you with the necessary skills to conduct comprehensive security assessments, adeptly navigate the risk assessment and authorization process, and prepare effectively for security audits. These skills are crucial for ensuring that the security measures and controls in place are not just theoretically sound but are also effective in the real-world scenarios they are intended to safeguard against.

In this chapter, we will cover the following main topics:

- Conducting security assessments
- The risk assessment and authorization process
- Preparing for security audits

Through these sections, you will gain a deeper understanding of how to assess security controls, manage risks, and ensure compliance with relevant standards and regulations. By the end of this chapter, you will not only comprehend the theoretical underpinnings of these processes but also be able to apply these principles in practical scenarios, thereby enhancing the security posture of your organization. This knowledge is not just a regulatory checkbox but a cornerstone in the foundation of any robust cybersecurity strategy.

Conducting security assessments

Security assessments are critical for identifying vulnerabilities, evaluating risks, and ensuring that the security controls are effectively mitigating those risks. This section delves into the methodologies and best practices for conducting thorough security assessments, as outlined in the NIST RMF and supported by other authoritative sources.

Understanding the scope of security assessments

The scope of a security assessment is foundational to its effectiveness, accuracy, and relevance. Defining this scope is a multi-dimensional task, requiring meticulous planning, stakeholder involvement, and a nuanced understanding of the organization's assets, systems, and the broader business context.

In initiating the scoping process, the first critical step is **identifying assets and systems**. This encompasses creating a comprehensive inventory of all organizational assets and categorizing them based on functionality, sensitivity, and criticality. This categorization is not static; it evolves as organizational priorities shift and new assets are introduced or retired. The aim is to prioritize assessment efforts in alignment with the potential impact on the organization.

Parallel to asset identification is **defining the organizational context**. This involves aligning the scope with the organization's business objectives and ensuring that legal, regulatory, and compliance requirements are thoroughly considered. Understanding how each asset and system supports the organization's objectives is crucial. It's about embedding the assessment within the business fabric of the organization, thus ensuring that the outcomes are not just technically sound but also strategically relevant.

Stakeholder involvement is another cornerstone of defining the scope. This includes identifying and engaging a diverse group of stakeholders – from IT staff and business unit leaders to legal and compliance officers. Their insights are crucial, providing a rounded perspective that encompasses technical, operational, and strategic considerations. Engaging these stakeholders early and continuously ensures that the scope is grounded in practical realities and organizational aspirations.

The **organization's risk appetite** and **tolerance levels** play a pivotal role in scoping the assessment. Understanding the level of risk the organization is willing to accept guides the depth and focus of the assessment. It's about balancing the need for security with operational realities and resource constraints. Defining specific risk tolerance levels for different assets and systems helps in prioritizing where the assessment efforts are most needed and where they can have the most significant impact.

Delineating boundaries is also essential. This includes not only internal systems and processes but also external services, third-party interactions, and the interfaces between them. In the context of increasing reliance on cloud services and third-party vendors, it becomes critical to establish what aspects fall within the assessment's purview. This delineation ensures that the assessment is comprehensive and covers all areas of potential vulnerability.

The defined scope must then be meticulously documented and regularly reviewed. This documentation serves as a reference point for all stakeholders and forms the basis for future assessments. It should be revisited regularly to reflect any changes in the organizational environment, asset inventory, and risk landscape. Continual evaluation and adjustment of the scope ensure that the assessment remains relevant and effective over time.

In summary, understanding and defining the scope of a security assessment is a critical process that sets the stage for the entire assessment. It requires a balanced approach that incorporates asset and system identification, organizational context, stakeholder involvement, risk assessment, and clear documentation. A well-defined scope ensures that the security assessment is not only comprehensive and compliant but also aligned with the organization's strategic goals and risk tolerance.

Selecting assessment methods

Selecting assessment methods is a crucial step in the security assessment process as it defines how the assessment will be conducted and what types of vulnerabilities and risks will be identified. This step requires a strategic approach, where the choice of methods aligns with the defined scope and the organization's broader security objectives. It involves a careful evaluation of various assessment techniques and tools, each offering unique insights into the organization's security posture.

In choosing the right assessment methods, it's important to consider a variety of techniques, each suited to uncover different types of vulnerabilities and risks. This often involves a combination of automated and manual methods, ensuring a comprehensive evaluation. Automated tools, such as vulnerability scanners and security software, are efficient for identifying known vulnerabilities and providing a broad overview of the security landscape. However, they often lack the depth and context that manual methods, such as penetration testing and code reviews, provide. Manual methods are more time-consuming but offer a detailed, nuanced understanding of specific vulnerabilities, particularly in complex systems and environments.

The selection process also involves considering the nature of the systems and data involved. For systems that handle sensitive or critical data, more rigorous and thorough assessment methods are needed. This may include in-depth penetration testing, security audits, and compliance checks. These methods are essential for ensuring that the security controls in place are robust and capable of protecting sensitive information against sophisticated threats.

Another key factor in selecting assessment methods is the regulatory and compliance landscape. Different industries and sectors have specific regulatory requirements that dictate certain assessment methods and standards. For example, organizations handling credit card information will need to comply with **Payment Card Industry Data Security Standard** (PCI-DSS) requirements, which specify particular security assessment methodologies. Ensuring compliance not only helps in avoiding legal and financial repercussions but also in maintaining customer trust and business integrity.

The organization's risk tolerance and appetite also influence the choice of assessment methods. Organizations with a lower risk tolerance may opt for more comprehensive and frequent assessments, while those willing to accept higher levels of risk might choose less rigorous methods. This decision should be aligned with the organization's overall risk management strategy and should consider the potential impact of security incidents on the organization's operations and reputation.

Collaboration and communication with stakeholders are essential in this selection process. Engaging with IT staff, security experts, business unit leaders, and other relevant personnel ensures that the chosen methods are feasible, effective, and aligned with operational realities. This collaborative approach also fosters a culture of security awareness and shared responsibility, which is crucial for the successful implementation of security measures.

Finally, the selection of assessment methods should be a dynamic process that can adapt to changes in the organizational environment, emerging threats, and technological advancements. Regular reviews and updates of the assessment methods ensure that they remain effective and relevant in the face of evolving cyber threats and security landscapes.

In conclusion, selecting the right assessment methods is a critical and nuanced process that requires a balance between technical efficacy, regulatory compliance, risk management, and operational feasibility. It involves a strategic combination of various techniques, tailored to the organization's unique security needs and objectives. A well-chosen set of assessment methods not only identifies current vulnerabilities and risks but also strengthens the organization's overall security strategy.

Developing an assessment plan

Developing an assessment plan is a critical phase in the security assessment process, where the strategic vision for the assessment is transformed into a practical and actionable roadmap. This plan serves as a guide, detailing the objectives, methodologies, timelines, and responsibilities associated with the assessment. Its development requires careful planning coordination, and a clear understanding of the organization's security goals and constraints. Let's look at the steps:

1. **Craft objectives and goals**: The first step in developing an assessment plan is to establish clear objectives and goals. These should align with the organization's broader security strategy and the specific scope of the assessment. Objectives might include identifying vulnerabilities, assessing the effectiveness of current security controls, or ensuring compliance with specific regulatory standards. These goals should be *smart*, providing a clear direction for the assessment activities.

2. **Methodology and techniques**: Once the objectives have been set, the next step is to select the appropriate methodologies and techniques that will be used in the assessment. This selection should be based on the scope of the assessment and the types of systems and data involved. The methodology section of the plan should detail the specific processes, tools, and techniques that will be employed, such as vulnerability scans, penetration tests, or compliance checks. It should also outline the criteria for evaluating the security controls and the benchmarks against which they will be measured.

3. **Define roles and responsibilities**: An effective assessment plan clearly defines the roles and responsibilities of everyone involved in the assessment process. This includes internal staff, such as IT personnel and security analysts, as well as external entities such as third-party auditors or consultants. Assigning clear roles and responsibilities ensures accountability and facilitates effective coordination among different teams and individuals.

4. **Timeline and phases**: The assessment plan should outline a detailed timeline, including the start and end dates and the key milestones. It should also break down the assessment into distinct phases, such as preparation, execution, reporting, and follow-up. This phased approach helps in managing the assessment more effectively and ensures that each stage receives the appropriate focus and resources.

5. **Resource allocation**: Allocating the necessary resources is critical for the successful execution of the security assessment. The plan should detail the human, technical, and financial resources required for each phase of the assessment. This includes staffing needs, technical tools and equipment, and any budgetary considerations. Proper resource allocation ensures that the assessment team has everything they need to conduct a thorough and effective assessment.

6. **Communication and risk management**: Effective communication and reporting mechanisms are essential components of the assessment plan. This includes regular updates to stakeholders, interim reports, and the final assessment report. The plan should specify the formats and channels for communication, as well as the frequency and content of the updates and reports. Clear communication ensures transparency and keeps all stakeholders informed throughout the assessment process.

7. **Contingency and risk management**: The assessment plan should also include contingency plans and risk management strategies. This involves identifying potential risks and challenges that could arise during the assessment and outlining strategies to mitigate them. Contingency planning ensures that the assessment can proceed smoothly, even in the face of unforeseen challenges or disruptions.

In conclusion, developing an assessment plan is a comprehensive process that sets the stage for a successful security assessment. It involves defining clear objectives, selecting appropriate methodologies, assigning roles and responsibilities, planning timelines and resources, and establishing communication and contingency plans. A well-developed assessment plan not only guides the assessment team through a structured process but also aligns the assessment activities with the organization's overall security objectives. Let's look at the steps:

1. **Execute the assessment**: The execution phase of the security assessment is where the planning and preparation come to fruition. It is the actionable stage where the assessment team applies the chosen methodologies to evaluate the security controls, identify vulnerabilities, and assess compliance with relevant standards. This phase requires meticulous execution, adherence to the established plan, and flexibility to adapt to emerging findings.

2. **Initiate the assessment**: The execution phase begins with initiating the assessment, as outlined in the plan. This involves setting up the necessary tools and resources, briefing the assessment team, and ensuring that all participants are clear on their roles and responsibilities. It's essential to confirm that all logistical aspects are in place, such as access to systems, availability of necessary credentials, and alignment with operational schedules.

3. **Systematic evaluation of security controls**: A key component of this phase is the systematic evaluation of security controls. This involves testing the effectiveness of technical controls, such as firewalls, intrusion detection systems, and encryption protocols. It also includes reviewing administrative controls such as policies, procedures, and training programs. The assessment should be thorough and unbiased, providing an accurate picture of the security posture.

4. **Vulnerability identification and analysis**: As vulnerabilities are identified, they should be carefully analyzed to understand their impact and severity. This analysis involves considering the likelihood of exploitation, the potential impact on the organization, and the ease of remediation. The team should prioritize vulnerabilities based on this analysis, focusing on those that pose the greatest risk to the organization.

5. **Compliance checks**: In addition to identifying vulnerabilities, the execution phase should also include compliance checks. This involves evaluating the organization's adherence to relevant laws, regulations, and industry standards. Compliance checks are critical for ensuring that the organization meets its legal and ethical obligations and avoids potential penalties or reputational damage.

6. **Document your findings**: Throughout the execution phase, it's crucial to document the findings meticulously. This documentation should include details of the vulnerabilities identified, the effectiveness of existing controls, and any deviations from compliance standards. The findings should be recorded in a clear, organized, and accessible manner, forming the basis for the subsequent reporting phase.

7. **Adapt to your findings**: The assessment team must be prepared to adapt their approach based on the findings. If significant vulnerabilities or compliance issues are discovered, the team may need to adjust their focus or methodology to ensure that these critical areas are thoroughly evaluated. Flexibility and adaptability are key in responding to the dynamic nature of the assessment process.

8. **Stakeholder engagement**: Engaging stakeholders throughout the execution phase is essential for maintaining transparency and support. Regular updates on the progress and preliminary findings should be provided to relevant stakeholders, ensuring that they are aware of any significant issues or challenges.

9. **Conclude the execution phase**: The execution phase concludes once all planned assessment activities are completed. This involves a final review of the documentation, ensuring that all findings are accurately and comprehensively recorded. The team should also ensure that all tools and resources are properly accounted for and that any temporary changes made to systems or processes during the assessment are reverted.

In summary, executing the assessment is a critical phase that demands thoroughness, accuracy, and adaptability. It involves systematically evaluating security controls, identifying and analyzing vulnerabilities, compliance checks, and meticulously documenting your findings. Effective execution not only provides a clear understanding of the organization's security posture but also lays the foundation for the subsequent phases of reporting and remediation.

Reporting and analysis

The reporting and analysis phase is a critical component of the security assessment process where the findings from the execution phase are compiled, analyzed, and communicated. This stage transforms raw data and observations into actionable insights, providing a comprehensive view of the organization's security posture. It involves meticulous documentation, thorough analysis, and effective communication of the assessment findings. Let's look at the steps:

1. **Compile your findings**: The first step in this phase is to compile all findings from the assessment. This includes vulnerabilities identified, assessment of security controls, and observations related to compliance. The compilation should be organized and detailed, ensuring that all relevant information is captured. This comprehensive collection forms the basis for the in-depth analysis that follows.

2. **Analyze your findings**: Analyzing the findings involves a deeper dive into the data to understand the implications of each identified vulnerability and control deficiency. The analysis should consider the severity of vulnerabilities, their potential impact on the organization, and the effectiveness of existing security controls. It's important to contextualize the findings within the organization's specific operational environment and risk landscape.

3. **Prioritize risks**: A key aspect of the analysis is prioritizing identified risks. This involves ranking vulnerabilities and issues based on their severity, likelihood of occurrence, and potential impact. Prioritization helps in focusing remediation efforts on the most critical areas, ensuring efficient allocation of resources.

4. **Develop recommendations**: Based on the analysis, the assessment team should develop recommendations for addressing the identified vulnerabilities and compliance gaps. These recommendations should be practical, feasible, and tailored to the organization's context. They might include technical fixes, policy updates, training programs, or changes to governance structures.

5. **Draft the assessment report**: The culmination of this phase is drafting the assessment report. This report should be clear, concise, and structured, providing a summary of the findings, analysis, and recommendations. It should include an executive summary for high-level stakeholders and detailed sections for technical teams. The report should be accessible to all intended audiences, ensuring that the findings and recommendations are clearly understood.

6. **Stakeholder communication**: Effective communication with stakeholders is crucial during this phase. The assessment team should present the findings and recommendations to relevant stakeholders, including senior management, IT teams, and other affected parties. This communication should be open and transparent, ensuring that all stakeholders are aware of the security posture and the steps needed to enhance it.

7. **Feedback and iteration**: Once the report has been communicated, it's important to gather feedback from stakeholders. This feedback may lead to further refinement of the recommendations or additional analysis. The iterative nature of this process ensures that the final report is comprehensive and aligned with the organization's needs and expectations.

8. **Finalization and approval**: The final step is the formal finalization and approval of the assessment report. This involves incorporating any feedback, making final edits, and obtaining formal sign-off from authorized personnel. The approved report then serves as an official record of the assessment and a guide for future remediation efforts.

In summary, the reporting and analysis phase is essential in translating the findings of the security assessment into actionable insights and recommendations. It involves thoroughly compiling and analyzing findings, prioritizing risks, developing recommendations, drafting the assessment report, stakeholder communication, and iterative refinement. This phase not only provides a clear understanding of the organization's security posture but also sets the stage for effective remediation and enhancement of security measures.

Recommending improvements

The recommending improvements phase is a pivotal part of the security assessment process that focuses on converting the insights gained from the assessment into practical, actionable steps to enhance the organization's security posture. This phase involves synthesizing the findings and analyses into coherent, strategic recommendations that address identified vulnerabilities and compliance gaps. It is characterized by a forward-looking approach, aiming to not just remedy current issues but also to bolster the overall resilience and security of the organization. Let's look at the steps:

1. **Synthesize your findings into actionable recommendations**: The first step in this phase is to synthesize the findings from the assessment into a set of clear, actionable recommendations. These recommendations should directly address the vulnerabilities and deficiencies that were identified during the assessment. They should be specific, measurable, and achievable, with a clear indication of how they will improve security and compliance.

2. **Tailor recommendations to the organization**: The recommendations must be tailored to the specific context and needs of the organization. This includes considering the organization's size, complexity, industry, regulatory environment, and available resources. Tailoring ensures that the recommendations are not only effective but also feasible and relevant to the organization's unique circumstances.

3. **Prioritize recommendations**: Given that resources are often limited, prioritizing the recommendations is essential. This involves ranking the recommendations based on factors such as the severity of the associated risk, the potential impact of implementation, and the urgency of addressing certain vulnerabilities. Prioritization helps in focusing efforts and resources on the most critical areas first.

4. **Develop an implementation roadmap**: Once the recommendations have been prioritized, the next step is to develop a detailed implementation roadmap. This roadmap should outline the steps needed to implement each recommendation, along with timelines, responsible parties, and required resources. The roadmap serves as a practical guide for the organization to follow in enhancing its security posture.

5. **Integrate with the overall security strategy**: The recommendations should be integrated with the organization's overall security strategy. This involves aligning them with existing security policies, procedures, and controls, and ensuring they contribute to the strategic security objectives of the organization. Integration ensures that the recommendations not only address immediate vulnerabilities but also strengthen the broader security framework.

6. **Stakeholder engagement and buy-in**: Engaging with key stakeholders is critical in this phase. Presenting the recommendations to stakeholders, including senior management, IT teams, and other relevant personnel, ensures awareness and buy-in. Their feedback and perspectives can further refine the recommendations and enhance their effectiveness.

7. **Documentation and communication**: Documenting and communicating the recommendations is an important step. This involves creating a comprehensive report or presentation that lays out the recommendations, their rationale, and the implementation roadmap. Effective communication ensures that all relevant parties understand the recommended actions and their role in implementation.

8. **Continuous improvement and feedback loop**: Finally, establishing a continuous improvement and feedback loop is vital. This involves monitoring the implementation of the recommendations, assessing their effectiveness, and adjusting as necessary. The feedback loop ensures that the security posture remains dynamic and adaptable to evolving threats and changing organizational needs.

In summary, the recommending improvements phase is about transforming assessment findings into strategic, actionable steps to enhance the organization's security. It involves synthesizing findings into tailored recommendations, prioritizing them, developing an implementation roadmap, integrating them with the overall security strategy, engaging stakeholders, documenting and communicating the recommendations, and establishing a continuous improvement loop. This phase is crucial for turning insights into impactful actions that strengthen the organization's security and resilience.

Follow-up and review

The follow-up and review phase is the final and ongoing component of the security assessment process. It focuses on implementing the recommended improvements and continuously evaluating their effectiveness. This phase ensures that the actions that are taken in response to the assessment findings are not only executed but also contribute to the long-term enhancement of the organization's security posture. It involves monitoring, reviewing, and updating security measures in line with evolving threats and organizational changes. Let's look at the steps:

1. **Monitor the implementation of recommendations**: The first step in this phase is to diligently monitor the implementation of the recommendations. This involves ensuring that the actions outlined in the implementation roadmap are being carried out as planned. Regular check-ins and progress reports are essential for tracking the implementation status and addressing any issues or delays that may arise.

2. **Assess the effectiveness of the implemented changes**: Once the recommendations have been implemented, assessing their effectiveness is crucial. This assessment can be achieved through various means, such as security audits, testing, or performance metrics. The goal is to determine whether the implemented changes have effectively addressed the identified vulnerabilities and improved the security posture.

3. **Regular reviews and updates**: The security landscape is dynamic, with new threats emerging and organizational environments evolving. Therefore, regularly reviewing and updating security measures is essential. This includes revisiting the security assessment plan, methodologies, and findings, and adjusting them as necessary. Regular reviews ensure that the organization's security measures remain relevant and effective.

4. **Engage stakeholders in the review process**: Engaging stakeholders in the review process is important for maintaining a collaborative approach to security. This engagement can take the form of meetings, reports, or feedback sessions. Stakeholder involvement ensures that different perspectives are considered and that there is organizational buy-in for ongoing security efforts.

5. **Document lessons learned**: An important aspect of the follow-up and review phase is documenting lessons learned from the assessment process and its aftermath. This documentation should capture what worked well, what challenges were encountered, and how they were overcome. Lessons learned are invaluable for improving future security assessments and overall security management practices.

6. **Continuous improvement**: The essence of this phase is the commitment to continuous improvement. This means not only addressing current security issues but also proactively identifying and mitigating potential future risks. Continuous improvement involves staying informed about new threats, technologies, and best practices, and integrating this knowledge into the organization's security strategy.

7. **Feedback loop**: Establishing a feedback loop is key to continuous improvement. This loop allows for the ongoing collection and analysis of feedback from various sources, including security

assessments, stakeholder input, and industry developments. The feedback loop facilitates adaptive and responsive security management, ensuring the organization remains resilient against evolving cyber threats.

8. **Prepare for the next assessment**: Finally, this phase sets the stage for the next security assessment. It involves evaluating the overall process, identifying areas for improvement, and planning for the next assessment cycle. This preparation ensures that the organization remains vigilant and proactive in its approach to cybersecurity.

This follow-up and review phase is about ensuring that the security improvements are effectively implemented, continuously evaluated, and updated in response to new challenges. It involves monitoring the implementation of recommendations, assessing their effectiveness, regularly reviewing and updating security measures, engaging stakeholders, documenting lessons learned, committing to continuous improvement, establishing a feedback loop, and preparing for the next assessment. This phase ensures that the security assessment process leads to sustained enhancements in the organization's security posture.

As we work through the process of conducting security assessments, we will begin to see the bigger picture of vulnerabilities that affect our organization, and more importantly, if we have an understanding of our business, the risk that we are potentially subjecting our business to. In the next section, we'll dive more into the risk assessment process.

The risk assessment and authorization process

The risk assessment and authorization process is a critical component of the NIST RMF that focuses on evaluating the risks associated with an organization's information systems and authorizing them for operation based on this evaluation. This process is integral to maintaining the security and integrity of systems and data and involves a thorough assessment of potential threats, vulnerabilities, and impacts, followed by a formal decision-making process.

Understanding the risk assessment in the RMF context

The **risk assessment**, as conceptualized within the NIST RMF, is a fundamental process that serves as the backbone of an organization's cybersecurity strategy. It is a systematic and comprehensive approach to identifying, evaluating, and managing the risks to organizational assets, operations, and individuals. It allows organizations to make smart resource decisions and achieve mission outcomes at acceptable, managed risk levels. This subsection explores the intricacies of the risk assessment within the RMF context, underscoring its significance, methodology, and integration with broader cybersecurity objectives:

- **Significance of the risk assessment in RMF**: The risk assessment is not merely a compliance exercise but a strategic endeavor that informs decision-making at all levels of the organization. It is instrumental in identifying security vulnerabilities and potential threats, evaluating the potential impacts of these threats, and prioritizing the risks based on their severity and likelihood. This assessment is crucial for developing an informed, proactive stance toward managing cybersecurity risks. It provides ongoing visibility into changing risk landscapes through periodic assessments.

- **Integrating the risk assessment with organizational goals**: An effective risk assessment within the RMF framework necessitates alignment with the organization's broader goals and objectives. It should reflect the organization's mission, operational context, and the value of the assets it seeks to protect. This alignment ensures that the risk assessment process is not only technically sound but also strategically relevant, addressing risks that are most critical to the organization's success and sustainability.

- **Comprehensive threat and vulnerability identification**: A key aspect of the risk assessment in RMF is the comprehensive identification of threats and vulnerabilities. This involves an extensive examination of all potential sources of risk, including cyber threats, natural disasters, system failures, and human errors. It also entails a thorough analysis of vulnerabilities within information systems, encompassing technical flaws, process weaknesses, and human factors.

- **Risk impact analysis and prioritization**: Once threats and vulnerabilities have been identified, the next step is to analyze the potential impact of these risks on the organization. This analysis should consider the consequences of security breaches in terms of operational disruption, financial loss, legal liabilities, and reputational damage. Risk prioritization is then conducted, categorizing risks based on their potential impact and the likelihood of occurrence, which guides the allocation of resources and efforts in risk mitigation.

- **Risk tolerance and appetite assessment**: Understanding the organization's risk tolerance and appetite is fundamental in the RMF risk assessment process. It involves determining the level of risk the organization is willing to accept in pursuit of its objectives. This assessment guides the development of risk thresholds and influences the selection of appropriate security controls and mitigation strategies. This should be done by interviewing key stakeholders, understanding the industry and what items are part of the risk appetite, validating the appetite statements and developing them into key risk indicators, and finally, monitoring.

- **Regulatory and compliance considerations**: The risk assessment process in RMF also encompasses regulatory and compliance considerations. Organizations must ensure that their risk management practices align with legal and industry-specific cybersecurity standards. This compliance aspect is crucial for avoiding legal penalties, maintaining customer trust, and fulfilling contractual obligations.

- **Continuous risk assessment and adaptation**: RMF advocates for a continuous, adaptive approach to risk assessment. Cybersecurity threats are dynamic, and the risk landscape evolves constantly. Therefore, organizations need to regularly review and update their risk assessments to reflect changes in the threat environment, technological advancements, and shifts in organizational priorities.

- **Stakeholder engagement and communication**: An effective risk assessment within RMF requires active engagement and communication with stakeholders across the organization. This involves including all key personnel in the risk assessment process, ensuring that their insights and expertise inform the assessment. Effective stakeholder communication enhances the comprehensiveness and accuracy of the risk assessment and fosters a culture of cybersecurity awareness and responsibility.

In conclusion, understanding the risk assessment within the RMF context is about appreciating its strategic importance, aligning it with organizational goals, comprehensively identifying threats and vulnerabilities, analyzing and prioritizing risks, assessing risk tolerance, considering regulatory compliance, embracing a continuous and adaptive approach, and engaging stakeholders effectively. This comprehensive understanding is crucial for developing robust, resilient cybersecurity strategies that protect organizational assets and ensure operational continuity.

Conducting the risk assessment

Conducting the risk assessment involves several key steps:

1. **Threat identification**: Identifying potential threats that could exploit vulnerabilities in information systems or processes.

2. **Vulnerability identification**: Determining weaknesses in systems, processes, or controls that could be exploited by threats.

3. **Impact analysis**: Assessing the potential impact of threats that are exploiting vulnerabilities in terms of the confidentiality, integrity, and availability of information and systems.

4. **Likelihood determination**: Evaluating the probability that a given threat will exploit a vulnerability.

5. **Risk determination**: Combining the impact and likelihood assessments to determine the level of risk for each threat and vulnerability pair.

Documenting and reporting risk assessment findings

The documentation and reporting phase is an essential component of the risk assessment process within the NIST RMF. This phase involves meticulously recording and effectively communicating the findings from the risk assessment. Proper documentation and reporting are crucial for ensuring that the insights gained from the risk assessment are understood and actionable and that they contribute to the informed decision-making process regarding the organization's cybersecurity posture.

Key elements of documentation and reporting

The following key elements of good documentation are crucial as you work through the risk management process:

- **Comprehensive documentation**: The documentation process should capture all significant details of the risk assessment. This includes the scope of the assessment, methodologies used, detailed descriptions of identified threats and vulnerabilities, the impacts and likelihoods of these risks, and the overall risk levels. The documentation should be clear, accurate, and thorough, serving as a definitive record of the assessment findings.

- **Risk assessment report**: The culmination of the documentation process is the risk assessment report. This report should be structured and comprehensive, presenting the findings in an organized manner. It typically includes an executive summary for senior management, detailed findings for technical teams, and recommendations for risk mitigation. The report should be tailored to its audience, ensuring that it is both informative and accessible to all stakeholders.

- **Effective communication**: Reporting involves effectively communicating the risk assessment's findings to relevant stakeholders. This can include presentations, meetings, or distributing the risk assessment report. The goal is to ensure that decision-makers, security teams, and other relevant personnel are fully informed about the organization's risk profile and understand the implications of the findings.

- **Actionable insights**: The documentation and reporting should not only provide a snapshot of the current risk landscape but also offer actionable insights. This includes prioritizing risks, suggesting potential mitigation strategies, and highlighting areas that require immediate attention. The aim is to provide a clear path forward for addressing identified risks.

- **A basis for decision-making**: The documented findings and the risk assessment report form the basis for strategic decision-making regarding cybersecurity. They inform the development of risk mitigation plans, security control implementations, and overall cybersecurity strategy. Therefore, the report should be seen as a foundational document that guides the organization's response to cybersecurity risks.

- **Record keeping and compliance**: Proper documentation and reporting also serve as a record for compliance purposes. It demonstrates the organization's due diligence in assessing risks and can be critical in the event of a security incident or audit. Maintaining these records is essential for demonstrating adherence to regulatory requirements and industry standards.

In summary, documenting and reporting risk assessment findings are vital steps in the risk management process. They involve creating detailed, structured documentation of the risk assessment process and findings, effectively communicating these findings to stakeholders, providing actionable insights for risk mitigation, and providing a basis for informed decision-making and compliance. This phase ensures that the valuable insights gained from the risk assessment are utilized effectively to enhance the organization's cybersecurity posture.

Risk mitigation strategy development

Based on the risk assessment's findings, a risk mitigation strategy should be developed. This strategy involves identifying and selecting appropriate controls to reduce identified risks to an acceptable level. The strategy should align with the organization's risk tolerance and involve a cost-benefit analysis to ensure that the mitigation efforts are proportionate to the risks.

System authorization process

The system authorization process, often referred to as the **Authorization to Operate (ATO)**, is the formal decision by a senior official to authorize the operation of an information system. This decision is based on the risk assessment findings and the implementation of required security controls:

- **Authorization package preparation**: Develop an authorization package that includes the system security plan, the risk assessment report, and a plan of action and milestones for any unresolved security issues
- **Review and decision**: The senior official reviews the authorization package and makes an informed decision about whether to authorize the system, deny authorization, or require additional risk mitigation measures

Continuous monitoring and authorization maintenance

Once a system has been authorized, continuously monitoring the security controls and the risk posture is essential. This involves regularly assessing the effectiveness of the implemented controls, monitoring changes in the threat landscape, and updating the risk assessment and mitigation strategies as needed. Continuous monitoring supports the ongoing authorization of the system and ensures that security risks are managed effectively over time.

In summary, the risk assessment and authorization process is a systematic approach to understanding, assessing, and managing risks in the context of the NIST RMF. It involves conducting comprehensive risk assessments, documenting and reporting findings, developing risk mitigation strategies, making informed authorization decisions, and maintaining authorization through continuous monitoring. This process is crucial for ensuring the security and resilience of information systems within the organization.

Preparing for security audits

In the ever-evolving landscape of cybersecurity, security audits have become an indispensable tool for organizations to ensure the integrity, confidentiality, and availability of their information systems. This introductory section aims to provide you with a fundamental understanding of security audits, their importance, and the various types that organizations might encounter. Additionally, it offers an overview of common audit frameworks and standards, setting the stage for a comprehensive approach to preparing for these critical evaluations.

Understanding the purpose and importance of security audits

Security audits are structured evaluations of an organization's information systems and processes to ascertain whether they comply with the established security policies, standards, and regulatory requirements. The primary purpose of these audits is to identify vulnerabilities, assess risks, and ensure that appropriate controls are in place to mitigate those risks. They are critical for several reasons:

- **Ensuring compliance**: Audits help organizations comply with legal, regulatory, and industry standards, thereby avoiding potential fines and legal issues

- **Enhancing security posture**: By identifying vulnerabilities and gaps, audits enable organizations to strengthen their security measures

- **Building trust**: By demonstrating adherence to security best practices, audits help in building trust among customers, partners, and stakeholders

Types of security audits

Organizations may undergo various types of security audits, each with its specific focus and methodology:

- **Internal audits**: Conducted by the organization's audit team to internally assess the effectiveness of security measures

- **External audits**: Performed by independent third-party entities to provide an objective assessment of security practices

- **Regulatory audits**: Aimed at ensuring compliance with specific legal and regulatory requirements

- **Compliance audits**: Focused on adherence to industry standards and best practices, such as ISO 27001 or NIST frameworks

Overview of common audit frameworks and standards

Different frameworks and standards guide the process and expectations of security audits. Some of the most widely recognized are as follows:

- **ISO/IEC 27001**: An international standard that provides a framework for **Information Security Management Systems (ISMS)**

- **NIST SP 800 series**: A set of guidelines provided by NIST for improving the security of information systems

- **PCI-DSS**: The **Payment Card Industry Data Security Standard**, which is crucial for organizations handling credit card transactions

- **HIPAA**: The **Health Insurance Portability and Accountability Act**, which is vital for healthcare organizations in protecting patient data

In this subsection, we will delve into strategies and practical steps to effectively prepare for these diverse types of security audits. Our focus will be on helping organizations develop a robust, audit-ready posture that not only meets compliance requirements but also significantly enhances their overall security infrastructure. By understanding the nuances and expectations of security audits, organizations can approach these evaluations with confidence and a clear sense of purpose.

Audit preparation strategies

Preparing for a security audit is a critical task for any organization committed to maintaining a robust cybersecurity posture. Effective preparation not only facilitates a smoother audit process but also significantly enhances the likelihood of a favorable outcome. This subsection outlines key strategies and steps that organizations should undertake to prepare efficiently for security audits.

Establishing an audit preparation team

Let's look at the steps involved:

1. **Form a cross-functional team**: Assemble a team comprising members from various departments such as IT, security, legal, and operations. This diversity ensures that all aspects of the audit are covered.

2. **Define roles and responsibilities**: Assign specific roles and responsibilities to team members, ensuring clarity in who does what during the preparation phase.

3. **Regular meetings and coordination**: Schedule regular meetings for the preparation team to track progress, address challenges, and ensure alignment of efforts.

Understanding the audit's scope and objectives

Let's look at the steps involved:

1. **Clarify the scope**: Engage with the auditors or review audit standards to understand the scope of the audit. Knowing what systems, processes, and controls will be evaluated helps focus preparation efforts.

2. **Identify audit objectives**: Determine the specific objectives of the audit, whether it's compliance, security validation, or both. This understanding helps tailor the preparation to meet these objectives.

Reviewing previous audit reports and action items

Let's look at the steps involved:

1. **Analyze past findings**: Review previous audit reports to identify recurring issues or unresolved items. Addressing these areas can significantly improve the current audit's outcome.

2. **Implement past recommendations**: Ensure that recommendations from previous audits have been implemented and documented. This demonstrates an ongoing commitment to improving security practices.

In summary, effective audit preparation involves a structured and strategic approach that includes forming a dedicated team, understanding the audit scope, reviewing past audits, conducting self-assessments, updating policies and procedures, enhancing internal communication, planning logistics, and establishing a primary point of contact. By following these strategies, organizations can approach audits with confidence, ensuring they are well-prepared to showcase their commitment to cybersecurity and compliance.

Conducting a pre-audit self-assessment

A **pre-audit self-assessment** is a critical step in preparing for a security audit. It involves evaluating the organization's current security posture against the expected audit criteria. This self-assessment helps identify and address gaps before the external audit, thereby enhancing the organization's readiness and potentially improving the audit outcomes. This section outlines the steps and considerations for conducting an effective pre-audit self-assessment.

Tools and techniques for self-assessment

Let's look at this in detail:

1. **Utilize assessment frameworks**: Leverage established frameworks such as NIST or ISO checklists (the one for NIST is available at the National Checklist Program) to guide the self-assessment. These frameworks provide a comprehensive basis for evaluating security controls.

2. **Automated assessment tools**: Employ automated tools for vulnerability scanning and configuration checks. These tools can efficiently identify technical deficiencies in systems and networks.

Identifying and addressing gaps in security controls

Let's look at this in detail:

1. **Gap analysis**: Compare current security practices against the audit standards to identify gaps. This analysis should cover all areas that the audit will touch upon, including technical, administrative, and physical controls.

2. **Prioritize findings**: Prioritize the gaps that were identified based on their potential impact and the likelihood of them being flagged in the audit. Focus on addressing high-priority gaps first.

Documentation review and verification

Let's look at this in detail:

1. **Policy and procedure review**: Thoroughly review all relevant security policies and procedures. Ensure they are up-to-date, accurately reflect current practices, and align with audit standards.

2. **Evidence gathering**: Collect evidence demonstrating that security controls are implemented and effective. This evidence might include logs, reports, policy documents, and records of security incidents and their resolution.

In summary, conducting a pre-audit self-assessment is a proactive approach to understanding and improving an organization's security posture. It involves utilizing assessment frameworks and tools, conducting gap analysis, reviewing documentation, engaging stakeholders, conducting mock audits, developing action plans, and continually reviewing and updating security practices. This thorough preparation not only sets the stage for a successful audit but also contributes to the overall strengthening of the organization's cybersecurity defenses.

Updating policies and procedures

A critical aspect of preparing for a security audit is ensuring that all security policies and procedures are current, comprehensive, and effectively implemented. This subsection focuses on the steps and considerations necessary for updating these crucial elements to meet the standards expected in a security audit.

Comprehensive review of existing policies and procedures

Let's look at the steps involved:

1. **Evaluate the current documentation**: Begin by conducting a thorough review of all existing security policies and procedures. Assess whether they accurately reflect the current operational environment and security practices.

2. **Align with standards and best practices**: Ensure that these policies and procedures align with the relevant security standards and best practices, such as those outlined by NIST, ISO, or industry-specific regulations.

Identifying areas for improvement

Let's look at the steps involved:

1. **Gap analysis**: Identify areas where policies and procedures are lacking or outdated. Pay particular attention to areas that have undergone recent changes, such as new technologies, business processes, or regulatory requirements.

2. **Stakeholder input**: Gather feedback from various departments and teams to understand practical challenges and operational insights. This input is invaluable for making policies and procedures both comprehensive and practical.

Developing and refining security procedures

Let's look at the steps involved:

1. **Procedure updates**: Update existing procedures or develop new ones to address identified gaps. Ensure that these procedures are clear, actionable, and tailored to the specific needs and context of the organization.

2. **Consistency across the organization**: Strive for consistency in security procedures across different departments and functions to ensure a unified security posture.

The role of training and awareness in policy implementation

Let's look at the steps involved:

1. **Employee training programs**: Develop comprehensive training programs to educate employees about the updated policies and procedures. This training should cover the rationale behind the policies, the role of employees in compliance, and the implications of non-compliance.
2. **Ongoing awareness initiatives**: Implement ongoing awareness initiatives to keep security at the forefront of organizational culture. Regular updates, newsletters, and workshops can be effective tools.

Documentation and accessibility

Let's look at the steps involved:

1. **Accessible documentation**: Ensure that updated policies and procedures are documented in an accessible format. This includes maintaining them in a centralized repository where employees can easily access and reference them.
2. **Version control and record keeping**: Maintain proper version control of all documents and keep records of updates and changes. This practice is crucial for demonstrating continuous improvement and compliance in audits.

Policy and procedure approval process

Let's look at the steps involved:

1. **Review and approval**: Once updates are made, have the revised policies and procedures reviewed and approved by the appropriate authority within the organization, such as the security team, legal department, or executive leadership
2. **Official communication**: Communicate the updates officially within the organization, ensuring that all employees are aware of the new policies and procedures

In summary, updating policies and procedures is a vital step in preparing for a security audit. It involves a comprehensive review and alignment with standards, identifying areas for improvement, developing and refining procedures, incorporating emerging threats and technologies, emphasizing training and awareness, ensuring documentation accessibility, and undergoing a formal approval process. This thorough approach ensures that an organization's policies and procedures are not only compliant but also effective in safeguarding against cybersecurity risks.

Enhancing security controls

When preparing for a security audit, enhancing existing security controls is a critical step. This process involves evaluating, strengthening, and, where necessary, implementing new controls to ensure a robust defense against security threats. This subsection outlines key strategies for enhancing security controls to meet and exceed the standards expected in a security audit.

Reviewing and strengthening technical controls

Let's look at the steps involved:

1. **Assess the current controls**: Begin with a thorough assessment of the existing technical controls, such as firewalls, intrusion detection systems, encryption, and access controls. Evaluate their effectiveness in the current security landscape.

2. **Upgrades and improvements**: Based on the assessment, upgrade or improve technical controls to address any deficiencies. This might include updating software, patching vulnerabilities, or deploying advanced security technologies.

Implementing administrative and physical security measures

Let's look at the steps involved:

1. **Administrative controls**: Strengthen administrative controls, which include security policies, procedures, and employee training programs. Ensure these controls are effectively implemented and adhered to within the organization.

2. **Physical security measures**: Evaluate and enhance physical security measures. This includes secure access to facilities, protecting critical infrastructure, and monitoring physical access points.

Continuous monitoring and incident response planning

Let's look at the steps involved:

1. **Real-time monitoring**: Implement or enhance continuous monitoring systems to detect and respond to security incidents in real time. These systems should be capable of alerting relevant personnel to potential security breaches.

2. **Incident response plan**: Review and update the incident response plan. Ensure it is comprehensive and allows for a swift, coordinated response to security incidents. Regularly test and refine the plan through drills and simulations.

Vendor and third-party security management

Let's look at the steps involved:

1. **Vendor risk assessment**: Conduct thorough security assessments of vendors and third-party service providers. Ensure they adhere to the same security standards as the organization.

2. **Contractual agreements and compliance**: Review contractual agreements for compliance with security requirements. Include clauses that mandate adherence to specific security standards and practices.

In summary, enhancing security controls is an essential step in preparing for a security audit. It involves reviewing and strengthening technical, administrative, and physical controls, integrating advanced technologies, managing vendor and third-party security, conducting regular audits and assessments, and ensuring compliance with legal and regulatory standards. These efforts not only prepare the organization for a successful audit but also significantly contribute to the overall strengthening of its cybersecurity posture.

Data management and protection

Effective data management and protection are crucial components of an organization's cybersecurity strategy, especially in the context of preparing for a security audit. This subsection focuses on establishing and enhancing practices that ensure the integrity, confidentiality, and availability of data, which are key areas of focus in security audits.

Data classification and handling protocols

Let's look at the steps involved:

1. **Develop a data classification scheme**: Implement a data classification system to categorize data based on sensitivity and the level of protection required. Common classifications include public, internal, confidential, and highly confidential.

2. **Handle protocols for each classification**: Establish and document handling protocols for each data classification level. This includes access controls, encryption standards, and transmission protocols.

Ensuring data integrity and confidentiality

Let's look at the steps involved:

1. **Data integrity measures**: Implement measures to ensure data integrity, such as checksums, digital signatures, and version controls. Regular data integrity checks can help in the early detection of unauthorized data alterations.

2. **Encryption and access controls**: Utilize encryption for data at rest and in transit. Strengthen access controls to ensure that only authorized personnel can access sensitive data.

Backup and recovery procedures

Let's look at the steps involved:

1. **Regular data backups**: Establish a routine for regular data backups. This includes determining what data to back up, how often, and using what methods.

2. **Disaster recovery planning**: Develop a comprehensive disaster recovery plan that includes procedures for restoring data in the event of a loss. Regularly test and update the disaster recovery plan to ensure its effectiveness.

In summary, data management and protection are critical to ensuring an organization's readiness for a security audit. Key aspects include establishing data classification and handling protocols, ensuring data integrity and confidentiality, implementing effective backup and recovery procedures, complying with data protection regulations, managing the data life cycle, overseeing third-party data management, training employees, and conducting regular monitoring and internal audits. These practices not only help in passing security audits but also play a vital role in safeguarding the organization's most valuable asset: its data.

Stakeholder engagement and communication

Effective stakeholder engagement and communication are vital in preparing for and conducting a successful security audit. This subsection outlines strategies for involving relevant stakeholders in the audit process, ensuring clear communication, and fostering a collaborative approach to cybersecurity within the organization.

Identifying and engaging key stakeholders

Let's look at the steps involved:

1. **Stakeholder identification**: Identify all relevant stakeholders who have a role or interest in the security audit. This group may include senior management, IT staff, department heads, legal and compliance teams, and external partners.

2. **Engagement strategies**: Develop strategies to engage these stakeholders, such as regular meetings, briefings, and collaborative workshops. Ensure their concerns and insights are considered in the audit preparation process.

Roles and responsibilities during an audit

Let's look at the steps involved:

1. **Clear role definition**: Clearly define and communicate the roles and responsibilities of each stakeholder in the audit process. This clarity helps in efficient coordination and ensures that all necessary tasks are covered.

2. **Responsibility for remediation actions**: Assign specific stakeholders the responsibility for addressing any identified issues during the audit. This assignment should be based on their expertise and authority within the organization.

Effective communication with audit teams

Let's look at the steps involved:

1. **Audit team liaison**: Designate a primary point of contact for the audit team. This person will be responsible for facilitating communication between the auditors and the organization.

2. **Transparent and open communication**: Encourage transparent and open communication with the audit team. Providing complete and accurate information can facilitate a more effective and thorough audit.

Preparing employees for audit participation

Let's look at the steps involved:

1. **Employee briefings**: Conduct briefings for employees to explain the purpose and process of the audit. Inform them about what to expect and how they can contribute to a successful audit.

2. **Training sessions**: Offer training sessions to employees, particularly those who will be directly involved in the audit process. Focus on areas such as data handling, security protocols, and answering auditors' questions.

In summary, stakeholder engagement and communication are key to the successful preparation and execution of a security audit. This involves identifying and engaging key stakeholders, defining roles and responsibilities, ensuring effective communication with the audit team, preparing employees, utilizing communication channels effectively, building a culture of security awareness, and transparently sharing post-audit results and action plans. Engaging stakeholders in this manner not only contributes to a smoother audit process but also strengthens the overall cybersecurity framework of the organization.

Logistics and operational readiness

Properly managing logistics and ensuring operational readiness are essential components of preparing for a security audit. This subsection outlines the steps organizations should take to ensure that all logistical aspects are addressed and operations are aligned to support the audit process effectively.

Coordinating audit schedules and resources

Let's look at the steps involved:

1. **Schedule the audit**: Coordinate with the audit team to schedule the audit at a time that minimizes disruption to normal operations. Consider factors such as business cycles, project deadlines, and availability of key personnel.

2. **Resource allocation**: Ensure that adequate resources, including staff time, equipment, and space, are allocated for the audit. This might involve setting aside dedicated rooms for auditors or ensuring the availability of necessary technology resources.

Physical and technical resources for auditors

Let's look at the steps involved:

1. **Provide the necessary equipment**: Prepare the physical space where the audit will take place. Provide necessary equipment such as computers, internet access, and printing facilities.

2. **Access to systems and data**: Ensure that auditors have the required access to systems, data, and documentation they need to conduct the audit efficiently. This access should be controlled and monitored in line with security policies.

Contingency planning for audit disruptions

Let's look at the steps involved:

1. **Develop contingency plans**: Develop contingency plans for potential disruptions or challenges that may arise during the audit. This includes technical issues, personnel unavailability, or unforeseen operational challenges.

2. **Communication plan**: Have a communication plan in place to quickly address and resolve any issues, keeping all relevant parties informed.

In summary, logistics and operational readiness play a crucial role in the smooth execution of a security audit. This involves carefully planning schedules and resources, providing necessary physical and technical resources, making operational adjustments, developing contingency plans, conducting pre-audit checks, establishing a dedicated point of contact, and reviewing operational impacts post-audit. Proper management of these elements ensures that the audit is conducted efficiently and with minimal disruption to the organization's operations.

Post-audit activities

The completion of a security audit is not the end but a critical juncture in an organization's ongoing journey toward cybersecurity excellence. Post-audit activities are essential for capitalizing on the audit's findings, driving improvements, and reinforcing a culture of continuous cybersecurity enhancement. This subsection outlines the key activities to undertake after a security audit.

Reviewing and analyzing audit findings

Let's look at the steps involved:

1. **Detailed analysis of the report**: Begin with a thorough analysis of the audit report. Understand the findings, including both the strengths and weaknesses identified.
2. **Identify key areas for improvement**: Focus on the key areas that require improvement, particularly those that pose the highest risk to the organization.

Developing a remediation plan for identified issues

Let's look at the steps involved:

1. **Action plan development**: Develop a detailed action plan to address the audit findings. This plan should include specific measures to remediate identified deficiencies.
2. **Prioritize actions**: Prioritize actions based on risk, with high-risk areas addressed first. Consider the resources and time required to implement these actions.

Implementing the remediation plan

Let's look at the steps involved:

1. **Resource allocation**: Allocate the necessary resources, including budget, personnel, and tools, for implementing the remediation plan.
2. **Execution of remediation actions**: Implement the actions as planned, ensuring that each step is executed thoroughly and effectively.

Continuous improvement based on audit feedback

Let's look at the steps involved:

1. **Incorporate feedback into practices**: Use the insights gained from the audit to refine and improve security policies, procedures, and practices.
2. **Ongoing security enhancements**: Treat the audit as a learning opportunity for continuous security enhancement, rather than a one-time event.

In summary, post-audit activities are crucial for leveraging the insights gained from the audit to strengthen the organization's cybersecurity posture. This involves reviewing and analyzing audit findings, developing and implementing a remediation plan, continuous improvement based on audit feedback, effective communication with stakeholders, regular monitoring and adjustments, meticulous documentation, and preparing for future audits. These activities not only address immediate security concerns but also contribute to the long-term resilience and security maturity of the organization.

Summary

In concluding this chapter, it is clear that the journey through the realms of conducting security assessments, navigating the risk assessment and authorization process, and preparing for security audits is both comprehensive and essential for an organization's cybersecurity resilience. These processes are not isolated activities but interconnected elements of a robust cybersecurity framework. By diligently following the guidelines and strategies outlined in each section, organizations can achieve not only compliance and readiness for audits but also a strengthened security posture that safeguards their digital assets against evolving threats. The skills and knowledge imparted in this chapter empower organizations to perform thorough security assessments, adeptly manage risk, and effectively prepare for and respond to security audits.

Looking ahead, the next chapter, *Continuous Monitoring and Incident Response*, builds upon these foundations. It delves into the critical aspects of maintaining ongoing vigilance through continuous monitoring of security controls and preparing for timely and effective incident response. This progression is a natural extension of the groundwork laid in this chapter, highlighting the dynamic nature of cybersecurity and the need for an adaptive, proactive approach to protecting an organization's information assets in an ever-changing cyber landscape.

Part 3:
Advanced Topics
and Best Practices

Here we are – the final part. So far, we've covered the entire framework, but you may be asking, "*How do we put it all together? What if my environment is radically different than what has been described so far?*" That's what this part is all about. We're going to discuss how to monitor your environment and your own practices so that you and your organization can continue to get better. Your implementation of the framework should be a living, breathing document. You'll need to figure out what is working in your environment and what is not and make the appropriate changes as you go.

Too many times we write a policy only to never revisit it. In cybersecurity, that cannot be the case. Nor can it be that we're learning new technology, policies, and so on after hours. There must be time in the workday, and cybersecurity must be a priority enough that you can do the research, implementation, and analysis during that time.

That all being said, cybersecurity has to be a business enabler, not a blocker. Security has to go along with business needs, and how best to do that than to understand how to implement frameworks, rules, and regulations in the context of your business?

This part will cover how to monitor for improvement, what to do when you have a bad day, and how this whole framework could be implemented in the cloud; we're even going to get into real-life case studies, examples, and where I think this whole thing is heading in the future.

This part has the following chapters:

- *Chapter 8, Continuous Monitoring and Incident Response*
- *Chapter 9, Cloud Security and the NIST RMF*
- *Chapter 10, NIST RMF Case Studies and Future Trends*
- *Chapter 11, A Look Ahead*

8

Continuous Monitoring and Incident Response

In the evolving landscape of cybersecurity, the ability to not only respond to but also anticipate threats is crucial. This chapter is focused on empowering organizations (and you!) with the knowledge and tools necessary to establish robust continuous monitoring processes and develop effective **incident response plans** (**IRPs**). These are indispensable elements of an adaptive security program. By implementing continuous monitoring, organizations can achieve real-time visibility into their security status, enabling the early detection of vulnerabilities and threats. This proactive approach is pivotal in mitigating risks before they escalate into full-blown security incidents. Meanwhile, a well-developed IRP ensures that when an incident does occur, the response is swift, organized, and effective, thereby minimizing impact and supporting a speedy recovery.

Through the lessons in this chapter, you will learn how to leverage tools, technologies, and best practices to set up a continuous monitoring strategy that aligns with your organization's risk tolerance and security objectives. You'll also gain insights into creating a structured IRP that includes clear roles, responsibilities, and procedures for managing and recovering from security incidents. Furthermore, we will delve into techniques for managing and recovering from security incidents. We'll wrap up by discussing best practices for analyzing security incidents to extract lessons learned and improve your future security posture.

In this chapter, we're going to cover the following main topics:

- Implementing continuous monitoring
- Developing an IRP
- Analyzing security incidents

Implementing continuous monitoring

Continuous monitoring is a critical component of a dynamic risk management strategy. It involves the ongoing observation, assessment, and analysis of security controls and risks to ensure that an organization's information systems remain within acceptable risk levels. This section outlines the steps and considerations necessary for implementing an effective continuous monitoring program.

Understanding continuous monitoring

Continuous monitoring stands as a foundational pillar in the architecture of modern cybersecurity strategies. It is predicated on the understanding that the cyber threat landscape is not static; it evolves constantly, as do the technologies and practices designed to mitigate these threats. In this context, continuous monitoring offers a dynamic approach to security management, enabling organizations to keep pace with these changes by providing real-time insights into their security posture.

The purpose of continuous monitoring

The primary goal of continuous monitoring is to ensure that the effectiveness of security controls and risk management strategies remains high over time. This is achieved through the ongoing assessment of security controls, the identification of vulnerabilities, and the detection of unauthorized activities within an organization's networks and systems. Continuous monitoring serves not just as a defensive mechanism against external threats but also as a proactive tool for internal risk management.

Key components of continuous monitoring

Continuous monitoring is comprised of several key components, each contributing to the overarching goal of maintaining an acceptable level of cybersecurity risk:

- **Security control assessment**: Regular evaluations of security controls to ensure they are functioning as intended and to identify areas where they may be strengthened
- **Vulnerability management**: The continuous identification, assessment, and mitigation of vulnerabilities within the organization's systems and networks
- **Threat detection**: Monitoring for signs of malicious activity or unauthorized access attempts, enabling rapid response to potential security incidents
- **Configuration management**: Ensuring that system configurations adhere to security policies and standards, thereby reducing potential attack surfaces

The role of continuous monitoring in risk management

In the framework of risk management, continuous monitoring acts as a feedback loop, providing ongoing insights into the effectiveness of risk strategies and the organization's adherence to its risk tolerance levels. It enables risk managers to make informed decisions based on current data, adjusting their strategies to address emerging threats and vulnerabilities. This dynamic approach to risk management is critical in a landscape where threats can emerge rapidly and without warning.

Integrating continuous monitoring with the NIST risk management framework

The **National Institute of Standards and Technology Risk Management Framework (NIST RMF)** provides a structured approach to managing cybersecurity risk, and continuous monitoring is integral to its execution. Within the RMF, continuous monitoring ensures that security controls are continuously reviewed and assessed, facilitating the timely update of security documentation and authorization packages. This integration underscores the necessity of continuous monitoring in achieving compliance with regulatory requirements and in fostering a resilient cybersecurity posture.

Establishing a continuous monitoring strategy

Developing a comprehensive continuous monitoring strategy is essential for maintaining an effective cybersecurity posture. This strategy serves as the blueprint for how an organization will continuously observe, assess, and manage its security risks. Drawing from decades of experience in cybersecurity and risk management, this sub-section provides a detailed guide on establishing a continuous monitoring strategy that aligns with organizational objectives and the NIST RMF.

Defining objectives and scope

The first step in establishing a continuous monitoring strategy is to define its objectives and scope clearly. This involves understanding what you aim to achieve with continuous monitoring and determining which assets, systems, and data are critical to the organization's operations and therefore must be monitored. Objectives typically include detecting and responding to threats in real time, ensuring compliance with regulatory requirements, and maintaining an acceptable level of risk.

Identify critical assets. Start by identifying and classifying the organization's assets based on their criticality and sensitivity. This includes everything from physical devices and software applications to data and network infrastructure.

Determine monitoring needs. Based on the critical assets, determine what needs to be monitored, such as network traffic, user activities, access logs, and system configurations.

Selecting tools and technologies

The selection of tools and technologies for continuous monitoring is not just about choosing the most advanced solutions available; it's about finding the right fit for your organization's specific needs, infrastructure, and cybersecurity goals. This process involves careful consideration of various factors, including compatibility, scalability, user-friendliness, and the ability to integrate with existing systems and workflows. Ahead, we delve deeper into the selection process, highlighting the use of these tools and outlining best practices for their utilization.

Security information and event management systems

Security information and event management (SIEM) systems are central to continuous monitoring efforts, aggregating log data from various sources across the organization's network, analyzing this data in real time, and generating alerts based on predefined criteria. They are invaluable for identifying potential security incidents by correlating events from different systems and providing a comprehensive view of the organization's security posture.

Here are some best practices to keep in mind when choosing and implementing a SIEM:

- **Customization**: Customize SIEM rules and dashboards to reflect your organization's specific security policies and threat models. This ensures that the system is tuned to detect the most relevant threats.

- **Integration**: Ensure your SIEM system can integrate seamlessly with other security tools, such as **intrusion detection systems (IDS)/intrusion prevention systems (IPS)**, firewalls, and vulnerability management solutions, to enhance its analytical capabilities. Properly configure and extensively test the SIEM integrations to validate seamless log collection abilities.

- **Regular updates**: Keep the SIEM system up to date with the latest threat intelligence and security patches to improve its effectiveness in detecting new and evolving threats. Schedule ongoing maintenance for the platform's background engine, including event rule updates, patches, and backups so that it continues to operate in a peak state.

IDS

IDS are critical for detecting unauthorized activities and attacks within the network. **Network-based IDS (NIDS)** are best at focusing on suspicious activity between devices, while **host-based IDS (HIDS)** will detect intrusions on the individual computers, or endpoints, in your network. Both play a crucial role in identifying malicious activities early in the attack chain.

Here are some best practices to keep in mind when choosing an IDS:

- **Placement**: Strategically deploy NIDS sensors at key points within the network to monitor inbound and outbound traffic. For HIDS, ensure coverage across all critical systems.

- **Tuning**: Regularly tune IDS signatures and rules to minimize false positives and false negatives, ensuring that the system accurately identifies threats without overwhelming analysts with irrelevant alerts.

- **Integration**: Integrate IDS alerts with your SIEM system for enhanced event correlation and analysis, facilitating a more comprehensive understanding of potential security incidents.

- **Scalability**: Assess infrastructure requirements for IDS sensors and management servers to handle expected network growth and log loads.

Vulnerability scanning tools

Vulnerability scanning tools automate the process of identifying security weaknesses in systems, software, and networks. These tools scan for known vulnerabilities and provide detailed reports on findings, including severity ratings and remediation recommendations.

Some best practices for deciding on and using a vulnerability scanning tool are the following:

- **Regular scans**: Conduct vulnerability scans regularly and after any significant changes to your IT environment to ensure continuous visibility into your security posture

- **Prioritization**: Use the severity ratings provided by scanning tools to prioritize vulnerabilities for remediation, focusing first on those that pose the greatest risk to your organization

- **Remediation tracking**: Implement a process for tracking and verifying the remediation of identified vulnerabilities to ensure that security gaps are effectively closed

Configuration management tools

Configuration management tools help ensure that systems are configured in line with established security policies and standards. These tools can automate the process of configuring new devices, monitoring for unauthorized changes, and reverting systems to a secure state.

These tools are not very well understood in the industry but can be crucial for detecting changes to your systems. Some best practices for configuration management tools are the following:

- **Baseline configurations**: Establish secure baseline configurations for all types of systems and devices within your organization. Use configuration management tools to enforce these baselines across your IT environment.

- **Continuous monitoring**: Set up continuous monitoring of system configurations to detect and alert on unauthorized changes, helping to prevent security breaches resulting from misconfiguration.

- **Integration**: Integrate configuration management tools with your **incident response** (**IR**) platform to automate the response to detected configuration issues, such as isolating affected systems or rolling back unauthorized changes.

- **Backup and redundancy**: Build backups and redundancies for configuration repositories to avoid losing sensitive system settings and data in case of outages.

Selecting the right tools and technologies for continuous monitoring is a strategic process that requires a deep understanding of your organization's unique environment and security challenges. By following these best practices and focusing on integration, customization, and regular maintenance, organizations can significantly enhance their ability to detect, respond to, and prevent security threats.

Developing metrics and thresholds

Developing precise metrics and setting appropriate thresholds is a pivotal step in the continuous monitoring process. These metrics and thresholds serve as benchmarks for evaluating the security posture and operational health of an organization's IT environment. They enable security teams to measure the effectiveness of their security controls, identify trends over time, and detect anomalies that could indicate potential security incidents. This sub-section delves into the intricacies of selecting these metrics and thresholds, ensuring they offer actionable insights and drive informed decision-making.

Identifying relevant metrics

Metrics should be carefully chosen to reflect the organization's specific security objectives, risk appetite, and compliance requirements. They must be quantifiable, relevant, and capable of providing insights into the effectiveness of security practices and controls. Common metrics include the number of detected vulnerabilities, the average time to patch critical vulnerabilities, the number of unauthorized access attempts, and the frequency and types of security incidents.

Keep the following tips in mind when identifying relevant metrics:

- **Alignment with objectives**: Ensure metrics align with your cybersecurity objectives and provide insights into your organization's security posture

- **Comprehensive coverage**: Utilize a balanced mix of metrics that cover various aspects of security, including preventive, detective, and responsive capabilities

- **Regular review**: Periodically review and adjust metrics to ensure they remain relevant and aligned with evolving security strategies and threat landscapes

Setting thresholds

Thresholds define the point at which normal activity becomes suspicious or indicative of a potential security issue, triggering alerts or further investigation. Setting these thresholds too low may result in an overwhelming number of alerts, many of which may be false positives. Conversely, setting them too high might lead to missed detections of actual security incidents.

Here are some thoughts to keep in mind when setting thresholds:

- **Baseline establishment**: Establish baselines of normal activity for your organization to inform threshold settings. Baselines should consider factors such as normal network traffic patterns, user behavior, and system performance.

- **Dynamic adjustment**: Implement mechanisms for dynamically adjusting thresholds based on historical data and trends. **Machine learning** (**ML**) algorithms can be particularly effective in learning from past behavior to fine-tune threshold settings.

- **Contextual awareness**: Consider the context when setting thresholds. For example, repeated login failures from a known administrative IP address during maintenance windows may not warrant the same response as similar failures from an unknown external IP address.

Utilizing metrics and thresholds for continuous improvement

Metrics and thresholds are not only tools for detection and alerting but also for continuous improvement. By analyzing the data derived from these benchmarks, organizations can identify areas of strength and weakness, adjust security controls, and refine their continuous monitoring strategies.

Metrics and thresholds can be the make-or-break item when it comes to continuous improvement, as without accurate metrics, you won't know what to focus on. Here are some things to keep in mind:

- **Trend analysis**: Use metrics to perform trend analysis, identifying improvements or deteriorations in security posture over time. This can help in forecasting potential security challenges and proactively addressing them.

- **Feedback loops**: Create feedback loops where insights from metric analysis inform the refinement of security policies, procedures, and controls. This includes adjusting metrics and thresholds themselves to better align with the organization's changing security landscape.

- **Incident post-mortem**: Incorporate metrics and threshold data into post-mortem analyses of security incidents to identify root causes and prevent recurrence. This can lead to more effective and targeted adjustments to thresholds and security controls.

Developing meaningful metrics and appropriately setting thresholds are critical for the success of a continuous monitoring program. They provide the data and alerts necessary to maintain situational awareness, respond to potential security incidents promptly, and continuously enhance the organization's cybersecurity posture. By adhering to these best practices, organizations can ensure their continuous monitoring efforts are both effective and efficient.

Integration and configuration

Successfully integrating and configuring the selected tools and technologies is a critical phase in operationalizing your continuous monitoring strategy. This process ensures that the tools not only work well within your existing IT infrastructure but also communicate effectively with each other to provide a unified view of your security posture. Ahead, we explore a detailed approach to achieving optimal integration and configuration, focusing on practical steps and considerations.

Ensuring system compatibility

Before integration, and even before procuring, verify that the chosen tools are compatible with your existing systems, software, and network configurations. This step is crucial to avoid potential conflicts that could impair system performance or result in data silos.

Effective tool integration is essential for correlating data across systems, facilitating comprehensive monitoring, and automating response processes. This requires a strategic approach to ensure seamless interoperability. Some best practices for integrating tools follow:

- **Use of application programming interfaces (APIs)**: Leverage APIs to facilitate communication between different tools and systems. Ensure that the APIs provide robust support for data exchange and can handle the volume and frequency of data you plan to share.

- **Central management console**: Where possible, utilize a central management console that can aggregate data from various sources. This console should offer a comprehensive dashboard for real-time monitoring and alerting.

- **Automation platforms**: Consider employing automation platforms that can integrate with multiple tools to orchestrate workflows, particularly for IR and remediation processes.

Configuring for efficiency

Proper configuration of your monitoring tools is vital to ensure they are focused on the right areas, generating meaningful alerts, and not overwhelming your team with false positives. While some of these are restated in the criteria for procuring tools earlier, they deserve repeating here and are as follows:

- **Customize alerts**: Tailor alert settings to prioritize critical issues and reduce noise. This might involve setting different priority levels based on the severity of vulnerabilities or the sensitivity of the assets involved.

- **Define actionable responses**: Configure automated response actions for common scenarios, such as isolating a compromised system from the network or automatically applying patches to known vulnerabilities.

- **Continuous configuration review**: Regularly review and adjust configurations to adapt to changes in the IT environment and threat landscape. This includes updating rulesets for IDS/IPS systems, refining SIEM correlation rules, and tweaking vulnerability scanner settings.

Validation and testing

After integration and initial configuration, conduct comprehensive testing to validate that the tools are functioning as expected and that the data flows correctly between systems. When testing, the use of virtual networks or cyber ranges to provide a **proof of concept** (**PoC**) for your tools can be critical to ensuring their success. Some best practices are the following:

- **Simulation exercises**: Perform simulation exercises to test the system's ability to detect and respond to simulated attacks. This can help identify any gaps in coverage or issues with alerting and response processes.

- **Performance benchmarking**: Benchmark the performance of your systems before and after integration to ensure that the monitoring tools have not introduced significant latency or resource overhead.

- **Feedback loop**: Establish a feedback loop with your security operations team to gather insights on the effectiveness of the tools and configurations in real-world scenarios. Use this feedback to make continuous improvements.

Integrating and configuring your continuous monitoring tools and technologies is a complex but critical task. By focusing on compatibility, strategic integration, effective configuration, and thorough validation, you can ensure that your continuous monitoring strategy is robust, efficient, and capable of supporting your organization's cybersecurity objectives.

Developing an IRP

In today's digital age, where cyber threats loom large and data breaches can have significant financial, operational, and reputational impacts, having a robust IRP is not just advisable; it's imperative. This plan is your organization's blueprint for responding effectively to cyber incidents, ensuring that you can quickly contain threats, minimize damage, and recover operations with minimal disruption. An effective IRP not only helps in managing the immediate challenges posed by a security incident but also in mitigating potential long-term consequences.

The purpose of an IRP

The primary goal of an IRP is to provide a structured and systematic approach to addressing and managing the aftermath of a security breach or cyber attack. The plan outlines the processes and procedures your organization should follow to effectively respond to and recover from security incidents. It aims to ensure clarity of action, minimize information loss and infrastructure damage, and reduce recovery time and costs. Moreover, a well-conceived IRP is crucial for maintaining trust and confidence among stakeholders, including customers, partners, and regulatory bodies.

Key elements of an IRP

A comprehensive IRP includes the following:

1. **Preparation**: Building and training the **IR team** (**IRT**), along with developing the necessary capabilities to support IR efforts
2. **Identification**: Detecting and determining the nature and scope of an incident
3. **Containment**: Limiting the spread and impact of the incident
4. **Eradication**: Removing the threat and any associated vulnerabilities from the environment
5. **Recovery**: Restoring and returning affected systems and services to normal operations
6. **Lessons learned**: Analyzing the incident and the response to improve future readiness and response actions

The value of an IRP

An IRP is invaluable for several reasons. It ensures that when an incident occurs, there's no confusion about who should do what; response actions are swift and coordinated, minimizing downtime and operational impact. It also helps organizations to meet legal and regulatory obligations related to cybersecurity breaches. Furthermore, by having a plan that is regularly updated and tested, organizations can adapt to the evolving cyber threat landscape, enhancing their overall security posture and resilience against future attacks.

Getting started

Developing an IRP begins with a commitment from the top, ensuring that adequate resources are allocated and that cybersecurity is recognized as a critical component of the organization's risk management strategy. The subsequent sections of this chapter will guide you through the essential steps of forming an IRT, creating a communication plan, selecting the right tools and resources, understanding legal considerations, and, importantly, testing and updating your plan to keep it effective.

Embarking on this journey will not only prepare your organization to respond to incidents more effectively but also strengthen your defenses against the myriad of cyber threats in the digital landscape.

Understanding the IR life cycle

The IR life cycle is a framework that outlines the phases an organization goes through in preparing for, responding to, and recovering from a cyber incident. This life cycle is critical to developing an effective IRP, as it provides a structured approach for managing incidents. By understanding and implementing this life cycle, organizations can ensure a coordinated and comprehensive response to security threats, minimizing their impact and reducing recovery time. The life cycle typically consists of the following phases.

Preparation

The foundation of effective IR lies in thorough preparation. This phase involves establishing the IRT, developing policies and procedures, and ensuring that necessary tools and technologies are in place. Preparation also includes training and awareness for the IRT and broader organization, as well as conducting regular exercises to test the effectiveness of the IRP.

Some key portions of this phase include the following:

- Develop and document the IRP
- Form the IRT and assign roles and responsibilities
- Equip the team with the necessary tools and resources
- Conduct regular training and simulation exercises

Identification

Identification is the process of detecting and determining whether an event is indeed a security incident. This phase relies heavily on monitoring tools and the vigilance of the IRT and staff to quickly spot potential security issues. The sooner an incident is identified, the more effectively it can be contained and resolved.

Key items accomplished in this phase are the following:

- Monitor systems and networks for signs of unauthorized activity
- Analyze alerts to distinguish false positives from genuine incidents
- Initiate the IRP once an incident is confirmed

Containment

Once an incident is identified, the immediate goal is to contain it to prevent further damage. Containment strategies may vary depending on the incident but typically involve isolating affected systems, blocking malicious traffic, or temporarily shutting down certain services.

In this phase, the IRT accomplishes the following:

- Executes short-term containment measures to limit the spread
- Plans for long-term containment to ensure the threat is fully neutralized

Eradication

With the threat contained, the focus shifts to removing the cause of the incident and any related vulnerabilities from the organization's environment. This might involve deleting malicious files, disabling breached user accounts, or applying patches to vulnerable systems.

With the shift to removing artifacts and vulnerabilities from the network, the following tasks are pursued:

- Identify and remove all components of the threat
- Address underlying vulnerabilities to prevent recurrence

Recovery

In the recovery phase, affected systems and services are restored and returned to normal operations in a controlled manner, ensuring no remnants of the threat remain. This phase also involves monitoring for any signs of the threat re-emerging.

These tasks include the following:

- Carefully restore systems and verify their integrity
- Monitor for anomalies that suggest the threat persists

Lessons learned

Perhaps the most critical phase for improving future response efforts, the lessons learned phase involves reviewing and analyzing the incident and the effectiveness of the response. This review should lead to tangible improvements to the IRP and other security measures.

This phase is often overlooked but is extremely important for continuous improvement. Items completed in this phase include the following:

- Conduct a post-incident review with all stakeholders involved
- Document findings, including what worked well and areas for improvement
- Update the IRP and training programs based on these insights

Understanding and implementing the IR life cycle allows organizations to manage and mitigate the impact of cyber incidents effectively. Each phase plays a crucial role in ensuring that the organization can respond swiftly and efficiently, minimizing damage and reducing the likelihood of future incidents.

Forming your IRT

An effective IRT is the cornerstone of a successful IRP. The formation of this team is a critical step that involves selecting individuals with the right mix of skills, expertise, and roles to handle and recover from security incidents efficiently. This sub-section guides you through the process of assembling your IRT, defining roles and responsibilities, and ensuring the team's effectiveness through training and resources.

Defining core roles

The first step in forming your IRT is to define the core roles required for IR. These roles typically include the following:

- **Incident manager/leader**: The leader of the team, responsible for overseeing the IR process, making critical decisions, and serving as the primary point of contact
- **Incident reporter**: This is an extremely key role and is typically the second-most senior person, responsible for keeping a timeline of events and gathering key information about the event from the rest of the team
- **Security analysts**: Specialists who investigate and analyze incidents, manage containment efforts, and assist with recovery and eradication

- **IT specialists**: Professionals focused on maintaining and restoring IT systems, applying patches, and implementing technical measures to recover affected systems

- **Communications coordinator**: The individual responsible for managing internal and external communications, including notifications to stakeholders, employees, and possibly the public or media

- **Legal advisor**: A role that provides legal guidance on IR activities, ensuring compliance with laws and regulations, and managing legal risks

Selecting team members

When selecting members for your IRT, consider individuals' expertise, experience, and ability to work under pressure. It's also important to ensure that the team includes members from various departments (IT, legal, HR, PR, and so on) to address all aspects of IR.

Following are some important items to keep in mind for your team's composition:

- **Skills and expertise**: Choose individuals with a deep understanding of your organization's IT infrastructure, cybersecurity threats, and legal obligations

- **Availability**: Ensure team members are available to respond to incidents at any time, considering the creation of an on-call rotation for after-hours emergencies

- **Training**: Select individuals who are committed to ongoing learning and can adapt to the evolving cybersecurity landscape

Assigning responsibilities

Clearly define the responsibilities for each role within the IRT. Responsibilities should cover the entire IR life cycle, from identification through to recovery and post-incident analysis.

Following are some of the roles to expect as a part of the IRT:

- **Incident manager**: Coordinates the team's activities, ensures resources are available, and communicates with senior management

- **Security analysts**: Conduct technical analyses of the incident, identify compromised systems, and recommend containment strategies

- **IT specialists**: Implement technical fixes, restore services, and apply security measures to prevent future incidents

- **Communications coordinator**: Develops communication plans, drafts notifications, and serves as the liaison for internal and external communications

- **Legal advisor**: Advises on legal requirements, assists with regulatory reporting, and manages any legal implications of the incident

Training and resources

Provide your IRT with the training, tools, and resources they need to respond effectively to incidents. This includes regular training sessions, access to the latest cybersecurity tools and technologies, and opportunities for professional development:

- **Regular exercises**: Conduct simulated IR exercises to test the team's readiness and improve their response capabilities

- **Access to tools**: Ensure the team has access to and training on the IR tools and technologies they will use

- **Continuous learning**: Encourage team members to stay informed about the latest cybersecurity threats, trends, and best practices through ongoing education and professional development

Forming your IRT is a critical step in preparing your organization to handle cybersecurity incidents. By carefully selecting team members, clearly defining roles and responsibilities, and providing the necessary training and resources, you can ensure that your IRT is ready and able to manage and mitigate the impacts of security incidents effectively.

IR communication plan

An **IR communication plan** (**IRCP**) is an essential component of an organization's broader IRP. It outlines how communication should be handled during and after a cybersecurity incident, ensuring that information is disseminated quickly, accurately, and to the appropriate audiences. This plan minimizes confusion, maintains trust, and ensures compliance with regulatory requirements.

Developing the communication plan

Developing an effective IRCP involves several key steps and considerations:

1. **Identify stakeholders**: Begin by identifying all potential stakeholders who may need to be informed during a cybersecurity incident. This includes internal stakeholders such as employees, management, and board members, as well as external ones such as customers, partners, regulatory bodies, and possibly the public.

2. **Define communication channels**: When setting up communication channels, work with your stakeholders to determine what is most efficient for them. This could include email, internal messaging systems, press releases, social media, and direct phone calls. Ensure that backup communication methods are in place in case primary systems are compromised.

3. **Assign communication roles**: Assign specific team members to handle communications. This typically involves designating a primary spokesperson to ensure messages are consistent. The communications coordinator role within the IRT is critical here.

4. **Develop message templates**: Prepare templates for various scenarios to speed up the response time. Templates can be customized during an incident but should outline the basic structure of the message, including acknowledgment of the incident, steps being taken, and where to find further information.

5. **Legal and regulatory considerations**: Include guidelines for complying with legal and regulatory requirements related to incident communication. This involves understanding what needs to be reported, to whom, and within what timeframe.

6. **Review and approval processes**: Establish processes for reviewing and approving communications before they are released. This ensures accuracy, consistency, and compliance with legal requirements.

The importance of a communication plan

The importance of having a dedicated IRCP cannot be overstated. It serves several critical functions:

- **Maintaining trust**: Effective communication helps maintain trust with customers, partners, and the public by demonstrating that the organization is handling the incident responsibly.

- **Reducing confusion**: Clear, consistent messaging helps reduce confusion and panic among employees and other stakeholders.

- **Compliance**: Many regulatory frameworks require timely notification of security incidents to affected individuals and regulatory bodies. A well-defined communication plan ensures compliance, helping avoid legal penalties and reputational damage.

Regulatory requirements

Several regulatory bodies have specific requirements regarding the communication of cybersecurity incidents. Organizations must be familiar with and adhere to these requirements based on their geographic location and industry. These regulations are discussed in a later section and are important to consider when developing your communication plan.

Developing an IRCP is a vital step in preparing for and managing cybersecurity incidents. By ensuring clear, timely, and compliant communication, organizations can significantly mitigate the impact of incidents on their operations, reputation, and legal standing.

Testing and updating the IRP

An IRP is a living document that requires regular testing, evaluation, and updates to ensure its effectiveness in the face of evolving cyber threats and organizational changes. This dynamic approach enables organizations to adapt their IR capabilities to new threats, technologies, and business processes, ensuring they can respond swiftly and effectively when a real incident occurs.

Testing the IRP

Testing the IRP is crucial for identifying gaps in response capabilities, understanding the roles and responsibilities of the IRT, and improving coordination and communication during an incident. Various testing methods can be employed, each serving different objectives:

- **Tabletop exercises**: These are discussion-based sessions where the IRT reviews specific scenarios to walk through the IRP step by step. Tabletop exercises help assess the plan's comprehensiveness and the team's understanding of their roles and responsibilities.

- **Simulated attacks**: More technical and involved than tabletop exercises, simulated attacks (or drills) test the organization's operational capability to respond to an incident. This can range from deploying malware in a controlled environment to simulating a phishing attack to see how quickly and effectively the team can respond. By far, simulated attacks in an environment that utilizes similar size and tooling to your production environment, such as a cyber range, (for example, those provided by leading best-in-class vendors such as Cloud Range (`https://www.cloudrangecyber.com`)), are highly recommended. By utilizing a cyber range, your cybersecurity IRT can exercise its full playbook on realistic attacks that match the threat landscape and, in many cases, utilize the same or similar tooling.

- **Full-scale exercises**: These are comprehensive drills that simulate a real-life cyber incident as closely as possible, involving not just the IRT but also other organizational functions such as PR, legal, and HR. Full-scale exercises test the coordination and communication between different parts of the organization under stress. Again, the use of a cyber range in these integrated simulation-to-tabletop exercises cannot be overstated.

Evaluating test outcomes

After each test, it's essential to conduct a thorough debriefing session to evaluate the performance of the IRT and the effectiveness of the IRP. Key questions to consider include the following:

- Were there any delays in identifying or responding to the incident?

- Did any communication issues arise?

- Were there any gaps in roles or responsibilities that caused confusion?

- How effective were the containment and eradication strategies?

- Were the recovery procedures adequate and timely?

Updating the IRP

Based on the outcomes of these tests and the lessons learned, the IRP should be updated to address any identified weaknesses or gaps. Updates might also be necessitated by changes in the organization's IT infrastructure, new threats, business processes, or regulatory requirements. Key areas to focus on include the following:

- **Roles and responsibilities**: Adjust roles based on personnel changes or insights gained from exercises on how to better distribute responsibilities

- **Communication protocols**: Refine communication strategies both internally and externally, based on what was learned during testing

- **Technical procedures**: Update technical response strategies to address new threats or vulnerabilities identified since the last iteration of the IRP

- **Recovery strategies**: Enhance recovery procedures to ensure quicker restoration of services with minimal data loss

- **Compliance requirements**: Incorporate any changes in legal or regulatory obligations regarding IR and reporting

Continuous improvement

The process of testing and updating the IRP should be viewed as an ongoing cycle of improvement. Regular reviews and updates help ensure that the organization remains prepared to respond to cyber incidents effectively. This cycle of continuous improvement not only enhances the organization's cybersecurity posture but also builds resilience against future threats.

Incorporating feedback from real incidents, along with insights from regular testing and exercises, ensures that the IRP evolves in line with the threat landscape and the organization's changing risk profile. This proactive approach to IR planning is vital for maintaining the security, integrity, and resilience of the organization's information systems and networks.

Legal considerations and compliance

In the context of IR, navigating the complex landscape of legal considerations and compliance requirements is crucial. Cybersecurity incidents often involve data breaches that can lead to significant legal consequences, including regulatory penalties, litigation, and reputational damage. This sub-section outlines key legal considerations and compliance obligations that organizations must be aware of when developing and executing their IRP.

Understanding regulatory requirements

Various industries and jurisdictions have specific regulations governing how organizations must respond to and report cybersecurity incidents. Familiarity with these regulations is essential for ensuring compliance and avoiding penalties. Key regulatory frameworks include the following:

- **General Data Protection Regulation (GDPR)**: For organizations operating in or handling data from the European Union, GDPR mandates strict data protection and privacy standards, including timely notification of data breaches to both supervisory authorities and affected individuals.

- **Health Insurance Portability and Accountability Act (HIPAA)**: In the United States, healthcare organizations must comply with HIPAA rules, which include requirements for protecting patient health information and reporting breaches.

- **California Consumer Privacy Act (CCPA)/California Privacy Rights Act (CPRA)**: These laws require businesses that handle California residents' data to implement specific security measures and report certain types of data breaches.

- **U.S. Securities and Exchange Commission (SEC)**: On July 26, 2023, the SEC released new rules standardizing the process of disclosing cybersecurity incidents. These regulations apply to publicly traded companies. Under the new rules, when a company has a cyber incident that has been determined to be material, it now must disclose it with an 8-K filing within 4 days. This is filed under form 6-K for foreign businesses. In this filing, the nature of the event, scope, and anticipated impact must also be discussed.

Legal implications of IR

The manner in which an organization responds to a cybersecurity incident can have significant legal implications. Key considerations include the following:

- **Documentation and evidence preservation**: Proper documentation of the IR process is critical for legal defense and regulatory compliance. This includes preserving evidence that could be crucial for investigations or litigation.

- **Privacy and confidentiality**: When handling incidents involving personal data, it's essential to maintain the privacy and confidentiality of affected individuals to comply with data protection laws.

- **Communication**: Public statements and notifications about a security incident must be carefully crafted to avoid admitting liability or making statements that could be used against the organization in court.

Contractual obligations

Organizations must also consider contractual obligations related to cybersecurity incidents. This includes obligations to notify business partners, customers, or other third parties in the event of a breach that may affect their data or operations.

Staying informed

Laws and regulations related to cybersecurity and data protection are continually evolving. Organizations must stay informed about changes to ensure their IRP remains compliant. This may involve regular legal consultations and subscribing to updates from regulatory bodies.

Legal considerations and compliance are integral to the IR planning and execution process. By understanding and adhering to the relevant laws and regulations, organizations can not only mitigate the risks associated with cybersecurity incidents but also protect themselves from legal and regulatory repercussions. Incorporating these considerations into the IRP ensures that the organization's response is not just effective but also legally sound.

Analyzing security incidents

In the evolving landscape of cybersecurity, the ability to not only respond to but also thoroughly analyze security incidents is paramount. This analysis is crucial for understanding how breaches occur, the extent of their impact, and the effectiveness of the response deployed. This section is designed to guide organizations through the intricate process of dissecting and learning from cybersecurity events to fortify their defenses against future threats.

The importance of incident analysis

The post-mortem analysis of a security incident is a critical step that goes beyond immediate containment and eradication efforts. It provides deep insights into threat actors' **tactics, techniques, and procedures** (**TTPs**), revealing vulnerabilities within the organization's security posture. This analysis is fundamental to identifying the root causes of incidents, preventing recurrence, and enhancing the organization's resilience to new and evolving cyber threats.

Objectives of incident analysis

The primary objectives of analyzing security incidents include the following:

- **Understanding the incident**: Comprehensive analysis helps clarify the sequence of events, the methods used by attackers, and the vulnerabilities exploited. This understanding is vital for developing more effective defenses.

- **Improving IR**: By evaluating the response to an incident, organizations can identify strengths and weaknesses in their IRP, leading to more efficient and effective future responses.

- **Enhancing security measures**: Analysis provides actionable intelligence that can be used to strengthen security measures, patch vulnerabilities, and implement more robust security controls.

- **Regulatory compliance and reporting**: Detailed incident analysis supports compliance with legal and regulatory requirements, guiding the reporting process to authorities and affected parties.

- **Educating and preparing**: Sharing lessons learned from incident analysis within the organization promotes a culture of security awareness and preparedness among all employees.

Analyzing security incidents is a multifaceted process that involves various steps, from initial identification and reporting to post-incident review and continuous improvement. Each step is designed to extract valuable insights from the incident, turning adverse events into opportunities for strengthening cybersecurity measures.

As we delve deeper into this section, we'll explore the methodologies and best practices for each phase of the incident analysis process. Organizations will learn how to conduct effective assessments, utilize forensic techniques, develop and apply **indicators of compromise** (**IoCs**), and, ultimately, translate findings into strategic improvements in their security posture. This guide aims to empower organizations with the knowledge to not just react to incidents but to proactively evolve their cybersecurity defenses in alignment with the dynamic nature of cyber threats.

Assessment and decision-making processes

Once a security incident is identified and reported, the next critical step is to assess its scope, impact, and severity. This assessment informs the decision-making process, guiding the IRT in determining the most appropriate response actions. Effective assessment and decision-making are pivotal for minimizing damage and recovering from an incident efficiently. This section outlines the processes involved in assessing security incidents and making informed decisions.

Conducting an initial assessment

The following are key components of conducting an initial assessment. Guidelines, flowcharts, and other items to help your response team should be a part of your IRP:

- **Determining the nature of the incident**: Quickly identify what type of incident has occurred, whether it's a malware infection, unauthorized access, data breach, or another form of attack. Understanding the nature of the incident is crucial for selecting the appropriate response strategy.

- **Scope of impact**: Evaluate how widespread the incident is within the organization's systems and networks. This includes identifying affected assets, systems, data, and users to understand the full extent of the impact.

- **Severity evaluation**: Assess the severity of the incident based on its potential impact on business operations, data integrity, and confidentiality. Severity levels help prioritize response efforts and resource allocation.

Decision-making framework

A decision-making framework is a flowchart designed with pre-planned responses. This should be clearly laid out in your IRP. Some things to keep in mind are listed here:

- **Predefined response protocols**: Develop a set of predefined response protocols for different types of incidents and severity levels. These protocols should outline recommended actions for containment, eradication, and recovery, ensuring a swift and organized response.

- **IRT involvement**: The IRT should convene quickly to review the initial assessment findings and decide on the next steps. This team should have the authority to make critical decisions regarding IR actions.

- **Communication and escalation pathways**: Define clear communication and escalation pathways within the organization. This ensures that all relevant stakeholders, including senior management, are informed about significant incidents and can contribute to decision-making when necessary.

Prioritizing response actions

Let us look at some strategies for prioritizing response actions:

- **Based on impact and severity**: Prioritize response actions based on the assessed impact and severity of the incident. High-impact incidents that threaten critical assets or operations require immediate attention.

- **Legal and regulatory considerations**: Consider any legal and regulatory implications of the incident in the decision-making process. This includes compliance with data protection laws, which may dictate specific response and notification requirements.

- **Business continuity (BC)**: Factor in the importance of affected systems and data to BC. Efforts should be focused on ensuring that critical operations can be maintained or quickly restored.

Continuous assessment and adaptation

While responding to an incident, it's important for the incident commander/manager to continue to adapt their response based on the events unfolding. The following are things to keep in mind. Take care to consider this from a high-level perspective, and consider additional training on IR management, such as a specific incident commander course:

- **Dynamic situation analysis:** Recognize that security incidents are dynamic situations. Continuous assessment of the incident and its impact is necessary, as new information may require adjusting the response strategy.

- **Feedback loops:** Implement feedback loops within the IR process. Information gathered during response actions can provide valuable insights, leading to adjustments in the strategy to more effectively contain and mitigate the incident.

Effective assessment and decision-making processes are essential for navigating the complexities of security IR. By quickly understanding the nature, scope, and severity of an incident, the IRT can make informed decisions that prioritize the organization's security, compliance, and operational continuity. This approach ensures that response actions are both strategic and adaptable, key factors in successfully managing and recovering from cybersecurity incidents.

Containment, eradication, and recovery strategies

Once a security incident has been identified and assessed, the focus shifts to containing the threat, eradicating it, and then recovering from the incident to restore normal operations. These phases are critical in minimizing damage, preventing the spread of the incident, and ensuring a swift return to business as usual. This combined sub-section provides a high-level overview of containment, eradication, and recovery strategies that form the core of effective IR.

Containment strategies

The primary goal of containment is to limit the impact of the incident and prevent it from spreading to unaffected areas of the network or systems. Containment strategies vary depending on the type and severity of the incident but generally include the following:

- **Isolating affected systems**: Disconnecting or isolating affected systems from the network to prevent the spread of the threat. This may involve physically unplugging devices, blocking network access, or using firewall rules to isolate parts of the network.

- **Segmentation**: Implementing network segmentation to contain the incident within a controlled environment, reducing the risk to the broader network.

- **Temporary controls**: Applying temporary controls or patches to vulnerable systems to mitigate the threat while a more permanent solution is developed.

Eradication techniques

Eradication involves removing the threat from the organization's systems and repairing any damage. This phase ensures that the incident is fully resolved before recovery begins. Key eradication techniques include the following:

- **Removing malware**: Utilizing antivirus software and malware removal tools to detect and remove malicious software from affected systems.

- **Patching vulnerabilities**: Applying patches to software and systems to fix vulnerabilities that were exploited during the incident. This helps prevent future occurrences of the same or similar incidents.

- **Strengthening defenses**: Enhancing security measures based on the insights gained from the incident analysis to fortify defenses against future attacks.

Recovery and restoration

The recovery phase focuses on restoring affected systems and services to their fully operational states while ensuring no remnants of the threat remain. Effective recovery strategies include the following:

- **System restoration**: Restoring systems from backups after confirming they are free from threats. This step must be executed carefully to avoid reintroducing vulnerabilities.

- **Service resumption**: Gradually resuming business operations while maintaining heightened monitoring to detect any signs of incident recurrence.

- **Post-recovery monitoring**: Implementing an enhanced monitoring regime following the incident to quickly identify any anomalies that could suggest the presence of undetected threats or the recurrence of the incident.

The containment, eradication, and recovery phases are interconnected components of a comprehensive IR process. Effective execution of these strategies is essential for minimizing the impact of security incidents, ensuring a thorough resolution, and restoring normal operations with confidence. Organizations must continuously refine these strategies based on lessons learned from past incidents and evolving best practices in cybersecurity, ensuring resilience against future threats.

Post-incident analysis and review

After navigating through the containment, eradication, and recovery phases of IR, organizations must not overlook the critical step of conducting a post-incident analysis and review. This process is essential for extracting valuable lessons from the incident, improving future response efforts, and ultimately strengthening the organization's cybersecurity posture. At a high level, the post-incident analysis and review involve a thorough examination of the incident, the response to it, and the outcomes, aiming to identify both successes and areas for improvement.

Objectives of post-incident analysis

The main objectives of conducting a post-incident analysis and review include the following:

- **Identifying root causes**: Understanding the underlying vulnerabilities or flaws that allowed the incident to occur, with the aim of preventing similar incidents in the future

- **Evaluating response effectiveness**: Assessing how effectively the IRT managed the incident, including the speed of response, decision-making processes, and the effectiveness of containment and eradication efforts

- **Improving IRPs**: Using insights gained from the analysis to refine the organization's IRP, enhancing preparedness for future incidents

Conducting the review

The post-incident review process typically involves the following steps:

1. **Gathering data**: Compile all relevant data from the incident, including logs, reports, and team member accounts, to create a comprehensive overview of the incident and the response.

2. **Meeting with the IRT**: Convene a meeting with the IRT and other stakeholders involved in the response to discuss the incident and gather feedback on response efforts.

3. **Analyzing the incident life cycle**: Review the entire life cycle of the incident, from detection to recovery, identifying any gaps in procedures, tools, or skills that could be addressed to improve future responses.

4. **Documenting lessons learned**: Clearly document the lessons learned from the incident, including both what worked well and what did not. This documentation should be accessible to relevant parties within the organization to inform future cybersecurity strategies.

Implementing improvements

Based on the findings from the post-incident analysis, organizations should do the following:

- **Update policies and procedures**: Revise the IRP and related policies and procedures to incorporate lessons learned, ensuring that improvements are effectively integrated into the organization's IR framework

- **Enhance training and awareness**: Identify any training needs highlighted by the incident and implement targeted training and awareness programs to address these gaps

- **Invest in technology and tools**: Consider investing in additional technologies or tools that could help prevent future incidents or improve the response to them

The post-incident analysis and review process is a cornerstone of continuous improvement in cybersecurity. By systematically analyzing incidents and integrating lessons learned into the organization's cybersecurity practices, organizations can adapt to the evolving threat landscape and enhance their resilience against future threats. This iterative process ensures that the organization's cybersecurity measures remain effective and responsive to new challenges.

Utilizing forensic analysis

Forensic analysis plays a crucial role in the aftermath of cybersecurity incidents, offering a methodical approach to investigating and understanding the how and why behind a breach. By meticulously examining digital evidence and reconstructing events, forensic analysis aids organizations in identifying the root causes of incidents, ensuring that vulnerabilities are addressed, and enhancing defenses against future attacks. This section highlights the importance of forensic analysis in the context of IR and provides guidance on its application, along with references to reputable resources for further exploration.

The role of forensic analysis

Forensic analysis involves the collection, preservation, examination, and analysis of digital evidence from computers, networks, and other digital devices. This process is essential for the following:

- **Identifying attack vectors**: Understanding the methods attackers use to penetrate defenses, move laterally across the network, and exfiltrate data

- **Determining the scope of the incident**: Establishing the full extent of the compromise, including which systems were affected and what data may have been accessed or stolen

- **Supporting recovery efforts**: Providing insights that inform the recovery process, ensuring that systems are cleaned and restored securely

- **Facilitating legal and regulatory compliance**: Collecting evidence in a manner that maintains its integrity, ensuring it can be used in legal proceedings or regulatory investigations

Best practices for forensic analysis

When conducting forensic analysis, it is important to follow the best practices in the industry. Some of those are discussed as follows:

- **Establishing a forensic capability**: Organizations should develop a forensic capability as part of their broader IR framework. This includes training staff in forensic techniques, acquiring necessary tools, and establishing procedures for evidence collection and analysis. For organizations that cannot afford this, outsourcing is a possible option.

- **Preservation of evidence**: The integrity of digital evidence is paramount. Organizations must ensure that evidence is collected in a manner that preserves its integrity, following established guidelines for evidence handling and documentation, otherwise known as a **chain of custody (CoC)**.

- **Analysis and reporting**: Forensic analysis should be thorough and methodical, leading to a detailed report that outlines the findings, supports conclusions with evidence, and provides actionable recommendations for preventing future incidents.

References from reputable organizations

For organizations looking to deepen their understanding of forensic analysis and integrate best practices into their IR efforts, the following resources from reputable organizations are invaluable:

- **NIST**: *NIST Special Publication 800-86, Guide to Integrating Forensic Techniques into Incident Response*, offers comprehensive guidance on incorporating forensic analysis into IR strategies

- **Cybersecurity and Infrastructure Security Agency (CISA)**: CISA provides a range of resources and tools designed to assist organizations in strengthening their cybersecurity posture, including aspects related to forensic analysis and incident handling

Forensic analysis is an indispensable component of a comprehensive IR strategy, providing the depth of insight required to fully understand and recover from cybersecurity incidents. By utilizing forensic analysis effectively, organizations can not only address the immediate impacts of an incident but also fortify their defenses against future threats. Leveraging resources from NIST, CISA, and other reputable organizations can help organizations establish and refine their forensic analysis capabilities, ensuring they are well prepared to respond to and recover from cybersecurity incidents.

Developing IoCs

IoCs are crucial forensic artifacts used to detect cybersecurity threats, breaches, or other malicious activities. By identifying and analyzing IoCs, organizations can enhance their detection capabilities, improve IR actions, and strengthen their overall cybersecurity posture. This section outlines the process of developing IoCs and emphasizes their importance in early threat detection and prevention strategies.

Understanding IoCs

IoCs are pieces of information used as signs of unauthorized or malicious activity within a system or network. Common types of IoCs include malicious IP addresses, URLs involved in cyber attacks, unusual outbound network traffic, unexpected spikes in data usage, and files with known malicious signatures. By monitoring these signs, organizations can detect potential security incidents before they escalate.

Process of developing IoCs

Developing IoCs typically takes a **cyber threat intelligence (CTI)** team using a dedicated platform. However, the following general process is followed:

- **Collection and analysis**:

  - **Incident analysis**: Following a cybersecurity incident, conduct a thorough analysis to gather data on how the intrusion occurred, the tactics used by attackers, and the systems or data targeted.

  - **Artifact identification**: Identify and document artifacts related to the incident, such as malicious file hashes, suspicious IP addresses, and unusual patterns of behavior that could serve as IoCs.

- **Standardization**: Utilize standardized formats for documenting IoCs, such as the **Structured Threat Information eXpression (STIX™)**. This facilitates the sharing of IoCs with **threat intelligence platforms (TIPs)** and other cybersecurity tools.

- **Validation and testing**: Before deploying IoCs in detection tools, validate their accuracy to minimize false positives. This can involve testing IoCs in a controlled environment to ensure they accurately identify malicious activity without overwhelming the system with false alerts.

Utilizing IoCs

IoCs are a key component of attribution in cybersecurity attacks. With the plethora of tools in the environment, it's important to follow several best practices for efficiently using them. The following practices are suggested:

- **Integration with security tools**: Integrate IoCs into security monitoring tools, such as SIEM systems, IDS, and **endpoint detection and response (EDR)** solutions. This enables real-time detection of threats based on the identified IoCs.

- **Sharing with the community**: Share IoCs with industry partners, **Information Sharing and Analysis Centers (ISACs)**, and cybersecurity communities. Sharing helps others protect against known threats and contributes to collective cybersecurity resilience.

Importance of IoCs in cybersecurity

IoCs play a pivotal role in enhancing an organization's threat detection and response capabilities. By systematically developing, updating, and utilizing IoCs, organizations can do the following:

- **Detect threats early**: IoCs enable organizations to identify and respond to threats at an early stage, often before significant damage occurs

- **Improve IR**: With accurate IoCs, IRTs can quickly understand the nature of an attack, making it easier to contain and eradicate threats

- **Enhance threat intelligence**: Collecting and analyzing IoCs over time contributes to a richer understanding of threat actors and their evolving TTPs

Developing and effectively utilizing IoCs is a continuous process that requires collaboration, standardization, and a proactive approach to threat detection and response. Organizations that prioritize this practice not only safeguard their own assets for the immediate period after, but as IoCs are directly indicative of tools used and specific TTPs, they're also safeguarding their assets for the long haul.

Summary

In this chapter, we explored the essentials of cybersecurity through three pivotal sections: *Implementing continuous monitoring*, *Developing an IRP*, and *Analyzing security incidents*. These sections collectively highlighted the importance of real-time monitoring for early threat detection, the creation of a structured response plan for effective **incident management (IM)**, and the critical analysis of incidents to bolster future defenses. These strategies ensure organizations are well equipped to proactively identify, respond to, and learn from cybersecurity threats, enhancing their resilience in the digital landscape. Moving forward, the next chapter, *Cloud Security and the NIST RMF*, will transition our focus toward applying these foundational cybersecurity principles within cloud environments, addressing the unique challenges and opportunities of securing cloud-based operations.

9

Cloud Security and the NIST RMF

As organizations increasingly leverage the cloud's flexibility and scalability, securing these environments against evolving threats becomes paramount. The **National Institute for Standards and Technology (NIST) Risk Management Framework (RMF)** offers a proven structure for managing cybersecurity risk, but adapting it to the cloud's unique landscape requires insight and strategy. This chapter, *Cloud Security and the NIST RMF*, aims to bridge this gap, guiding you through the nuances of applying the RMF in cloud environments. You'll learn how to tailor RMF principles to address the shared responsibilities, dynamic resources, and service models that define cloud computing. Additionally, we'll navigate the complexities of cloud compliance, detailing how to meet regulatory requirements and manage risks effectively in cloud settings.

By exploring common cloud security challenges and presenting practical solutions, this chapter empowers you to enhance data protection, manage access controls, and ensure a secure cloud adoption journey. You'll emerge with the skills to apply RMF principles strategically within cloud environments, ensuring a robust security posture that aligns with compliance mandates and industry best practices.

In this chapter, we're going to cover the following main topics:

- Adapting RMF for cloud environments
- Ensuring cloud compliance
- Challenges and solutions

Adapting RMF for cloud environments

As organizations increasingly adopt cloud computing, the need to secure cloud-based systems and data becomes paramount. The NIST RMF offers a structured approach to managing cybersecurity risk, but its principles must be adapted to address the unique characteristics of cloud environments. This adaptation requires an understanding of cloud service models, the shared responsibility model, and how to apply RMF steps effectively in the cloud. This section explores how to tailor RMF to the cloud, ensuring organizations can leverage cloud computing's benefits while minimizing security risks.

Understanding cloud service models

Cloud computing has revolutionized how organizations deploy and manage IT resources, offering flexibility, scalability, and cost-efficiency. However, securing cloud environments necessitates an understanding of the various cloud service models, each with its own set of security considerations and challenges:

- **Infrastructure as a service (IaaS)**: This is a type of computing that offers the hardware as a platform – typically in a pay-as-you-go model, with discounts associated with various commitments. In an IaaS model, the **cloud service provider (CSP)** manages the backend infrastructure and the customer is responsible for building everything from that point up, including the operating systems, applications, runtime, and data. Security considerations for IaaS environments include securing virtual machines, managing network traffic, and protecting stored data.

- **Platform as a service (PaaS)**: A PaaS combines an IaaS with the complete environment that developers would need to build, run, and manage their products. This could include servers, operating systems, and all of the networking, storage, and tools that the customer would need.

- **Software as a service (SaaS)**: SaaS is simply a platform for delivering the software your company has built over the internet, typically by being centrally hosted and accessed via a web browser. The CSP manages everything from infrastructure to applications, with the customer only managing user access and data. Security challenges in SaaS include data privacy, user access controls, and secure data transmission.

- **RMF adaptation for each model**: Adapting RMF for cloud environments starts with recognizing the responsibility shifts in these service models. For IaaS, organizations retain significant control over the security of their operating systems, applications, and data, necessitating a focus on securing these elements. In PaaS, the emphasis shifts toward securing the applications and data managed by the organization, while in SaaS, the focus is primarily on managing access and protecting data privacy.

Understanding these service models and their inherent security responsibilities is crucial for effectively applying the RMF in cloud environments. It enables organizations to identify which security controls they are responsible for implementing and which controls are managed by the CSP, ensuring comprehensive coverage of security risks across the cloud ecosystem.

The shared responsibility model

A foundational concept in cloud security is the shared responsibility model, which delineates the security obligations of the CSP and the customer. Understanding this model is crucial for organizations looking to adapt the NIST RMF to cloud environments, as it directly impacts the application of security controls, risk assessment, and overall cybersecurity strategy.

Defining shared responsibility

In the **shared responsibility model**, the CSP is responsible for securing the infrastructure that runs all of the services offered in the cloud. This includes the physical security of data centers, the security of hardware and software that power cloud services, and the networking infrastructure. On the other hand, the customer's responsibility varies depending on the cloud service model utilized (IaaS, PaaS, or SaaS), ranging from securing operating systems and applications in IaaS to managing user access and data in SaaS.

Implications for RMF

The shared responsibility model significantly influences how organizations apply the RMF steps in cloud environments:

- **Categorization of information systems**: Customers must categorize their systems and data based on the level of impact on confidentiality, integrity, and availability. This step becomes nuanced in the cloud, as customers need to understand the data types processed or stored through cloud services and categorize systems accordingly, considering the CSP's underlying security measures.

- **Selection of security controls**: While CSPs may offer a range of security controls, customers need to assess these controls' adequacy against their specific requirements and the RMF standards. Customers may need to supplement CSP controls with additional measures to meet their security and compliance needs.

- **Implementation of controls**: Implementing security controls in a cloud environment often requires collaboration with the CSP. Customers should leverage CSP tools and services where appropriate and implement additional controls as needed to secure their applications and data.

- **Assessment of security controls**: Assessing the effectiveness of security controls in a cloud context requires an understanding of which controls are managed by the CSP and which are managed by the customer. Customers may need to rely on CSP audits, certifications, and reports for controls managed by the provider.

- **Authorization of information systems**: The authorization process must take into account the shared responsibility model, with customers ensuring that all necessary security controls are in place and effective, including those managed by the CSP.

- **Monitoring security controls**: Continuous monitoring in cloud environments involves both CSP-provided tools and customer-implemented tools. Customers need to establish processes for monitoring the effectiveness of controls across this shared landscape.

Navigating shared responsibility

Successfully navigating the shared responsibility model requires clear communication and understanding between the customer and the CSP. Organizations should do the following:

- Carefully review CSP security documentation and contracts to understand the scope of the provider's responsibilities

- Clearly document their own responsibilities and ensure that appropriate security controls are implemented and maintained

- Engage in regular dialogue with the CSP to stay informed about changes to services or security practices that may affect their security posture

By comprehensively understanding and effectively managing their part of the shared responsibility model, organizations can ensure that the RMF is appropriately adapted for cloud environments, leading to enhanced security and compliance.

Integrating RMF steps in cloud environments

Integrating the NIST RMF steps into cloud environments involves a nuanced approach that accommodates the dynamic and distributed nature of cloud computing. This process ensures that the security controls and risk management practices are effectively aligned with the cloud's unique operational models and the shared responsibility model. Ahead, we outline how each RMF step can be adapted and applied in cloud settings.

Categorization of information systems

When considering how to categorize information systems, working in the cloud requires a whole different mindset. From containers to data lakes to S3 buckets (data stores in Amazon Web Services), there are some special considerations to keep in mind. The following are some of them:

- **Cloud-specific considerations**: In cloud environments, categorizing information systems must take into account the data's sensitivity stored or processed in the cloud and the services' impact level. Organizations should consider the cloud service models (IaaS, PaaS, or SaaS) and data residency issues, as these factors can influence the potential impact levels of **confidentiality, integrity, and availability (CIA)**.

- **Collaboration with CSPs**: Engage with CSPs to understand the baseline security features and controls they offer. This information can help in accurately categorizing cloud-based systems by aligning the CSP's capabilities with the organization's specific requirements.

Selection of security controls

Just like categorization, selecting security controls is going to be different in the cloud. These controls could be more granular due to the nature of the infrastructure. In my Google Cloud account at work, there are over 9,000 different permissions. Keep the following in mind:

- **Adapting to cloud models**: The selection of security controls in cloud environments requires a thorough understanding of the shared responsibility model. Organizations must identify which security controls are managed by the CSP and which controls they must implement. This differentiation is crucial for ensuring comprehensive coverage without duplicating efforts.

- **Leveraging cloud-specific controls**: Many CSPs offer a range of security controls designed specifically for cloud deployments. Organizations should take advantage of these controls, supplementing them with additional measures as necessary to meet their specific security requirements.

Implementation of controls

When actually going about the implementation of security controls, keep the following at the forefront of your mind to make your work more efficient:

- **Utilizing CSP tools and services**: Implement security controls using tools and services provided by the CSP wherever possible. This includes configuring security groups, access controls, and encryption services, and logging and monitoring services offered by the CSP.

- **Custom implementations**: For controls not covered by the CSP, implement custom solutions or third-party tools that integrate well with the cloud environment. This may include deploying additional security software or using cloud-compatible encryption for data at rest and in transit.

Assessment of security controls

When assessing security controls in the cloud, some challenges may arise, but there are also plenty of methods (and vendors) to assist you. Some items to keep in mind are as follows:

- **Assessment strategies**: Assessing security controls in the cloud can be challenging due to the limited visibility into the underlying infrastructure. Organizations should use CSP-provided security assessments, audits, and certifications (e.g., SOC 2 or ISO 27001) as part of their assessment strategy.

- **Continuous monitoring tools**: Leverage continuous monitoring tools that integrate with cloud environments to assess the effectiveness of security controls in real time. This includes using CSP monitoring services and third-party security solutions designed for cloud deployments.

Authorization of information systems

In cloud environments, the authorization process should focus on a risk-based approach, considering the cloud service model and the shared responsibility model. Documenting the CSP's controls and how they integrate with the organization's controls is essential for obtaining an **authorization to operate (ATO)**.

Monitoring security controls

Cloud environments have unique abilities for monitoring themselves that on-premises environments do not have. Here are some thoughts:

- **Leveraging cloud capabilities**: Utilize the advanced monitoring and logging capabilities offered by CSPs to facilitate continuous monitoring of security controls. This includes using cloud-native tools for real-time threat detection, anomaly detection, and security event logging.

- **Integrating third-party solutions**: Where necessary, integrate third-party **security information and event management (SIEM)** solutions that offer enhanced monitoring capabilities across cloud and on-premises environments.

Adapting and integrating the RMF steps into cloud environments requires careful planning and a deep understanding of both the RMF and the specific characteristics of cloud computing. By thoughtfully applying these steps, organizations can effectively manage cybersecurity risks in cloud deployments, ensuring robust security and compliance in their cloud operations.

Addressing cloud-specific risks

Cloud computing, while offering scalability, flexibility, and cost-efficiency, introduces unique security risks that organizations must address. These risks stem from the cloud's inherent characteristics, such as shared resources, dynamic provisioning, and reliance on third-party service providers. Adapting the NIST RMF to cloud environments involves not only understanding these risks but also implementing targeted strategies to mitigate them. This sub-section explores common cloud-specific risks and provides guidance on leveraging RMF to effectively address them.

Identifying cloud-specific risks

Key risks associated with cloud computing include the following:

- **Data breaches and loss**: The risk of unauthorized access to or leakage of sensitive data is amplified in the cloud due to the vast amount of data stored and the potential for misconfiguration.

- **Insufficient identity and access management**: Inadequate control over who has access to cloud resources can lead to unauthorized access, escalating the risk of data breaches and resource misuse.

- **Insecure interfaces and APIs**: Cloud services often rely on interfaces and APIs for management and integration. If these are insecure, they can become prime targets for exploitation.

- **Shared technology vulnerabilities**: The underlying infrastructure in cloud environments is shared among multiple users, potentially leading to cross-tenant attacks if the isolation controls fail.

- **Compliance challenges**: Ensuring compliance with regulatory standards can be more complex in the cloud, where data residency and sovereignty issues come into play.

Mitigating risks with RMF

To mitigate these risks, organizations should apply the RMF steps with a focus on cloud-specific considerations:

- **Categorization**: Clearly understand and categorize the types of data stored or processed in the cloud to assess potential impacts of breaches or loss.

- **Selection of controls**: Choose security controls that specifically address cloud risks, such as encryption of data at rest and in transit, and robust access control mechanisms. Leverage CSP-offered controls and integrate them with organizational controls for comprehensive coverage.

- **Implementation**: Implement the selected controls with an emphasis on automation and orchestration to keep pace with the dynamic nature of cloud environments. Utilize cloud-native security features and third-party security solutions that offer integration with cloud services.

- **Assessment**: Regularly assess the effectiveness of implemented controls, utilizing both internal assessments and external audits or certifications provided by CSPs. This helps ensure that controls remain effective in the ever-evolving cloud landscape.

- **Authorization**: Adapt the authorization process to account for the shared responsibility model, ensuring that all cloud-based systems and services are authorized for operation based on a comprehensive understanding of the risks and controls in place.

- **Monitoring**: Employ continuous monitoring strategies that leverage cloud-native tools for real-time visibility into security events and compliance status. Integrate these tools with organizational **security operations centers** (**SOCs**) for a unified security posture.

Leveraging cloud advantages

While addressing cloud-specific risks, organizations should also leverage the cloud's capabilities to enhance their security posture. Cloud environments offer advanced security features, such as automated patch management, scalability of security resources, and sophisticated threat intelligence platforms. By effectively integrating these capabilities into their RMF implementation, organizations can not only mitigate risks but also achieve a more resilient and proactive security stance.

Addressing cloud-specific risks through the adaptation of the RMF enables organizations to confidently navigate the complexities of cloud security. By systematically identifying, assessing, and mitigating these risks, organizations can harness the full potential of cloud computing while safeguarding their assets and maintaining compliance with relevant standards and regulations.

As we can see, the focus shifts toward integrating RMF within the dynamic and scalable nature of cloud computing. There is a unique service model and shared responsibility between CSPs and clients. This approach delineates the allocation of security tasks, highlighting the need for a collaborative effort in safeguarding data and infrastructure.

Ensuring cloud compliance

Navigating the cloud's expansive terrain requires more than just technical acumen; it demands a rigorous adherence to compliance standards. Ensuring cloud compliance isn't merely about ticking boxes–it's about safeguarding data, maintaining customer trust, and upholding the integrity of cloud operations against a backdrop of ever-evolving regulatory landscapes. This section delves into the critical aspects of cloud compliance, highlighting the challenges organizations face in aligning cloud operations with legal, regulatory, and industry standards. From understanding the shared responsibility model to addressing data sovereignty and preparing for compliance audits, we will explore strategies to ensure that cloud environments are not only efficient and scalable but also compliant and secure.

Understanding regulatory requirements

In the cloud, compliance is a moving target, influenced by a plethora of regulatory frameworks that vary by industry, region, and the type of data handled. Understanding these requirements is the first step in developing a compliance strategy that mitigates risk and aligns with business objectives.

Key regulatory frameworks

Here are some of the key regulatory frameworks you may encounter:

- **General Data Protection Regulation (GDPR)**: The GDPR is a data protection law that is designed to give European Union individuals more control over their data. This includes the right to access, correct, delete, and restrict processing, and strict rules on data breach notifications.

- **Health Insurance Portability and Accountability Act (HIPAA)**: This United States federal law is designed to protect patient health information from being disclosed without the patient's consent or knowledge. HIPAA established national standards for the protection of health information, applicable to healthcare providers, health plans, and clearinghouses. This also applies to all of their business associates.

- **Payment Card Industry Data Security Standard (PCI DSS)**: PCI DSS is a set of security standards to ensure that anyone handling credit card information in any form (accepting, processing, storing, or transmitting) maintains a secure environment. This is focused on preventing fraud and applies to almost anyone who handles credit card transactions in any manner.

- **Sarbanes-Oxley Act (SOX)**: SOX is a federal law in the United States that aims to enhance corporate governance and make for better accuracy and reliability of disclosures made pursuant to securities, such as stocks. This applies to all public companies in the U.S., as well as some others.

Staying informed and agile

As we work to implement RMF, staying informed of technological and regulatory changes is crucial. Here are some ways to do just that:

- **Continuous learning**: Regulatory frameworks are subject to change. Organizations must commit to ongoing education and vigilance to stay abreast of new developments and updates to existing laws.

- **Legal and compliance teams**: Engage these teams early in the cloud adoption process to interpret how regulatory requirements impact cloud operations. Collaboration with legal experts can provide clarity and direction in navigating the compliance landscape.

- **Industry resources**: Leverage resources from CSPs, industry groups, and regulatory bodies. Many CSPs offer compliance programs and tools designed to help customers meet specific regulatory requirements.

Strategic compliance planning

Developing a compliance strategy in the cloud involves mapping out regulatory requirements against the organization's cloud architecture and operations. This planning should consider the types of data stored or processed in the cloud, the cloud service models in use (IaaS, PaaS, or SaaS), and the geographical locations of cloud services. A strategic approach to compliance ensures that organizations can meet their regulatory obligations while maximizing the benefits of cloud computing.

Understanding regulatory requirements sets the foundation for cloud compliance, guiding organizations in the development and implementation of controls, policies, and procedures that ensure compliance across cloud environments. This proactive stance not only mitigates risks but also positions organizations to respond swiftly and effectively to changes in the regulatory landscape.

The shared responsibility model and compliance

The shared responsibility model is a cornerstone of cloud computing, defining the division of security obligations between CSPs and their customers. This model significantly influences compliance strategies, as both parties must understand their respective responsibilities to ensure regulatory requirements are fully met. Navigating compliance within this model requires a clear delineation of roles and a collaborative approach to implementing the necessary security controls and compliance measures.

Understanding shared responsibilities

In the shared responsibility model, CSPs are typically responsible for the security *of* the cloud, including physical infrastructure, network controls, and the virtualization layer. Conversely, customers are responsible for security *in* the cloud, which encompasses data protection, identity and access management, application security, and client-side encryption and data integrity authentication.

Compliance implications

To achieve compliance, it's essential for customers to clearly understand which aspects of compliance are managed by the CSP and which fall under their purview. This distinction can vary significantly across different cloud service models (IaaS, PaaS, and SaaS), with customers generally assuming more responsibility in IaaS compared to SaaS.

Many CSPs undergo independent certifications for common regulatory standards (e.g., ISO 27001, SOC 2, and GDPR compliance). Customers should leverage these certifications as part of their compliance strategy but also recognize the limits of CSP certifications, which may not cover all customer-specific compliance requirements.

Strategies for ensuring compliance

Now that we understand some of the facets of compliance, let's talk about some practical strategies to ensure that we remain so:

- **Comprehensive documentation**: Maintain detailed documentation of the CSP's and customers' security controls. This documentation is crucial for demonstrating compliance to auditors and regulatory bodies.

- **Leverage CSP tools and services**: Many CSPs offer tools and services designed to assist with compliance efforts, such as data encryption, access control, and logging services. Customers should fully utilize these offerings to enhance their compliance posture.

- **Regular compliance reviews**: Conduct regular reviews of the shared responsibility model in the context of compliance, especially when adopting new cloud services or when there are changes in regulatory requirements. This ensures that all compliance obligations are continuously met.

- **Collaboration and communication**: Establish clear lines of communication with the CSP to stay informed about any changes in their services or compliance offerings that may affect the customer's compliance status. Collaborative engagement can help address compliance gaps and foster a proactive approach to regulatory challenges.

Navigating multi-cloud environments

In multi-cloud environments, where services from multiple CSPs are used, managing compliance becomes more complex. Organizations must navigate different shared responsibility models and ensure a cohesive compliance strategy that addresses the specific requirements of each CSP.

The shared responsibility model underpins the approach to compliance in cloud computing, requiring a nuanced understanding of the division of responsibilities between CSPs and customers. By clarifying these roles, leveraging CSP certifications and tools, and engaging in ongoing collaboration and review, organizations can effectively navigate the compliance landscape in the cloud, ensuring that their operations remain secure and in alignment with regulatory requirements.

Compliance in different cloud service models

Cloud computing offers a range of service models, each presenting unique challenges and considerations for compliance. Understanding how compliance responsibilities shift across IaaS, PaaS, and SaaS is crucial for organizations aiming to secure their cloud deployments and meet regulatory standards. This sub-section explores the compliance nuances of these cloud service models and offers strategies for maintaining compliance within each.

IaaS

Compliance challenges in IaaS environments often revolve around data protection, network security, and access controls, as customers have significant control and responsibility over their deployed applications and data.

Strategies for compliance can include the following:

- Implementing robust access controls and encryption for data at rest and in transit to protect sensitive information

- Regularly updating and patching operating systems and applications to mitigate vulnerabilities

- Utilizing CSP-provided tools for security monitoring and compliance reporting to enhance visibility and control over the infrastructure

PaaS

The CSP manages the infrastructure and platforms, but the customer manages the applications and data.

Compliance in PaaS environments focuses on application security, including securing application code, managing user access, and protecting the data used by applications.

Strategies for compliance can include the following:

- Conducting regular security assessments and code reviews to identify and remediate vulnerabilities in application development

- Leveraging CSP services for identity and access management to ensure only authorized users can access application resources

- Employing data encryption and managing application secrets securely to protect sensitive data processed by the applications

SaaS

SaaS delivers software applications over the internet, with the CSP managing the infrastructure, platform, and software. Customers typically only manage their user accounts and the data within the SaaS applications.

The primary compliance challenge in SaaS environments is data privacy and security, as customers have limited control over the underlying application security but are still responsible for their data.

Strategies for compliance can include the following:

- Understanding the data privacy and security measures implemented by the SaaS provider, ensuring they align with compliance requirements

- Implementing strong data governance policies for managing and classifying data stored in SaaS applications

- Regularly reviewing user access rights and employing data loss prevention strategies to safeguard sensitive information

Navigating compliance across service models

With different service models come different ways to navigate compliance. Here are some strategies to keep in mind:

- **Clear understanding of responsibilities**: Regardless of the cloud service model, having a clear understanding of the shared responsibility model is essential. Know what aspects of compliance are managed by the CSP and which are the organization's responsibility.

- **Leverage CSP compliance programs**: Many CSPs offer compliance programs and certifications specific to their services. Utilize these programs to simplify compliance efforts, especially when operating across multiple service models.

- **Continuous monitoring and assessment**: Continuously monitor compliance status and conduct regular assessments to ensure ongoing adherence to regulatory standards. This is crucial as cloud environments are dynamic, and compliance requirements may evolve.

By tailoring compliance strategies to the specific characteristics and responsibilities associated with IaaS, PaaS, and SaaS, organizations can more effectively navigate the complexities of cloud compliance. This targeted approach ensures that regardless of the service model, cloud deployments remain secure, compliant, and aligned with organizational and regulatory standards.

Data sovereignty and compliance

Data sovereignty refers to the legal principle that digital data is subject to the laws of the country in which it is located. As cloud computing often involves storing and processing data across global data centers, understanding and adhering to data sovereignty laws become crucial for maintaining compliance in cloud environments. This sub-section explores the challenges posed by data sovereignty and offers strategies for ensuring compliance while navigating these complexities.

Challenges of data sovereignty in the cloud

When it comes to the cloud, you have to be aware of many different policies. Every CSP has its own third-party providers, for instance, and when you migrate to the cloud, you're opening yourself up to a whole world of people who now could potentially access your data. Let's discuss some of the challenges that you may face:

- **Cross-border data transfers**: Data stored in the cloud can physically reside in any of the CSP's global data centers, potentially crossing borders and becoming subject to multiple jurisdictions' laws and regulations. This can complicate compliance efforts, especially when laws conflict or impose strict data protection and privacy requirements.

- **Regulatory compliance**: Regulations such as the GDPR in the European Union impose strict rules on data transfer outside the EU. Organizations must ensure that their cloud deployments comply with such regulations to avoid hefty penalties.

- **Data localization requirements**: Some countries have enacted data localization laws requiring certain types of data to be stored within the country's borders. These laws aim to protect citizens' data from foreign surveillance and ensure legal jurisdiction over the data.

Strategies for ensuring compliance

Now that we've discussed the challenges, let's discuss the strategies to overcome them:

- **Understand applicable laws and regulations**: Organizations must thoroughly understand the data sovereignty laws and regulations applicable to their operations. This includes identifying the jurisdictions where data is stored and processed and understanding the implications for data privacy, protection, and cross-border transfers.

- **Data mapping and classification**: Implement a robust data mapping and classification process to identify where sensitive or regulated data resides in the cloud. This can help in applying appropriate controls and ensuring compliance with data sovereignty laws.

- **Leverage CSP data residency options**: Many CSPs offer data residency options, allowing customers to select specific regions or countries for data storage and processing. Utilize these options to comply with data localization laws and manage data sovereignty risks.

- **Negotiate data processing agreements**: Work with CSPs to negotiate data processing agreements that address compliance with data sovereignty laws. Ensure these agreements include clauses on data transfer, storage, and processing that align with legal requirements.

- **Implement encryption and access controls**: Use encryption for data at rest and in transit to protect data integrity and confidentiality. Implement strict access controls to ensure that only authorized personnel can access sensitive data, regardless of its location.

- **Regularly review and update compliance practices**: As data sovereignty laws can change, regularly review and update compliance practices to adapt to new requirements. Stay informed about legal developments in jurisdictions where your data is stored or processed.

Navigating the complexities of data sovereignty in cloud environments requires a proactive and informed approach. By understanding the legal implications of where data is stored and processed and implementing strategies to manage these challenges, organizations can ensure their cloud operations remain compliant with global data protection and privacy laws, safeguarding their data and maintaining trust with their customers and stakeholders.

Compliance audits and certifications

In the cloud computing environment, demonstrating compliance through audits and certifications becomes a critical component of an organization's security posture. Compliance audits provide a formal evaluation of how well an organization adheres to regulatory standards and best practices, while certifications offer a recognized benchmark of security excellence. This sub-section explores the role of compliance audits and certifications in cloud environments, detailing how organizations can prepare for audits and leverage certifications to enhance trust and security.

The role of compliance audits

Compliance audits in cloud environments serve several key purposes:

- **Verification of compliance**: Audits verify that an organization's cloud operations comply with relevant laws, regulations, and standards. This includes assessing the effectiveness of implemented security controls and procedures.

- **Identification of gaps**: Audits help identify compliance gaps or weaknesses in an organization's cloud security practices, providing an opportunity to address these issues proactively.

- **Enhancing credibility**: Successfully passing compliance audits enhances an organization's credibility, demonstrating to customers, partners, and regulators that it takes data security and privacy seriously.

Preparing for compliance audits

When preparing for compliance audits, there is a lot to keep in mind–from preparing all of your documentation to last-minute checks to make sure you're all set. Here are some ideas to keep you level-headed as you enter that preparation phase:

- **Understand audit requirements**: Familiarize yourself with the specific requirements of the audit, including the standards and regulations being assessed. This understanding guides the preparation process and ensures that all necessary documentation and evidence are ready for review.

- **Conduct internal reviews**: Regular internal reviews or self-assessments help identify potential compliance issues before the formal audit. Use these reviews to adjust practices and resolve any identified gaps.

- **Document policies and procedures**: Ensure that all security policies, procedures, and control implementations are well-documented. Auditors will review these documents to understand how compliance is maintained.

- **Engage with CSPs**: For aspects of compliance managed by your CSP, obtain the necessary documentation or attestations that demonstrate their compliance. This may include SOC 2 reports, ISO certifications, or other relevant compliance evidence.

Leveraging certifications

Certifications may play a large educational role in preparing you and your team for an audit. These may also help the auditors directly. Consider the following:

- **Industry-recognized certifications**: Obtaining certifications such as ISO 27001 and PCI DSS signifies that an organization meets high standards of security and compliance. These certifications can be pivotal in building trust with stakeholders and differentiating your services in the market.

- **Certification process**: Achieving certification typically involves an extensive audit by an independent third party, which assesses the organization's compliance with the standards' specific criteria. Preparation for certification involves a thorough review of security practices, policies, and controls, similar to preparing for compliance audits.

- **Continuous compliance**: Maintaining certifications requires ongoing adherence to the standards, necessitating continuous monitoring, regular reviews, and periodic recertification audits. This continuous compliance effort ensures that security practices remain robust over time.

Compliance audits and certifications play a vital role in establishing and maintaining the security and compliance posture of cloud-based operations. By thoroughly preparing for audits, addressing identified gaps, and leveraging industry-recognized certifications, organizations can demonstrate their commitment to security and compliance. This not only satisfies regulatory requirements but also builds trust with customers and partners, ensuring the organization's cloud environment is secure, compliant, and aligned with industry best practices.

Continuous compliance monitoring

In the dynamic landscape of cloud computing, where services and data flows evolve rapidly, maintaining continuous compliance is imperative. Traditional compliance checks, performed annually or semi-annually, are no longer sufficient to ensure that cloud environments always adhere to regulatory standards and internal policies. Continuous compliance monitoring emerges as a crucial strategy, enabling organizations to automatically detect and address compliance deviations in real time. This sub-section outlines the importance of continuous compliance monitoring in cloud environments and provides strategies for its implementation.

Continuous compliance monitoring in the cloud is essential for several reasons:

- **Dynamic cloud environments**: Cloud services and configurations change frequently, introducing new compliance risks that must be identified and mitigated promptly

- **Regulatory evolution**: Compliance standards and regulations are continually updated to address emerging security threats and privacy concerns, necessitating ongoing adjustments to compliance practices

- **Proactive risk management**: Continuous monitoring allows organizations to proactively identify compliance gaps and vulnerabilities, reducing the risk of data breaches and regulatory penalties

Implementing continuous compliance monitoring

To effectively implement continuous compliance monitoring in cloud environments, organizations should consider the following strategies:

- **Leverage cloud-native tools**: Many CSPs offer native tools designed to support continuous monitoring of security and compliance postures. These tools can automate the detection of non-compliant configurations, unauthorized access attempts, and other potential compliance issues.

- **Integrate third-party solutions**: For more comprehensive coverage, integrate third-party compliance monitoring tools that can work across multiple cloud platforms and on-premises environments. Choose solutions that offer real-time alerts, customizable compliance checks, and reporting capabilities.

- **Define compliance policies**: Clearly define compliance policies and rules that align with regulatory requirements and industry standards. These policies serve as the foundation for monitoring activities, guiding the automated detection of non-compliant actions or configurations.

- **Automate remediation processes**: Where possible, automate the remediation of detected compliance issues. Automated workflows can help correct non-compliant configurations and enforce compliance policies without manual intervention, speeding up the response to potential compliance violations.

- **Regularly review and update policies**: Compliance requirements and organizational needs evolve over time. Regularly review and update compliance policies and monitoring parameters to ensure they remain relevant and effective in addressing current compliance challenges.

- **Enhance visibility with dashboards**: Utilize dashboards and reporting tools to enhance visibility into the organization's compliance posture. These tools can aggregate data from continuous monitoring efforts, providing insights into compliance trends, risks, and the effectiveness of current compliance measures.

Benefits of continuous compliance monitoring

Implementing continuous compliance monitoring offers numerous benefits, including the following:

- **Enhanced compliance posture**: Continuous monitoring helps maintain an up-to-date compliance posture, reducing the risk of regulatory penalties and reputational damage

- **Increased operational efficiency**: Automating compliance monitoring and remediation processes increases operational efficiency, freeing up resources to focus on strategic initiatives

- **Improved security**: By continuously monitoring for compliance deviations, organizations can also enhance their overall security posture, as many compliance requirements are closely aligned with security best practices

Continuous compliance monitoring is a critical component of a robust cloud security and compliance strategy. By leveraging cloud-native and third-party tools to continuously assess and enforce compliance policies, organizations can ensure their cloud environments remain compliant, secure, and aligned with business objectives amidst the rapidly changing cloud landscape.

Managing compliance in multi-cloud environments

The adoption of multi-cloud environments, where organizations utilize services from multiple CSPs, has become increasingly common. While this approach offers benefits such as increased flexibility, redundancy, and avoidance of vendor lock-in, it also introduces significant challenges for maintaining compliance. Different CSPs may have varying compliance standards, tools, and reporting mechanisms, complicating the task of ensuring a consistent compliance posture across the entire cloud ecosystem. This sub-section discusses strategies for effectively managing compliance in multi-cloud environments, ensuring that regulatory requirements are met uniformly regardless of the CSP.

Understanding the complexity of multi-cloud compliance

In a multi-cloud environment, compliance complexities arise from the following:

- **Diverse compliance standards**: Each CSP may adhere to different compliance certifications and standards, necessitating a thorough understanding of what each CSP covers and where gaps may exist

- **Varied security controls**: Security controls and features can vary significantly between CSPs, requiring organizations to carefully tailor their security and compliance measures to each environment

- **Inconsistent reporting and monitoring tools**: The lack of standardized reporting and monitoring tools across CSPs can hinder visibility into compliance status and security events

Strategies for ensuring multi-cloud compliance

To navigate the compliance challenges of multi-cloud environments, organizations should employ the following strategies:

- **Centralized compliance management**: Establish a centralized compliance management function that oversees compliance efforts across all cloud environments. This includes standardizing compliance policies, controls, and procedures as much as possible to ensure consistency.

- **Leverage cloud-agnostic tools**: Utilize cloud-agnostic security and compliance tools that can integrate with multiple CSPs. These tools can provide a unified view of the compliance posture across different cloud environments, simplifying monitoring and management.

- **Automate compliance processes**: Implement automation for compliance-related tasks, such as configuration management, monitoring, and reporting. Automation helps maintain consistency in policy enforcement and reduces the risk of human error.

- **Regular compliance assessments**: Conduct regular compliance assessments for each cloud environment to identify and address compliance gaps. This should include reviews of CSP-provided security controls and any custom controls implemented by the organization.

- **Cross-cloud compliance frameworks**: Develop cross-cloud compliance frameworks that outline common compliance requirements applicable across all CSPs. This framework should also specify provider-specific considerations to address unique aspects of each cloud environment.

- **Collaboration with CSPs**: Engage in ongoing collaboration with CSPs to stay informed about changes to their services, security controls, and compliance certifications. This partnership can aid in swiftly addressing compliance issues as they arise.

- **Education and training**: Ensure that the teams responsible for managing cloud environments are well-versed in the compliance requirements and security controls of each CSP. Continuous education and training can help maintain a high level of compliance awareness and expertise.

Managing compliance in multi-cloud environments demands a proactive, strategic approach that accounts for the variability across different CSPs. By implementing centralized compliance management, leveraging cloud-agnostic tools, automating compliance processes, and fostering collaboration with CSPs, organizations can overcome the challenges of multi-cloud compliance. This comprehensive strategy ensures that regardless of how cloud services are deployed, the organization's compliance posture remains robust, consistent, and aligned with regulatory obligations, safeguarding the organization against compliance risks and enhancing its overall security framework.

Understanding key regulatory frameworks and staying informed about changes is crucial to remaining agile in compliance efforts and ensuring cloud compliance. Equally critical is strategic planning, alongside having a grasp on the shared responsibility model. We've also discussed the challenges of compliance audits and the use of certifications as well as continuous compliance monitoring. Let's dive deeper into the challenges you may face (and the solutions you could bring).

Challenges and solutions

As organizations increasingly migrate their operations to the cloud, the complexity and scope of securing these environments have grown exponentially. Cloud computing, while offering unparalleled scalability, efficiency, and flexibility, also introduces a host of unique security challenges that can compromise data integrity, privacy, and compliance. This section will present the most pressing security challenges faced by organizations in cloud environments and offer targeted solutions to mitigate these risks. From protecting sensitive data and ensuring robust access management to navigating legal and compliance hurdles, this section aims to arm organizations with the strategies and best practices needed to secure their cloud deployments effectively. By addressing these challenges head-on, organizations can not only safeguard their assets and data against emerging threats but also harness the full potential of cloud computing to drive business innovation and growth.

Data security and privacy

One of the foremost concerns in cloud security is the protection of sensitive data against unauthorized access, breaches, and leaks. In the cloud, where data is stored off-premises and potentially across global data centers, ensuring data security and privacy becomes a complex challenge. Here's how organizations can tackle these issues:

- **Implement encryption**: Encrypting data at rest and in transit is fundamental to protecting sensitive information in the cloud. Encryption acts as a last line of defense, ensuring that even if data is accessed without authorization, it remains unintelligible and secure.

- **Robust access controls**: Limit users on your network to only the sensitive data they are authorized for. This could be done by implementing **identity and access management (IAM)** solutions that support **multi-factor authentication** (**MFA**) and **role-based access control** (**RBAC**), minimizing the risk of unauthorized data access.

- **Data anonymization**: For data that is used in testing or development environments, consider data anonymization techniques. Anonymizing data ensures that personal or sensitive information is obfuscated or removed, reducing privacy risks.

- **Data loss prevention** (**DLP**): Utilize DLP tools to monitor and control data transfer, preventing sensitive data from being leaked or transferred outside the organization's cloud environments without authorization.

- **Regular audits and monitoring**: Conduct regular audits of data access and usage within cloud environments to detect unauthorized access or abnormal data usage patterns. Continuous monitoring allows for the early detection of potential data security and privacy issues.

- **Backup and recovery**: Implement a comprehensive data backup and recovery strategy to protect against data loss scenarios. Cloud-based backup solutions can offer automated, secure, and scalable options for backing up critical data.

- **Understand CSP security practices**: Gain a clear understanding of your CSP's security practices and policies. Ensure they align with your organization's data security and privacy requirements and leverage any CSP-offered tools and services designed to enhance data protection.

By prioritizing data security and privacy and implementing these solutions, organizations can significantly reduce the risk of data breaches and privacy violations in cloud environments. Protecting sensitive data not only complies with legal and regulatory requirements but also builds trust with customers and stakeholders, reinforcing the organization's reputation for security and reliability.

IAM

Effective IAM is pivotal in securing cloud environments, ensuring that only authorized users have access to resources and data. As organizations expand their cloud footprint, managing identities and access permissions becomes increasingly complex yet critical for preventing unauthorized access and potential security breaches. This section delves into the IAM challenge in cloud security and outlines strategic solutions for robust IAM implementation.

Challenges in IAM for cloud environments

IAM in the cloud is quite an undertaking. The Google Cloud Platform alone has nearly 9,000 individual permissions that can be assigned to a single account. When looking at cloud environments, keep the following in mind:

- **Scalability and complexity**: As organizations deploy services across various cloud platforms, managing user identities and permissions across disparate systems adds complexity and challenges in maintaining a consistent security posture

- **Privilege creep**: Without regular review and adjustment, users may accumulate access rights beyond their current job requirements, increasing the risk of insider threats and data breaches

- **Identity federation and single sign-on**: Integrating multiple cloud services and on-premises systems while providing users with seamless access requires effective identity federation and **single sign-on** (SSO) solutions, complicating IAM strategies

Strategies for effective IAM in cloud computing

Let's go over some strategies for navigating the complexities of access management in the cloud:

- **Implement MFA**: MFA is one more layer of security that is quickly becoming the online standard and should be enforced by default in cloud environments. The idea behind MFA is having multiple ways to prove who you are, and typically they come from different categories; for example, a password is something you know, while using an authenticator app requires something you already have.

- **Deploy least privilege access**: Assign users and services the minimum level of access rights they need to perform their tasks. Regularly review and adjust these permissions to prevent privilege creep and minimize the potential impact of a compromised account.

- **Utilize IAM tools and services**: Leverage cloud-native IAM tools provided by CSPs, which offer features such as automated permission management, activity monitoring, and detailed access policies tailored to cloud environments.

- **Regular access reviews and audits**: Conduct periodic reviews and audits of user access rights and permissions to ensure they remain aligned with current job roles and responsibilities. Automated tools can streamline this process by identifying inactive users and excessive permissions.

- **Adopt RBAC**: Organize access controls around roles and responsibilities within the organization. RBAC simplifies the management of permissions, making it easier to adjust access rights as roles change.

- **Implement identity federation and SSO**: For organizations using multiple cloud services or a hybrid cloud model, identity federation and SSO can simplify user access while maintaining security. These technologies allow users to authenticate once and access multiple services without logging in separately to each one.

- **Educate users on security best practices**: Regularly train users on the importance of security practices related to IAM, including the use of strong passwords, recognizing phishing attempts, and securing their authentication credentials.

A robust IAM strategy is essential for securing cloud environments against unauthorized access and potential security threats. By implementing comprehensive IAM practices, such as MFA, least privilege access, and utilizing cloud-native IAM tools, organizations can enhance their cloud security posture. Regular reviews and user education further reinforce IAM policies, ensuring that access to cloud resources is securely managed and aligned with the organization's security objectives.

Misconfiguration and insecure instances

Misconfigurations and insecure instances in cloud environments represent some of the most common yet avoidable security challenges. As cloud platforms offer extensive flexibility and control over settings, the risk of misconfiguring a service or resource can lead to significant security vulnerabilities, including unauthorized access, data breaches, and service disruptions. This sub-section explores the issue of misconfigurations and insecure instances in the cloud and provides strategies for mitigating these risks.

Understanding the risks

It's important to understand the risks associated with cloud IAM as they are very complex. Consider the following:

- **Excessive permissions**: Overly permissive configurations can expose cloud resources to unnecessary risk, allowing broader access than required for operations

- **Default settings**: Many cloud services come with default settings that may not align with an organization's security requirements, potentially leaving systems exposed

- **Improper data exposure**: Incorrect configurations can lead to unintended data exposure, making sensitive information accessible via the internet

Strategies for mitigating risks

Now, let's look at some strategies for mitigating said risks:

- **Implement configuration management**: Use configuration management tools to enforce and maintain desired configurations across cloud environments. These tools can automate the application of secure configurations and identify deviations in real time.

- **Regular audits and assessments**: Conduct regular security audits and assessments to identify and rectify misconfigurations. CSPs often offer tools to assess the security posture of your deployments and recommend improvements.

- **Adopt infrastructure as code**: **Infrastructure as code** (**IaC**) allows organizations to define and deploy cloud infrastructure through code, which can be versioned and audited. This approach ensures consistent application of secure configurations across all environments.

- **Use CSP security baselines and benchmarks**: Leverage security baselines and benchmarks provided by CSPs and industry organizations. These guidelines offer best practices for securing cloud services and resources.

- **Educate and train staff**: Ensure that all team members involved in configuring and managing cloud resources are aware of best practices for cloud security. Regular training sessions can help keep security top of mind.

- **Leverage automated compliance monitoring**: Utilize tools that continuously monitor compliance with security policies and standards. These tools can alert administrators to misconfigurations or insecure instances that need attention.

- **Practice least privilege access**: Limit the risk of misconfigurations leading to security breaches by adhering to the principle of least privilege. Ensure that only necessary permissions are granted for specific roles and tasks.

Misconfigurations and insecure instances in cloud environments can lead to serious security vulnerabilities, but they are preventable with the right strategies and tools. By implementing robust configuration management practices, conducting regular security audits, leveraging IaC, and educating staff, organizations can significantly reduce the risk of misconfigurations. Additionally, utilizing automated tools for compliance monitoring and adhering to the principle of least privilege access can further strengthen an organization's cloud security posture, ensuring that cloud resources are configured securely and in alignment with best practices.

Compliance and legal issues

Navigating the complex landscape of compliance and legal issues represents a significant challenge for organizations operating in cloud environments. The global nature of the cloud means that data can traverse international borders easily, subjecting organizations to a myriad of regulations and legal requirements that vary by jurisdiction. This sub-section explores the challenges associated with maintaining compliance and addressing legal issues in the cloud, and offers strategic approaches to manage these concerns effectively.

Understanding the challenge

When it comes to legal issues and compliance, it's best to involve the appropriate experts. Here are some challenges with the legalities of compliance:

- **Varied regulatory landscapes**: Organizations must contend with differing data protection laws, industry-specific regulations, and international standards, all of which can impact cloud operations

- **Data residency and sovereignty**: Certain regulations require data to be stored within specific geographical boundaries, posing challenges for cloud deployments that span multiple countries

- **Contractual obligations with CSPs**: The terms of service and data processing agreements with CSPs must be carefully managed to ensure they align with compliance and legal requirements

Strategies for managing compliance and legal issues

As discussed before, here are some strategies for those legal issues (again, get the lawyers when you have questions):

- **Develop a comprehensive compliance framework**: Create a unified compliance framework that addresses all relevant regulations and standards. This framework should guide the selection of CSPs, the configuration of cloud services, and the management of data across all cloud environments.

- **Leverage cloud compliance tools**: Utilize tools offered by CSPs designed to assist with compliance monitoring, reporting, and management. These tools can help automate compliance tasks and provide visibility into the compliance status of cloud resources.

- **Engage in due diligence with CSPs**: Conduct thorough due diligence when selecting CSPs to ensure that their services comply with necessary regulations and that they can provide adequate assurances and certifications, such as ISO 27001, SOC 2, or GDPR compliance.

- **Implement data governance policies**: Establish strict data governance policies that address data classification, data handling, and data residency requirements. These policies should be enforced across all cloud services to maintain compliance and protect sensitive information.

- **Regularly review and update compliance strategies**: Compliance requirements can evolve, necessitating regular reviews of compliance strategies and adjustments to cloud configurations, policies, and practices to ensure ongoing compliance.

- **Train staff on compliance and legal requirements**: Ensure that all team members are aware of compliance obligations and legal issues related to cloud computing. Regular training can help prevent unintentional breaches of compliance.

- **Plan for international operations**: For organizations operating internationally, develop strategies to address data residency, cross-border data transfers, and international regulatory compliance, leveraging legal expertise and CSP capabilities to navigate these complexities.

Compliance and legal issues in cloud computing demand a proactive and informed approach to ensure that organizations remain compliant with all applicable laws and regulations while leveraging the cloud's benefits. By developing a comprehensive compliance framework, engaging in due diligence with CSPs, implementing robust data governance policies, and staying informed about regulatory changes, organizations can navigate the compliance landscape confidently. These efforts not only protect the organization from legal and regulatory risks but also build trust with customers and partners by demonstrating a commitment to compliance and data protection.

Insider threats and advanced persistent threats

In the cloud security landscape, organizations face significant risks not only from external attackers but also from insider threats and **advanced persistent threats** (**APTs**). Insider threats can emerge from within the organization, involving employees, contractors, or partners who misuse their access to cloud resources, intentionally or unintentionally causing harm. APTs, on the other hand, are sophisticated, prolonged cyberattacks aimed at stealing information or disrupting operations, often orchestrated by nation-states or criminal organizations. This sub-section explores strategies to mitigate the risks associated with insider threats and APTs in cloud environments.

Insider threats – identification and mitigation

Insider threats are considered to be one of the more difficult areas to address. Consider the following:

- **Comprehensive access controls**: Implement strict access controls and regularly review access rights to ensure employees and contractors only have the permissions necessary to perform their job functions. Utilize RBAC and the principle of least privilege to minimize potential damage.

- **User entity and behavior analytics** (**UEBA**): Deploy UEBA tools to monitor for unusual activities that could indicate malicious insider actions. These tools can detect anomalies in user behavior, such as unusual access patterns or data exfiltration attempts.

- **Training and awareness programs**: Conduct regular security awareness training for all personnel to highlight the risks of insider threats and encourage the reporting of suspicious activities. Educate staff on the proper handling of sensitive data and the importance of adhering to security policies.

- **Insider threat detection programs**: Establish a formal insider threat detection program that includes a cross-functional team responsible for identifying, assessing, and responding to insider threat risks. This team should have clear procedures for investigating incidents and taking disciplinary actions.

APTs – identification and mitigation

When it comes to APTs that sometimes have more resources than your organization, depending upon its size, think about the following to help you identify and mitigate their presence:

- **Advanced threat detection solutions**: Utilize advanced threat detection and cybersecurity intelligence solutions to identify signs of APT activities. These solutions can analyze patterns and behaviors indicative of sophisticated attacks, providing early warning of potential threats.

- **Segmentation and zero trust**: Implement network segmentation and adopt a zero-trust security model to limit lateral movement within the cloud environment. These approaches ensure that even if attackers breach the perimeter, their access to sensitive resources is restricted.

- **Incident response and threat hunting**: Develop a robust incident response plan that includes provisions for dealing with APTs. Incorporate threat hunting into your security operations to proactively search for indicators of compromise and respond swiftly to mitigate threats.

- **Collaboration and information sharing**: Engage in information sharing with industry groups, security organizations, and law enforcement to stay informed about emerging APT tactics and indicators. Collaboration can enhance collective defense by providing access to shared threat intelligence.

Mitigating the risks posed by insider threats and APTs requires a multifaceted approach that combines advanced security technologies, strict access controls, continuous monitoring, and employee education. By understanding the characteristics and tactics of these threats, organizations can implement targeted strategies to detect and respond to malicious activities, protecting their cloud environments from compromise. Cultivating a culture of security awareness and maintaining vigilance are essential components of a comprehensive cloud security posture that can withstand the challenges posed by insider threats and APTs.

Vendor lock-in and cloud service dependency

Vendor lock-in and cloud service dependency represent significant strategic challenges for organizations leveraging cloud computing. Vendor lock-in occurs when an organization becomes overly reliant on a single CSP's technologies and services, making it difficult, costly, or disruptive to switch to another provider. This dependency can limit flexibility, hinder negotiation capabilities, and potentially expose the organization to increased risks if the CSP experiences downtime or discontinues certain services. This sub-section discusses the implications of vendor lock-in and cloud service dependency, along with strategies for mitigating these risks.

Understanding the risks

Risks around the cloud are in many ways similar to those around non-cloud environments but have their own *flavor* to keep in mind, especially between vendors. Consider the following:

- **Reduced flexibility**: Dependence on a single CSP can reduce an organization's ability to adapt to new technologies or services offered by competitors

- **Cost implications**: Organizations may face unexpected costs or unfavorable pricing structures when deeply integrated with a single vendor's ecosystem, with limited leverage to negotiate better terms

- **Operational risks**: Relying on a single CSP for critical services can expose organizations to operational risks, including service outages or data loss incidents affecting the provider

Mitigation strategies

Here are some strategies for mitigating risk in cloud environments – of course, these are not all-encompassing:

- **Adopt a multi-cloud strategy**: Utilizing multiple CSPs can help distribute risk and enhance flexibility. A multi-cloud approach allows organizations to leverage the best features and pricing from different providers, reducing dependency on any single vendor.

- **Standardize on open technologies**: Where possible, use open standards and technologies that are not proprietary to any single CSP. This can include containerization technologies such as Kubernetes, which can run across different cloud environments, and open source software that ensures portability.

- **Architect for portability**: Design cloud workloads and architectures with portability in mind. This involves abstracting applications from the underlying infrastructure and considering the use of cloud-agnostic tools and platforms that facilitate easier migration between providers.

- **Conduct regular vendor assessments**: Regularly evaluate the CSP's performance, service offerings, and costs against competitors. This assessment can inform strategic decisions about continuing, expanding, or changing cloud service relationships.

- **Negotiate flexible contracts**: Work to negotiate contracts with CSPs that include flexible terms, allowing for easier migration or exit strategies if needed. This can include clauses related to data portability, service levels, and termination processes.

- **Implement robust data backup and exit strategies**: Ensure that data backup practices that allow for data to be exported from the CSP's environment are in place. Develop a comprehensive exit strategy that outlines the steps and processes for migrating services away from the CSP if necessary.

While cloud computing offers numerous benefits, organizations must be mindful of the risks associated with vendor lock-in and cloud service dependency. By adopting a strategic approach that includes a multi-cloud strategy, standardization on open technologies, and careful vendor assessment, organizations can mitigate these risks, ensuring greater flexibility and resilience in their cloud operations. Planning for portability and negotiating flexible contracts are also key to maintaining operational agility and avoiding the pitfalls of becoming too reliant on a single CSP.

Disaster recovery and business continuity

In the context of cloud computing, ensuring robust **disaster recovery** (**DR**) and **business continuity** (**BC**) plans is crucial for minimizing downtime and maintaining operational resilience in the face of disruptions. Cloud environments offer scalable and flexible solutions for DR and BC, but they also require careful planning and management to effectively leverage these advantages. This sub-section explores the importance of DR and BC in cloud environments, outlining strategies to ensure organizations can quickly recover from disasters and maintain continuous business operations.

Cloud computing introduces both opportunities and challenges for DR and BC planning:

- **Opportunities**: The cloud provides on-demand resource scalability, geographic distribution of data centers, and cost-effective redundancy options, which are advantageous for implementing comprehensive DR and BC strategies.

- **Challenges**: Relying on cloud services introduces dependencies on external providers. Organizations must ensure their DR and BC plans account for potential cloud-specific risks, such as CSP outages or data loss incidents.

The strategies for ensuring DR and BC in cloud environments are as follows:

- **Risk assessment and planning**: Conduct a thorough risk assessment to identify potential threats to cloud-based resources and operations. This assessment should inform the development of a DR and BC plan that addresses identified risks and outlines recovery objectives, strategies, and procedures.

- **Leverage cloud-based DR solutions**: Utilize cloud-based DR solutions that offer data replication, automated failovers, and recovery orchestration. These solutions can significantly reduce **recovery time objectives** (**RTOs**) and **recovery point objectives** (**RPOs**), ensuring minimal data loss and downtime.

- **Implement data redundancy**: Store critical data across multiple geographically dispersed cloud regions or availability zones. This redundancy protects against data loss and ensures data availability, even if one location experiences an outage.

- **Regular testing and simulation**: Regularly test and simulate disaster scenarios to validate the effectiveness of the DR and BC plans. Testing helps identify gaps in the plans and provides an opportunity to train staff on their roles during a DR process.

- **Develop a communication plan**: Include a comprehensive communication plan that outlines how to notify employees, customers, and stakeholders in the event of a disaster. Clear communication is critical for managing expectations and coordinating recovery efforts.

- **Review and update plans regularly**: Cloud environments and organizational needs evolve, necessitating regular reviews and updates to DR and BC plans. Incorporate lessons learned from tests and actual incidents to continually improve recovery strategies.

- **Collaborate with CSPs**: Understand the DR and BC capabilities and responsibilities of your CSPs. Ensure that their offerings align with your organization's recovery objectives and that contractual agreements reflect these requirements.

DR and BC planning are essential components of a cloud security strategy, ensuring that organizations can quickly respond to and recover from disruptive events. By leveraging cloud-based DR solutions, implementing data redundancy, regularly testing recovery procedures, and collaborating with CSPs, organizations can enhance their resilience and maintain continuous operations, even in the face of unforeseen disasters. Effective DR and BC planning in cloud environments not only minimizes potential downtime and data loss but also supports the overall security and reliability of cloud-based operations.

Strengthening cloud security posture

As we conclude this exploration of challenges and solutions in cloud security, it's clear that securing cloud environments is a multifaceted endeavor, requiring diligent attention to data security, IAM, compliance, and resilience against threats both internal and external. This chapter has provided a roadmap for navigating the complexities of cloud security, offering practical solutions to the most pressing challenges that organizations face as they leverage cloud computing to drive their operations.

The strategies outlined across the various sections–from implementing robust encryption and access controls to navigating the intricacies of compliance and legal requirements, mitigating the risks of insider threats and APTs, avoiding vendor lock-in, and ensuring DR and BC–collectively contribute to strengthening an organization's cloud security posture.

Key takeaways include the following:

- **Proactive approach**: Security in the cloud is not a set-and-forget task but a continuous process of monitoring, assessment, and adjustment. Adopting a proactive approach to security, anticipating potential threats, and preparing for them in advance is crucial.

- **Shared responsibility**: Understanding and effectively managing the shared responsibility model is fundamental. Organizations must clearly delineate the security obligations that lie with the CSP and those that are their own, ensuring comprehensive coverage across all aspects of cloud security.

- **Adaptability and vigilance**: The cloud's dynamic nature demands adaptability and vigilance. As cloud technologies evolve and new threats emerge, organizations must be prepared to adjust their security strategies, adopt new tools and practices, and remain vigilant against potential security breaches.

- **Comprehensive planning**: Effective cloud security is underpinned by thorough planning, encompassing not just technical defenses but also strategic considerations such as compliance, legal requirements, and BC planning.

Moving forward

Strengthening your cloud security posture is an ongoing journey, one that benefits from continuous learning, sharing of best practices, and collaboration both within the organization and with CSPs. As cloud computing continues to evolve, so too will the strategies and technologies for securing it. Organizations that remain committed to enhancing their cloud security capabilities will be better positioned to harness the full potential of cloud computing while minimizing risks to their operations and data.

The path to robust cloud security is both challenging and rewarding. By applying the principles and strategies discussed in this chapter, organizations can build resilient, compliant, and secure cloud environments that support their business goals and protect their most valuable assets. As we move forward, the next chapters will continue to build on these foundations, exploring advanced topics in cloud security and emerging trends that will shape the future of cloud computing.

Summary

This chapter on *Cloud Security and the NIST RMF* delved into the intricacies of securing cloud environments, guided by the principles of the NIST RMF. Through a comprehensive exploration of adapting RMF for cloud environments, ensuring compliance, and addressing common security challenges, readers have gained a robust understanding of how to effectively navigate the complex landscape of cloud security. Key lessons covered include the adaptation of RMF steps to cloud-specific considerations, strategies for maintaining compliance amidst evolving regulations, and solutions to tackle challenges such as data security, IAM, and DR.

The skills and insights acquired in this chapter are invaluable for organizations seeking to leverage cloud computing's benefits while mitigating the associated risks. Understanding the shared responsibility model, implementing robust access controls, managing compliance in multi-cloud environments, and preparing for DR are crucial competencies that enhance an organization's cloud security posture. These practices not only safeguard sensitive data and systems but also ensure operational resilience and compliance with regulatory standards.

In the next chapter, *NIST RMF Case Studies and Future Trends*, we will build upon the foundational knowledge established in this chapter by examining real-world applications of the NIST RMF in various cloud environments. Through detailed case studies, readers will see how organizations have successfully navigated the challenges of cloud security and compliance, providing valuable insights and best practices that can be applied to their own cloud security strategies. Additionally, we will explore emerging trends in cloud computing and security, offering a glimpse into the future of cloud security and how organizations can prepare for the evolving threat landscape. This next chapter represents a natural progression from understanding cloud security principles to applying them in practical, real-world contexts, preparing readers to effectively address the security challenges of today and tomorrow.

NIST RMF Case Studies and Future Trends

As we delve deeper into the realm of cloud security and risk management, the practical application of the NIST **Risk Management Framework** (**RMF**) in real-world scenarios becomes invaluable. In this chapter, we aim to bridge the gap between theoretical principles and practical implementation by exploring how various organizations have navigated the complexities of cloud security using the RMF. Through a series of case studies, this chapter provides insights into the successes, challenges, and lessons learned from applying the RMF in diverse environments.

As the digital landscape continues to evolve at a rapid pace, staying abreast of emerging trends in cloud security is crucial for organizations looking to safeguard their organizations against future threats. This chapter not only highlights successful applications of the RMF but also delves into the future of cloud security, examining cutting-edge technologies, emerging threats, and the evolving regulatory environment. By understanding these trends, organizations can anticipate changes, adapt their security strategies accordingly, and ensure that they remain resilient in the face of new challenges.

In this chapter, we're going to cover the following main topics:

- Real-world case studies of successful RMF implementations

- Emerging trends in cybersecurity and RMF

- Preparing for the future of security operations

Real-world case studies of successful RMF implementations

In this section, we'll dive into several real-world case studies of organizations in various industry verticals that implemented the NIST RMF. We'll examine their background, why they chose to implement the NIST RMF, their successes, challenges, and lessons learned. *The names of the organizations have been modified for privacy.*

Case study 1 – healthcare

The organization, referred to as **HealthTech Innovations (HTI)**, is a leading healthcare provider specializing in advanced patient care and medical research. HTI operates a network of hospitals, clinics, and research facilities across the United States, serving millions of patients annually. With a strong emphasis on using cutting-edge technology to improve patient outcomes, HTI manages a vast amount of sensitive data, including **personal health information (PHI)**, research data, and financial records.

Why HTI chose to implement NIST RMF

HTI recognized the critical importance of safeguarding its information systems and data from increasing cybersecurity threats. The decision to implement the NIST RMF was driven by several factors:

- **Compliance requirements**: As a healthcare provider, HTI is subject to stringent regulatory requirements, including the **Health Insurance Portability and Accountability Act (HIPAA)**. The NIST RMF aligns with federal regulations and provides a structured approach to maintaining compliance.

- **Comprehensive security posture**: HTI sought a framework that offered a holistic approach to security, beyond mere compliance. The NIST RMF's focus on integrating security into the system development life cycle appealed to HTI as it looked to build security into its processes from the ground up.

- **Risk-based approach**: The NIST RMF emphasizes assessing and managing risk based on the impact on the organization. This approach resonated with HTI's strategic objectives, allowing it to prioritize resources effectively.

Successes

As a result of implementing the NIST RMF, HTI saw the following benefits and successes:

- **Enhanced security culture**: Implementing the NIST RMF fostered a culture of security awareness across the organization. Training programs and awareness campaigns increased the understanding of cybersecurity risks among staff at all levels.

- **Improved risk management**: HTI developed a more nuanced understanding of its risk landscape. The RMF's process of categorizing information systems, selecting appropriate security controls, and continuously monitoring for changes helped HTI to dynamically manage risks.

- **Streamlined compliance processes**: The RMF implementation streamlined HTI's compliance efforts. By integrating compliance activities with the RMF steps, HTI reduced redundancies and increased efficiency in meeting regulatory requirements.

Challenges

Implementing a framework isn't without its challenges, especially one as broad as the NIST RMF. Here is a summary of what HTI encountered:

- **Resource intensity**: The comprehensive nature of the NIST RMF required significant resources in terms of time, personnel, and budget. HTI faced challenges in allocating sufficient resources to fully implement the framework across its extensive network.

- **The complexity of integration**: Integrating the RMF into existing processes and systems was complex. HTI encountered difficulties in aligning the RMF steps with its legacy systems and workflows.

- **Change management**: The implementation of the RMF necessitated substantial changes in organizational processes and culture. Managing these changes, particularly in terms of staff buy-in and adapting to new security practices, was challenging.

Lessons learned

Every organization should document lessons learned, and thankfully, HTI did. The leadership at HTI had several lessons learned to pass along, summarized as follows:

- **Importance of executive support**: Strong backing from HTI's leadership was crucial in allocating resources and driving the cultural shift toward enhanced cybersecurity awareness.

- **Need for flexibility**: HTI learned the importance of being flexible in its implementation approach, allowing for adjustments as needed to fit the unique aspects of its operations and risk profile.

- **Value of continuous improvement**: The RMF is not a one-time effort but a continuous process of improvement. HTI recognized the need for ongoing evaluation and adaptation of security controls to address evolving threats and changes in the healthcare landscape.

HTI's implementation of the NIST RMF marked a significant step forward in its cybersecurity posture. Despite the challenges encountered, the successes that were achieved laid a solid foundation for continuous improvement in safeguarding the organization's critical information assets. HTI's experience underscores the value of adopting a structured, risk-based approach to cybersecurity, particularly in industries dealing with sensitive information such as healthcare.

Case study 2 – industrial control systems/operational technology

The organization, referred to here as **Industrial Solutions Corp** (**ISC**), is a leader in the **industrial control systems** (**ICS**) and **operational technology** (**OT**) sector. ISC specializes in designing, manufacturing, and implementing ICS and OT solutions for critical infrastructure sectors, including energy, water treatment, and transportation. With operations spanning globally, ISC's technologies and services are pivotal in ensuring the efficient, safe, and reliable operation of essential public and private sector utilities.

Why ISC chose to implement NIST RMF

ISC's decision to implement the NIST RMF was motivated by several key factors:

- **Growing cybersecurity threats**: The increasing prevalence of cyberattacks targeting critical infrastructure highlighted the need for enhanced security measures. ISC recognized the necessity of adopting a robust framework to protect its ICS and OT environments from potential threats.

- **Regulatory compliance**: ISC operates in a highly regulated environment, with stringent requirements for cybersecurity and risk management. Implementing the NIST RMF provided a structured and recognized approach to achieving compliance with industry standards and government regulations.

- **Risk management needs**: Given the critical nature of the services ISC provides, the organization sought a framework that emphasized a risk-based approach to security. The NIST RMF offered a comprehensive methodology for identifying, assessing, and mitigating risks across ISC's diverse and complex systems.

Successes

ISC had some successes that mirrored HTI, and some more to share:

- **Strengthened security posture**: The adoption of the NIST RMF significantly enhanced ISC's overall security posture. By following the RMF steps, ISC was able to systematically identify and address vulnerabilities, implement effective security controls, and reduce the likelihood of successful cyberattacks.

- **Improved operational resilience**: Implementing the RMF helped ISC to develop and refine business continuity and disaster recovery plans. This ensured that ISC could maintain or quickly restore critical operations in the event of a security incident.

- **Enhanced stakeholder confidence**: By adopting a recognized and respected framework, ISC was able to demonstrate its commitment to cybersecurity, thereby bolstering trust among clients, partners, and regulatory bodies.

Challenges

Challenges with OT and ICS environments will naturally be different than traditional IT environments as the focus of protecting the organization is about maintaining the availability of those systems as opposed to purely about confidentiality and integrity:

- **Integration with existing OT environments**: One of the primary challenges ISC faced was integrating the NIST RMF into existing OT environments, which often included legacy systems with limited modification capabilities. This required innovative approaches to implement security controls without disrupting operational integrity.

- **Balancing security and usability**: Ensuring that security measures did not impede the usability or performance of ICS and OT systems was a significant challenge. ISC had to carefully select and tailor security controls to maintain system efficiency and reliability.

- **Resource constraints**: The comprehensive nature of the NIST RMF meant that substantial resources were required for implementation. ISC encountered difficulties in allocating sufficient financial, technical, and human resources to fully embrace the framework's requirements.

Lessons learned

Just like HTI, ISC had some lessons learned to share, summarized here:

- **Importance of tailored security controls**: ISC learned the importance of customizing security controls to fit the specific needs and constraints of ICS and OT environments, rather than applying generic solutions.

- **Value of cross-functional collaboration**: Successful implementation of the RMF required close collaboration between cybersecurity teams, operational staff, and executive management. ISC found that fostering a culture of security awareness and collaboration across all levels of the organization was critical.

- **Continuous monitoring and improvement**: ISC recognized that cybersecurity is an ongoing process. Continuous monitoring, regular assessments, and the willingness to adapt security controls in response to new threats and technological changes were essential for maintaining resilience.

ISC's implementation of the NIST RMF marked a significant advancement in its approach to cybersecurity within the industrial control systems and operational technology sectors. Despite facing challenges related to integrating the framework into complex and varied environments, the organization achieved considerable success in enhancing its security posture, operational resilience, and stakeholder confidence. ISC's experience underscores the importance of a structured, risk-based approach to cybersecurity, particularly in sectors where the stakes for security are exceptionally high.

Case study 3 – financial sector

The organization, referred to as **Global Finance Group** (**GFG**), is a multinational corporation that provides a wide range of financial services, including banking, investment, and insurance, to millions of customers worldwide. With a vast network of branches and a significant online presence, GFG handles an enormous volume of sensitive financial data and personal information daily.

Why GFG chose to implement NIST RMF

GFG's decision to implement the NIST RMF was driven by several critical factors:

- **Evolving cybersecurity threats**: In the face of increasingly sophisticated cyber threats targeting the financial sector, GFG recognized the need for a more structured and comprehensive approach to managing cybersecurity risks.

- **Regulatory compliance**: As a key player in the global financial market, GFG is subject to a myriad of regulatory requirements designed to ensure the security and integrity of financial data. The NIST RMF aligns with many of these regulatory frameworks, offering a pathway to compliance.

- **Risk-based security strategy**: GFG sought a framework that would enable it to prioritize security efforts based on the risk to its operations and customer data. The NIST RMF's emphasis on risk assessment and management offered a strategic approach to aligning security investments with business objectives.

Successes

GFG had similar successes to other organizations, with some of the key points summarized here:

- **Improved risk management capabilities**: By adopting the NIST RMF, GFG enhanced its ability to identify, assess, and manage cybersecurity risks across its global operations. This led to a more proactive security posture and a reduction in the incidence and impact of security breaches.

- **Increased regulatory compliance**: The structured approach of the NIST RMF facilitated GFG's compliance with international and domestic financial regulations. This not only reduced legal and financial risks but also strengthened stakeholder confidence in GFG's commitment to security.

- **Enhanced security culture**: The implementation of the NIST RMF fostered a culture of security awareness within GFG. Employees at all levels became more engaged in security practices, contributing to a stronger defense against cyber threats.

Challenges

As GFG is a global organization and one that is highly regulated, they faced some special challenges, as discussed here:

- **Complexity and scale of implementation**: GFG faced significant challenges in applying the NIST RMF across its diverse and complex global operations, simply due to the sheer scale they were operating. Customizing the framework to accommodate different regulatory environments and business processes required substantial effort and expertise.

- **Integration with existing systems**: Integrating the NIST RMF with GFG's existing security infrastructure and legacy systems was a complex undertaking. This often required re-engineering processes and systems to align with the framework's requirements.

- **Resource allocation**: The comprehensive nature of the NIST RMF demanded significant resources, including time, budget, and skilled personnel. Balancing these resource demands with ongoing business operations was a constant challenge.

Lessons learned

Just like our previous discussions, there'd be no point in mentioning GFG without discussing the lessons learned here:

- **Executive support is crucial**: GFG learned that strong support from senior management was essential for the successful implementation of the NIST RMF. Executive backing helped secure the necessary resources and drive the cultural shift towards improved cybersecurity.

- **Tailored implementation strategy**: GFG found that a one-size-fits-all approach to implementing the NIST RMF was ineffective. Tailoring the implementation to the specific needs and risk profiles of different parts of the organization was key to overcoming challenges.

- **Continuous improvement process**: Implementing the NIST RMF is not a one-time project but an ongoing process. GFG recognized the importance of continuous monitoring, assessment, and adjustment of security controls to adapt to evolving threats and business changes.

GFG's implementation of the NIST RMF represented a pivotal step forward in its cybersecurity strategy. Despite facing challenges related to the framework's integration and the allocation of resources, the successes achieved in improving risk management capabilities, ensuring regulatory compliance, and fostering a culture of security awareness have had a lasting impact. GFG's experience underscores the value of adopting a structured, risk-based approach to cybersecurity in the financial sector, where the stakes for protecting sensitive financial data are exceptionally high.

Case study 4 – educational institution

The institution, referred to as **Tech University** (**TU**), is a prominent higher education institution known for its rigorous academic programs and cutting-edge research in technology and science. With a vast campus that hosts thousands of students, faculty, and staff, TU relies heavily on its information technology infrastructure to support its educational and administrative functions. This infrastructure includes a wide array of systems and networks that manage everything from academic records and research data to personal information of the university community.

Why TU chose to implement NIST RMF

TU's decision to implement the NIST RMF was influenced by several key considerations:

- **Increasing cybersecurity threats**: With the rise of cyber threats targeting educational institutions, TU recognized the need to enhance its cybersecurity measures to protect sensitive data and research information.

- **Compliance requirements**: TU is subject to various federal and state regulations governing the protection of student data, research information, and **personal identifiable information (PII)**. The NIST RMF provides a structured approach to achieving and maintaining compliance with these regulations.

- **Risk management focus**: TU sought a framework that would enable it to identify, assess, and manage cybersecurity risks in a structured and proactive manner. The NIST RMF's emphasis on a risk-based approach aligned with TU's strategic objectives to safeguard its information assets.

Successes

Some successes that TU had in their implementation of NIST RMF are as follows:

- **Strengthened security posture**: Implementing the NIST RMF allowed TU to significantly enhance its cybersecurity posture. The framework's systematic process of identifying, assessing, and addressing risks led to the implementation of robust security controls and measures.

- **Improved compliance**: The NIST RMF facilitated TU's compliance with regulatory requirements related to data protection and privacy. This not only reduced the risk of legal and financial penalties but also bolstered the institution's reputation for safeguarding student and faculty data.

- **Enhanced awareness and culture**: The implementation process raised awareness about cybersecurity risks and best practices among students, faculty, and staff. This cultural shift has been instrumental in promoting a more secure and responsible use of IT resources across the campus.

Challenges

Here are the challenges that TU faced when implementing the NIST RMF, in the context of their unique industry:

- **Resource constraints**: As with many educational institutions, TU faced challenges in allocating sufficient financial and human resources to the RMF implementation. Balancing budget constraints with the need for comprehensive cybersecurity measures was a constant struggle.

- **The complexity of the educational environment**: The diverse and open nature of TU's IT environment, characterized by a wide variety of devices and user needs, added complexity to the implementation of the NIST RMF. Tailoring security controls to accommodate academic freedom while ensuring security posed significant challenges.

- **Engagement across the institution**: Ensuring widespread engagement and buy-in from all parts of the university, including academic departments, administrative units, and research centers, was challenging. Overcoming skepticism and resistance to changes in IT practices required sustained communication and education efforts.

Lessons learned

As a university with different campuses, leadership among various academic departments, and support staff, TU had lessons learned that were different than the other industries. Let's explore those:

- **Importance of leadership support**: TU learned that strong support from university leadership was crucial for the successful adoption of the NIST RMF. High-level endorsement helped in securing resources and fostering a campus-wide commitment to cybersecurity.

- **Customization is key**: TU found that customizing the implementation of the NIST RMF to fit the unique needs and culture of the educational environment was essential. This involved adapting security controls and risk management practices to be both effective and minimally intrusive to academic activities.

- **Continuous improvement and adaptation**: The dynamic nature of cybersecurity threats and the evolving IT landscape at TU highlighted the need for ongoing monitoring, assessment, and adaptation of security practices. TU recognized that implementing the NIST RMF is not a one-time effort but a continuous process of improvement.

TU's journey in implementing the NIST RMF has significantly strengthened its ability to protect against cybersecurity threats while supporting its educational and research missions. Despite facing resource constraints and the complexities inherent in an educational setting, TU achieved notable successes in enhancing its cybersecurity posture, ensuring compliance, and fostering a culture of security awareness. TU's experience demonstrates the value of adopting a structured, risk-based approach to cybersecurity in the higher education sector, offering insights and lessons that can benefit other institutions facing similar challenges.

Emerging trends in cybersecurity and RMF

The landscape of cybersecurity is constantly evolving, shaped by technological advancements, emerging threats, and the shifting dynamics of the digital world. One of the most significant trends in recent years is the rise of generative **artificial intelligence** (**AI**) technologies. These AI systems, capable of producing content, solving complex problems, and automating decision-making processes, represent a frontier in innovation. However, they also introduce new vulnerabilities and challenges for cybersecurity frameworks, including the NIST RMF.

Generative AI, with its ability to generate realistic text, images, and data, allows for new avenues for cyberattacks, including sophisticated phishing campaigns, deepfake technologies, and the automation of malicious activities. The traditional cybersecurity measures, while still relevant, require adaptation to address the unique threats posed by AI technologies. Recognizing this, NIST is at the forefront of developing a new AI RMF, an extension of its traditional RMF, to specifically tackle the challenges presented by AI systems.

The AI RMF – a response to emerging threats

The AI RMF aims to provide a structured and comprehensive approach to managing risks associated with the development, deployment, and use of AI technologies. This initiative reflects a recognition of the dual-edged nature of AI: as much as it can enhance efficiency and innovation, it also can be exploited for malicious purposes or inadvertently introduce new vulnerabilities into systems.

Here are some of the key components of the AI RMF:

- **Ethical considerations**: The AI RMF emphasizes the importance of ethical considerations in AI development and deployment. This includes ensuring AI systems are transparent, equitable, and respectful of privacy and civil liberties.

- **Security by design**: Incorporating security considerations at the earliest stages of AI system development is a cornerstone of the AI RMF. This proactive approach ensures that AI systems are designed with robust security measures to mitigate potential risks from the outset.

- **Continuous monitoring**: Given the dynamic nature of AI technologies, the AI RMF advocates for continuous monitoring of AI systems. This involves regular assessments to identify and address emerging vulnerabilities and ensure that AI systems remain aligned with ethical guidelines and compliance requirements.

- **Collaboration and sharing**: The framework encourages collaboration among stakeholders in the AI ecosystem, including developers, users, and regulators. Sharing best practices, threat intelligence, and mitigation strategies is crucial for addressing the global challenges posed by AI technologies.

Implementing the AI RMF requires organizations to navigate a complex landscape of technical, ethical, and regulatory challenges. Here are some key considerations:

- **Technical expertise**: Organizations must cultivate or access technical expertise in AI and cybersecurity to effectively implement the AI RMF. This includes understanding the specific vulnerabilities associated with AI technologies and the measures required to mitigate these risks.

- **Regulatory compliance**: As regulatory bodies around the world begin to introduce laws and guidelines governing AI, organizations must ensure that their AI systems comply with an increasingly complex regulatory landscape. The AI RMF provides a framework for aligning AI deployments with regulatory requirements.

- **Ethical and social implications**: Beyond technical and regulatory considerations, organizations must also address the ethical and social implications of AI. This involves engaging with diverse stakeholders to understand the broader impacts of AI technologies on society and ensuring that AI systems are deployed responsibly.

The emergence of generative AI technologies represents a paradigm shift in the cybersecurity landscape. In response, NIST's development of an AI RMF underscores the need for a comprehensive and adaptive approach to risk management in the era of AI. As organizations navigate this evolving landscape, the principles and practices outlined in the AI RMF will be critical for managing the risks and harnessing the opportunities presented by AI technologies. This ongoing evolution of the RMF reflects a broader trend in cybersecurity: the need for continuous adaptation and innovation in the face of emerging threats and technological advancements.

Preparing for the future of security operations

As we navigate the complex and ever-evolving landscape of cybersecurity, preparing for the future of security operations has become a paramount concern for organizations worldwide. The advent of advanced technologies, such as generative AI, alongside the continuous evolution of cyber threats, necessitates a forward-looking approach to cybersecurity. This section outlines key strategies and considerations for organizations aiming to future-proof their security operations in alignment with the principles of the NIST RMF and its forthcoming AI extensions.

The pace of technological innovation presents both challenges and opportunities for security operations. To stay ahead of potential threats, organizations must embrace these advancements, integrating cutting-edge tools and techniques into their cybersecurity arsenals. This includes leveraging AI and machine learning for threat detection and response, adopting blockchain for secure transactions, and exploring quantum cryptography to safeguard against future threats. However, as new technologies are adopted, it is crucial to conduct thorough risk assessments in line with the NIST RMF, ensuring that security considerations are embedded from the outset.

The human element remains one of the most significant vulnerabilities in cybersecurity. Fostering a culture of security awareness and vigilance is essential for mitigating this risk. Organizations should invest in continuous education and training programs to keep staff informed about the latest cybersecurity threats and best practices. Engaging employees in regular security drills and simulations can also enhance preparedness for real-world incidents. By embedding security awareness into the organizational culture, employees become active participants in the defense against cyber threats.

No organization is an island in the vast sea of cybersecurity. Strengthening collaboration and information sharing among industry peers, government agencies, and international bodies is vital for a collective defense against cyber threats. Participating in **information sharing and analysis centers** (**ISACs**) and other collaborative initiatives can provide access to timely threat intelligence, best practices, and coordinated response efforts. The NIST RMF and AI RMF emphasize the importance of collaboration in managing cybersecurity risks, advocating for a shared approach to securing the digital ecosystem.

As cybersecurity threats evolve, so too do the policies and regulations designed to mitigate them. Organizations must remain agile, adapting their security operations to comply with the latest legal and regulatory requirements. This involves not only monitoring and implementing current regulations but also anticipating future legislative trends. Engaging with policymakers, contributing to public consultations, and participating in industry associations can provide insights into upcoming regulatory changes, ensuring that organizations are well-prepared to meet new compliance challenges.

In the dynamic field of cybersecurity, complacency can lead to vulnerability. Implementing mechanisms for continuous improvement is essential for staying ahead of threats. This includes regular reviews and updates of security policies, practices, and controls in line with the NIST RMF's iterative process. Leveraging analytics and feedback mechanisms can provide insights into the effectiveness of security operations, identifying areas for enhancement. Emphasizing adaptability and resilience, organizations can ensure that their security operations are robust and responsive to the changing threat landscape.

Summary

Preparing for the future of security operations requires a multifaceted approach that involves integrating technological innovation, fostering a culture of security awareness, strengthening collaboration, advancing compliance, and implementing continuous improvement mechanisms. By adhering to the principles of the NIST RMF and embracing its forthcoming AI extensions, organizations can navigate the complexities of the cybersecurity landscape with confidence. The future of security operations lies in a proactive, informed, and collaborative approach, ready to meet the challenges of tomorrow with the knowledge and tools of today. Let's turn the page to our final chapter and wrap up this story.

11

A Look Ahead

As we draw this book to a close, it's important to reflect on the journey we've embarked upon together. Implementing the NIST **Risk Management Framework** (**RMF**) is not merely about adopting a set of guidelines; it's about embracing a comprehensive approach to cybersecurity that will serve your organization now and in the future. Let's revisit the key insights we've gained, underscore the importance of cybersecurity, and look ahead to how we can continually evolve in our cybersecurity endeavors.

In this chapter, we're going to cover the following main topics:

- Key takeaways
- The ongoing importance of cybersecurity
- Encouragement for ongoing learning and improvement
- The NIST RMF as a lifelong tool
- The role of security leaders in cybersecurity excellence

Key takeaways

As we conclude our exploration of the NIST RMF, it's essential to discuss the key insights and lessons that have emerged from our discussions. The RMF represents a critical methodology for organizations seeking to navigate the complex and ever-evolving landscape of cybersecurity threats and compliance requirements. Here are the core takeaways from our journey through the implementation of the NIST RMF.

One of the RMF's most significant contributions to cybersecurity practices is its structured, systematic approach to managing risk. By dividing the risk management process into distinct steps – *Categorize, Select, Implement, Assess, Authorize,* and *Monitor* – the RMF provides organizations with a clear roadmap for securing their information systems and environments.

The RMF is designed to be flexible and scalable, accommodating the unique needs and risk profiles of different organizations. Whether you're a small nonprofit, a large multinational corporation, or a government agency, the RMF can be tailored to suit your specific operational context and security requirements. This adaptability is crucial in a world where technological landscapes and cyber threats are constantly changing.

The dynamic nature of cybersecurity risks is well recognized by the RMF, which places a strong emphasis on continuous monitoring. This proactive stance ensures that organizations can quickly identify and respond to new vulnerabilities, threats, and changes in their operational environments, maintaining a robust security posture over time.

Implementing the RMF does not occur in isolation. The framework is designed to integrate seamlessly with other compliance requirements and cybersecurity standards, such as ISO/IEC 27001, HIPAA, and GDPR. This integration capability simplifies the compliance process for organizations, enabling them to meet multiple regulatory requirements through a unified approach to risk management.

Central to the RMF is the principle of risk-based decision-making. By prioritizing risks based on their potential impact on the organization's operations and objectives, the RMF enables efficient allocation of resources to areas where they are most needed. This strategic approach to resource allocation is vital for organizations operating in resource-constrained environments.

Effective implementation of the RMF requires active engagement and communication with stakeholders across the organization. From senior executives to IT staff and end users, fostering a culture of cybersecurity awareness and collaboration is key to the successful adoption of the RMF. Stakeholder engagement ensures that cybersecurity is recognized as a shared responsibility, contributing to a more resilient organizational posture.

Lastly, the RMF underscores the importance of ongoing education and training in cybersecurity. Keeping abreast of the latest threats, technologies, and best practices is essential for cybersecurity professionals and the organization. The RMF encourages a culture of learning and improvement, recognizing that the human element plays a critical role in the effectiveness of cybersecurity measures.

These key takeaways underscore the comprehensive nature of the NIST RMF as a tool for managing cybersecurity risks. By adopting and adapting the RMF to their specific needs, organizations can enhance their security posture, ensure compliance with regulatory requirements, and build a resilient defense against cyber threats. As we look to the future, the principles and practices embodied in the RMF will continue to serve as a foundation for cybersecurity excellence, evolving alongside the technological and threat landscapes they aim to navigate.

The ongoing importance of cybersecurity

In the digital era, cybersecurity transcends the confines of IT departments, becoming a cornerstone of operational integrity, strategic planning, and organizational resilience. The persistent evolution of cyber threats, coupled with the increasing reliance on digital technologies, underscores the ongoing, critical importance of cybersecurity for organizations across all sectors. This section delves into the multifaceted reasons why cybersecurity remains imperative in safeguarding the future of organizations.

As organizations continue to undergo digital transformation, integrating technology into every facet of operations, the attack surface for potential cyber threats expands. From cloud computing and mobile connectivity to **Internet of Things (IoT)** devices and beyond, new technologies offer unprecedented opportunities for efficiency and innovation but also introduce new vulnerabilities. Cybersecurity measures must evolve in tandem with these technologies to protect organizational assets and data from exploitation.

Cyber threats have become increasingly sophisticated, with attackers employing advanced techniques such as AI and machine learning to bypass traditional security defenses. The rise of state-sponsored attacks and organized cybercrime syndicates further escalates the level of threat, making it imperative for organizations to adopt equally sophisticated cybersecurity measures. The ongoing importance of cybersecurity lies in its ability to evolve and respond to these advanced threats, ensuring the protection of critical infrastructure and sensitive data.

The regulatory landscape surrounding data protection and privacy continues to evolve, with laws such as the **General Data Protection Regulation (GDPR)** in Europe and the **California Consumer Privacy Act (CCPA)** in the United States setting stringent requirements for data handling and security. Organizations must navigate these regulations to avoid significant fines and reputational damage. Cybersecurity is integral to achieving compliance, demonstrating an organization's commitment to safeguarding stakeholder data against breaches and unauthorized access.

Cyber incidents can have profound economic and social impacts, from the direct costs associated with responding to breaches and recovering lost data to the indirect costs of operational downtime, loss of customer trust, and damage to brand reputation. The ongoing importance of cybersecurity is highlighted by its role in mitigating these impacts, protecting not only the financial health of organizations but also their relationships with customers and their standing in society.

In an environment where consumer and partner trust are paramount, robust cybersecurity measures can serve as a significant competitive advantage. Organizations that demonstrate a commitment to cybersecurity can differentiate themselves in the marketplace, attracting customers and partners who prioritize the security of their data. This strategic aspect of cybersecurity underscores its importance not just as a protective measure but also as a driver of business growth and sustainability.

Finally, the ongoing importance of cybersecurity is rooted in the human element. As cyber threats evolve, so too do the skills and knowledge required to combat them. Investing in cybersecurity is also an investment in people – training employees to recognize and respond to threats, cultivating a culture of security awareness, and building teams equipped to navigate the complex cybersecurity landscape.

The preceding imperatives highlight the multifaceted role of cybersecurity in ensuring the ongoing viability, competitiveness, and integrity of organizations. As we look to the future, the importance of cybersecurity will only continue to grow, driven by the accelerating pace of technological innovation, the evolving sophistication of cyber threats, and the increasing value of digital assets. *Cybersecurity is not a static goal but a dynamic process*, requiring continuous vigilance, adaptation, and commitment to protect the digital and physical worlds alike.

Encouragement for ongoing learning and improvement

The domain of cybersecurity is characterized by its rapid pace of change and evolution. New vulnerabilities, threat vectors, and defensive technologies emerge regularly, making continuous learning and improvement not just beneficial but essential for professionals in the field. This commitment to advancement is crucial for maintaining the efficacy of the NIST RMF and ensuring that cybersecurity measures remain robust and responsive to emerging challenges. In this section, we'll explore the importance of ongoing education and the pursuit of excellence in cybersecurity, providing encouragement and guidance for those dedicated to safeguarding their organizations in an ever-changing digital landscape.

Cybersecurity is a discipline where the learning journey never truly ends. The constant emergence of new technologies, attack methodologies, and security solutions demands that professionals continually update their knowledge and skills. Lifelong learning can take many forms, from formal education and certification programs to self-directed study and experiential learning. Embracing this journey not only enhances your capabilities but also contributes to the resilience and security of the organizations you serve.

The cybersecurity landscape is defined by innovation, both on the part of threat actors and those developing defenses against them. Staying abreast of the latest trends, tools, and techniques is crucial for anticipating and mitigating risks. This requires an openness to change and a willingness to experiment with new approaches and technologies. By fostering a culture of innovation within your organization, you can ensure that your cybersecurity practices remain at the cutting edge.

Cybersecurity is a collective endeavor, with individuals and organizations sharing the common goal of enhancing digital security. Engaging with the broader cybersecurity community can provide valuable insights, support, and collaboration opportunities. This can include participating in forums, attending conferences, and contributing to open source projects. Through community engagement, you can learn from the experiences of others, share your knowledge, and strengthen the collective defense against cyber threats.

Implementing the NIST RMF is an iterative process that involves continuously assessing, authorizing, and monitoring information systems. Establishing feedback loops within this process can facilitate ongoing improvement, allowing you to refine and adapt security controls in response to new information and evolving risks. Encourage open feedback within your organization and view each cybersecurity challenge as an opportunity for learning and growth.

The pursuit of ongoing learning in cybersecurity is not only a professional obligation but also an opportunity for personal and career development. Advancing your education and earning specialized certifications can open new career paths, increase your value to your organization, and affirm your commitment to excellence in the field. Consider setting specific professional development goals and seeking out resources and opportunities to achieve them.

Leaders within organizations play a critical role in encouraging ongoing learning and improvement in cybersecurity. By providing resources, creating opportunities for professional development, and modeling a commitment to continuous learning, leaders can cultivate an environment where cybersecurity excellence is the norm. This includes recognizing and rewarding initiative, curiosity, and innovation among team members.

In conclusion, the cybersecurity landscape's inherent dynamism and complexity call for an unwavering commitment to ongoing learning and improvement. By embracing this ethos, cybersecurity professionals can ensure they are equipped to meet the challenges of today and tomorrow, safeguarding their organizations against the ever-evolving threats of the digital age. Encouragement for continuous growth, coupled with the implementation of the NIST RMF, lays the foundation for achieving cybersecurity excellence and resilience.

The NIST RMF as a lifelong tool

The NIST RMF is not merely a set of guidelines to be implemented once and then forgotten. Instead, it should be viewed as a lifelong tool that evolves alongside the cybersecurity landscape, offering a structured approach to managing and mitigating risks over time. This perspective on the RMF emphasizes its lasting relevance and utility, providing a foundation upon which organizations can build a resilient and adaptive cybersecurity posture. Here, we'll explore how the RMF serves as a continuous resource for professionals committed to excellence in cybersecurity.

One of the RMF's core strengths is its adaptability to new technologies and emerging threats. As cybersecurity challenges evolve, so too can the application of the RMF. Its flexible framework is designed to accommodate changes in the operational environment, allowing organizations to reassess and adjust their security controls in response to the latest developments in the cyber landscape. This adaptability makes the RMF a vital tool for navigating the complexities of modern cybersecurity.

The RMF provides a comprehensive approach to risk management that extends beyond the technical aspects of cybersecurity. It encourages organizations to consider cybersecurity risks in the context of their broader operational and strategic objectives. By integrating risk management with business processes, the RMF enables organizations to make informed decisions about where to allocate resources, how to prioritize security initiatives, and when to accept, mitigate, or transfer risks. This strategic approach ensures that cybersecurity efforts are aligned with the organization's overall goals and objectives.

At its heart, the RMF embodies a philosophy of continuous improvement. Through its iterative process of categorization, selection, implementation, assessment, authorization, and monitoring, the RMF encourages organizations to regularly review and refine their security practices. This cyclical process ensures that cybersecurity measures remain effective and responsive to changing conditions, facilitating ongoing enhancement of the organization's security posture.

The implementation of the RMF contributes to the development of organizational resilience, preparing entities to withstand and recover from cybersecurity incidents. By emphasizing the importance of recovery planning and resilience strategies, the RMF helps organizations develop robust systems and processes that can adapt to and recover from disruptions. This focus on resilience is crucial for maintaining continuity of operations in the face of cyber threats.

Beyond its technical and strategic applications, the RMF plays a pivotal role in cultivating a culture of security within organizations. By involving stakeholders from across the organization in the risk management process, the RMF promotes awareness and shared responsibility for cybersecurity. This collaborative approach strengthens the organization's collective defense against cyber threats and reinforces the importance of cybersecurity as a shared organizational value.

In conclusion, the NIST RMF is a dynamic and enduring tool that offers more than just a methodology for securing information systems. It provides a comprehensive framework for managing cybersecurity risks, enhancing organizational resilience, and fostering a culture of continuous improvement and learning. Viewing the RMF as a lifelong resource empowers organizations and professionals to navigate the ever-changing cybersecurity landscape with confidence, ensuring that their security practices remain robust, responsive, and aligned with their strategic objectives.

The role of security leaders in cybersecurity excellence

The journey toward cybersecurity excellence is a continuous endeavor that requires leadership, vision, and unwavering commitment. Security leaders play a pivotal role in shaping the cybersecurity posture and culture of their organizations. Their responsibilities extend beyond managing technical defenses; they must also inspire, guide, and cultivate an environment where security is valued, understood, and practiced by everyone. In this final section, we'll explore the critical role of security leaders in driving cybersecurity excellence, leveraging the principles of the NIST RMF as a foundational element of their strategy.

Security leaders are the standard-bearers for cybersecurity within their organizations. They have the unique opportunity and responsibility to champion a culture of security that permeates every level of the organization. This involves communicating the importance of cybersecurity to all employees, fostering an environment where security awareness and hygiene are second nature, and ensuring that cybersecurity is considered in every business decision. By embodying and promoting a proactive security mindset, leaders can cultivate a culture where every team member is an active participant in safeguarding the organization's digital assets.

Effective security leaders understand the critical importance of aligning cybersecurity goals with the broader objectives of the organization. They work closely with executive leadership to ensure that cybersecurity strategies support business goals and do not impede operational efficiency or innovation. This strategic alignment requires a deep understanding of the organization's mission, industry dynamics, and the specific threats it faces. Security leaders must articulate how the NIST RMF and other cybersecurity initiatives contribute to the overall success and resilience of the organization, securing the necessary support and resources for their implementation.

Implementing the NIST RMF and maintaining a robust cybersecurity posture requires significant resources, including funding, technology, and skilled personnel. Security leaders must be adept advocates, making the case to executive management and boards for the resources needed to protect the organization effectively. This involves demonstrating the value of cybersecurity investments, articulating the potential costs and risks of inadequate security measures, and presenting a clear, strategic vision for the organization's cybersecurity future.

Cybersecurity is not the sole purview of the IT department; it requires collaboration across all parts of the organization. Security leaders must foster open lines of communication and collaboration between IT, operations, human resources, legal, and other departments. This collaborative approach ensures that cybersecurity considerations are integrated into all aspects of the organization's operations and that security policies and practices are understood and adhered to across the board.

The cybersecurity landscape is constantly evolving, with new threats and technologies emerging at a rapid pace. Security leaders must be forward-thinking, open to innovation, and committed to continuous improvement. They should encourage their teams to stay abreast of the latest cybersecurity trends, technologies, and best practices, fostering an environment where learning, experimentation, and adaptation are valued. This commitment to innovation and improvement is essential for staying ahead of cyber threats and ensuring the long-term security and resilience of the organization.

Finally, security leaders have a responsibility to mentor and develop the next generation of cybersecurity professionals. This involves providing opportunities for professional growth, offering guidance and support, and nurturing the skills and talents of their teams. By investing in the development of their people, security leaders not only enhance the capabilities of their organizations but also contribute to the strength and resilience of the broader cybersecurity community.

The role of security leaders in achieving cybersecurity excellence cannot be overstated. Through their vision, leadership, and dedication, they guide their organizations through the complexities of the digital age. By championing a culture of security, aligning cybersecurity goals with business objectives, advocating for resources, fostering collaboration, embracing innovation, and developing talent, security leaders lay the foundation for a secure, resilient, and successful future.

Summary

I'd like to conclude this book by acknowledging you, the reader. I know you because I'm one of you. I'm writing this summary after a long day of work, slogging through the cybersecurity industry. This, in addition to the continuous learning I do after hours just to keep up, as well as burnout, can become a real issue in this sector. The reason I wrote this book over the past 7 months was to enable each of you to hopefully have an easier go at understanding the RMF than I did. It's about enablement; a rising tide raises all ships.

I have faith the industry will turn. As it becomes harder to find people willing to put up with long hours, as culture shifts, such as the pivot to remote working, and other benefits become more important to the rising generations, I believe leaders in our industry will embrace quality of work over quantity; they'll embrace working smarter, not harder. Systems will be built with minimizing technical debt in mind, and more of us will be able to contribute to the security of the whole.

I'd love to hear your feedback. Please feel free to reach out; my contact information is as follows:

- **Email**: tom@thomasmarsland.com
- **Website**: https://thomasmarsland.com
- **Twitter**: @tmarsland
- **Bluesky**: @tmarsland.bsky.social

And – to my family once more – thank you.

Index

W

www.packtpub.com

Subscribe to our online digital library for full access to over 7,000 books and videos, as well as industry leading tools to help you plan your personal development and advance your career. For more information, please visit our website.

Why subscribe?

- Spend less time learning and more time coding with practical eBooks and Videos from over 4,000 industry professionals

- Improve your learning with Skill Plans built especially for you

- Get a free eBook or video every month

- Fully searchable for easy access to vital information

- Copy and paste, print, and bookmark content

Did you know that Packt offers eBook versions of every book published, with PDF and ePub files available? You can upgrade to the eBook version at packtpub.com and as a print book customer, you are entitled to a discount on the eBook copy. Get in touch with us at customercare@packtpub.com for more details.

At www.packtpub.com, you can also read a collection of free technical articles, sign up for a range of free newsletters, and receive exclusive discounts and offers on Packt books and eBooks.

Other Books You May Enjoy

If you enjoyed this book, you may be interested in these other books by Packt:

TLS Cryptography In-Depth

Dr. Paul Duplys, Dr. Roland Schmitz

ISBN: 978-1-80461-195-1

- Understand TLS principles and protocols for secure internet communication
- Find out how cryptographic primitives are used within TLS V1.3
- Discover best practices for secure configuration and implementation of TLS
- Evaluate and select appropriate cipher suites for optimal security
- Get an in-depth understanding of common cryptographic vulnerabilities and ways to
- mitigate them
- Explore forward secrecy and its importance in maintaining confidentiality
- Understand TLS extensions and their significance in enhancing TLS functionality

Practical Threat Detection Engineering

Megan Roddie, Jason Deyalsingh, Gary J. Katz

ISBN: 978-1-80107-671-5

- Understand the detection engineering process
- Build a detection engineering test lab
- Learn how to maintain detections as code
- Understand how threat intelligence can be used to drive detection development
- Prove the effectiveness of detection capabilities to business leadership
- Learn how to limit attackers' ability to inflict damage by detecting any malicious activity early

Packt is searching for authors like you

If you're interested in becoming an author for Packt, please visit `authors.packtpub.com` and apply today. We have worked with thousands of developers and tech professionals, just like you, to help them share their insight with the global tech community. You can make a general application, apply for a specific hot topic that we are recruiting an author for, or submit your own idea.

Share Your Thoughts

Now you've finished *Unveiling the NIST Risk Management Framework (RMF)*, we'd love to hear your thoughts! Scan the QR code below to go straight to the Amazon review page for this book and share your feedback or leave a review on the site that you purchased it from.

`https://packt.link/r/1835089844`

Your review is important to us and the tech community and will help us make sure we're delivering excellent quality content.

Download a free PDF copy of this book

Thanks for purchasing this book!

Do you like to read on the go but are unable to carry your print books everywhere?

Is your eBook purchase not compatible with the device of your choice?

Don't worry, now with every Packt book you get a DRM-free PDF version of that book at no cost.

Read anywhere, any place, on any device. Search, copy, and paste code from your favorite technical books directly into your application.

The perks don't stop there, you can get exclusive access to discounts, newsletters, and great free content in your inbox daily

Follow these simple steps to get the benefits:

1. Scan the QR code or visit the link below

https://packt.link/free-ebook/978-1-83508-984-2

2. Submit your proof of purchase
3. That's it! We'll send your free PDF and other benefits to your email directly